Patience Strong's
Thoughts for Every Day

Patience Strong's
Thoughts for
Every Day

Bounty
Books

This omnibus edition first published by Cresset Press

The right of Patience Strong to be identified
as the Author of this work has been asserted in
accordance with the Copyright, Designs and
Patents Act, 1988

This edition published 2004 by Bounty Books,
a division of Octopus Publishing Group Ltd,
2-4 Heron Quays, London E14 4JP

Reprinted in 2004, 2005, 2006 (twice), 2007, 2008 (twice)

The Bedside Book
First published in Great Britain by Frederick Muller Ltd
Copyright © 1953 Patience Strong

The Birthday Book
First published in Great Britain by Frederick Muller Ltd
Copyright © 1955 Patience Strong

The Friendship Book
First published in Great Britain by Frederick Muller Ltd
Copyright © 1962 Patience Strong

ISBN 978 0 753709 02 3

Printed and bound in Dubai

PATIENCE STRONG'S

BEDSIDE
BOOK

Daily readings in prose and verse

To Mary Bulloch
In gratitude and
affection

January 1st

THE NEW CALENDAR

IT is good to throw away the old calendar with its all too familiar picture and to hang something fresh on the wall. How clean and bright the new calendar looks ! It seems to symbolise the high hopes of this new morning of a new year. But as I flick through the crisp new pages of the months I am suddenly aware of the strange mystery of the future. These pages with their neat rows of dates represent unlived Time, the promise of seasons not yet come to fulfilment, days not yet granted, days that are still God's secret.

＊＊＊＊＊

January 2nd

THAT YOUR DAYS MAY BE BLESSED

WHAT shall I ask of the year that is dawning ? What shall I hope as I face the new day ? What shall I ask on the very first morning ? What shall I wish, and for what should I pray ? . . . Ask for an eye that is open to beauty. Ask for a faith that no bludgeon can break. Ask for the patience to do every duty — with a good humour that nothing can shake.

Now at this time of the year's new beginning. Pray for these gifts. They outweigh all the rest. For without these there is naught worth the winning. Ask for these things that your days may be blessed.

＊＊＊＊＊

January 3rd

THE STREAM OF PROVIDENCE

"THEY that are in the stream of Providence are borne continually to happiness no matter what the appearance of the means".

—*Swedenborg*

January 4th

LITTLE WORLDS

A BIRD lived in a painted cage beside a windowpane — knowing nothing of the wind, the sunlight and the rain. Poor little bird ! It was as well he did not realise — that his tiny wings were meant to beat against the skies.

A man lived in a little world of ready-made ideas — a cramping cage of prejudices and of doubts and fears. He did not know that out beyond the ranges of his thought — lay a strange and lovely world where miracles were wrought.

Year by year he lived content behind his prison bars — never looking up to seek for God amongst the stars. In many forms the Lord appeared and yet he could not see. Poor little man ! He lived and died in his captivity.

∽ ∽ ∽ ∽ ∽

January 5th

"THEREFORE all seasons shall be sweet to thee,
 Whether the summer clothe the general earth
With greenness, or the redbreast sit and sing
Betwixt the tufts of snow on the bare branch
Of mossy apple-tree, while the nigh thatch
Smokes in the sun-thaw."

—Coleridge

∽ ∽ ∽ ∽ ∽

January 6th

THE INN OF FRIENDSHIP

THE Inn of Friendship lights the way along life's winding path. The door stands ever open and a fire burns on the hearth. The lamp gives forth a glow of welcome where the long road ends. Who would fear the darkness in the company of friends ?

How sweet it is when sad at heart and weary and hard-pressed — to come upon an Inn of Friendship there awhile to rest. . . . And be it night or be it day within its walls you find — bread of comfort, wine of joy ; good fare for heart and mind.

January 7th

THE SECRET PLACE

"HE that dwelleth in the secret place of the most High shall abide under the shadow of the Almighty".
—*Psalm 91. 1*

~ ~ ~ ~ ~

January 8th

GROWING OLD

THERE are things that grow in beauty as the long years pass — growing lovelier day by day : oak, china, silver, glass. Towns of quaint old houses, weathered brick and mellowed stone — gather richly to themselves a beauty of their own. Often do we lose our looks when we have lost our youth. If we could but grow in virtue, kindliness and truth — we should face the sunset with tranquillity and grace — and lines of beauty Time would draw upon the ageing face.

~ ~ ~ ~ ~

January 9th

HOPE TRAVELS FAR

HOPE travels far.
Alone she goes into the darkness undismayed,
Where none has dared to tread before
She hastens forward, unafraid.
Pressing on and heeding not
The mocking voice that cries "Too late"
Striding on beyond the point
Where others halt and hesitate.

The lamp of God is in her hand,
Upon her brow a crown of light,
And where she walks a ray of glory
Makes a path into the night.
She needs no staff to lean upon,
No helping hand, no guiding star,
Over horizons lost to view,
Outstripping dreams,
Hope travels far.

January 10th

A WINTER MORNING

IT is a wonderful thing to think of the roots and bulbs waiting their hour under all this whiteness. Underneath the snow the earth is already pregnant with potential life. Beneath the winding sheet of the snow lies all the glory of summer : the blue steeples of the delphiniums, the crimson peonies, the lupins of May and the roses of June. It is no shroud of death that wraps the silent garden, but a warm feathery eiderdown, devised by Nature for her own secret purposes.

—From "The Glory Of The Garden"

~ ~ ~ ~ ~

January 11th

THE OLD VILLAGE

WHO could guess the century? It might be any year. Time, it seems, in passing by has left no footprint here. The village with its narrow street, the church, the mill, the pond. The ploughman on the furrowed slope, the Sussex Downs beyond.

~ ~ ~ ~ ~

January 12th

WHEN GRANNY DREAMS

I OFTEN wonder where she is when she has dropped asleep. I ask her when she wakes, but she replies, "Just counting sheep" . . . But from her smile I know she's been a long, long way from me — plucking secret roses in the lanes of memory.

THE HEART REMEMBERS

THE heart remembers everything although the mind forgets — the raptures and the agonies, the hopes and the regrets . . . The heart remembers April when the snows of winter fall, hearing on the bitter wind the sweetest song of all.

When Youth has had its shining hour and Love its golden day — Time may fade the colours and the glory turn to grey, but something of the magic lingers, never to depart — deep down in the secret places of the quiet heart.

You think you have forgotten but the heart remembers all. Suddenly, some strange and lovely thing it will recall — something that was buried long ago and far away : a kiss, a smile, a melody, a dream of yesterday.

＿ ＿ ＿ ＿ ＿

LOVING LIFE

"FOR he that will love life, and see good days, let him refrain his tongue from evil, and his lips that they speak no guile".

—1 Peter 3. 10

＿ ＿ ＿ ＿ ＿

TEMPTATION

IT is fatal to look at garden catalogues on a grey drizzly day in mid-January. Those fabulous roses ! Those monster delphiniums with their unbelievably tall steeples of incredible blue blooms ! Those rich, fat impossible-looking peonies ! Those fairy-story sunflowers with faces as big as pre-war dinner plates ! It doesn't matter about looking at the Dutch tulips or the lordly specimens of King Alfred daffodils because it's too late to do anything about them now. It's the herbaceous border section that makes you lose your head and reach for the order form.

OTHERS HAVE COME THIS WAY

THOUGH hard the road you have to tread and heavy be your cross — and the heart be breaking with a great and grievous loss. . . . Others have travelled ahead of you. Have groped through this same night. Have struggled through the darkness and come out into the light.

The track is marked with footprints where unnumbered souls have passed — through the Gates of Suffering and found their peace at last. . . . Remember this when sorrow comes and when for strength you pray. Others have walked the road before you. Others have come this way.

CHARITY

"AND though I bestow all my goods to feed the poor, and though I give my body to be burned, and have not charity, it profiteth me nothing".

—St. Paul

SPEAK NO ILL

SPEAK no ill of friend or neighbour. Let your words be fair and true. Speak of others as you would that other men should speak of you.

Tip the scales of your opinions on the side of sympathy. Temper justice with compassion, and the breath of charity.

Better silence than reproaches. Bitter words affections kill. If you cannot praise, say nothing. Cast no stones and speak no ill.

A SEAT IN THE SUN

IT'S known in the town as the Grandfathers' Seat, and on days that are sunny and fair, the same little group of old folks can be seen, sitting enjoying the air. Smoking and joking and nodding a bit — watching the crowds hurry on. Sifting old memories, thinking long thoughts. Talking of times that are gone. God grant all grandfathers joy and content — and peace when their life's work is done. For what could be better than this at the end? A pipe . . . and a seat in the sun.

〜　〜　〜　〜　〜

WINTER BLOSSOM

THE tree has blossomed overnight — for every twig is frozen white, and garlanded with crystal sprays that sparkle in the sun's bright rays. Each sprig is tipped with buds of rime. Strange burgeonings of wintertime. As lovely as a Spring display of flowering plum or snowy may. And on the window I can trace, where silver branches interlace, a picture on the pane embossed : a fairy orchard white with frost.

〜　〜　〜　〜　〜

NOW AND THEN

NOW and then in wintertime when all is grim and grey — in between the storms and gales, God sends a golden day. . . . A morning bright with skies of blue that seems too lovely to be true.

Now and then in life's dark times of sorrow and distress — in between the tears there comes a flash of happiness : a loving word, a tender smile, making everything worth while.

Now and then we're given glimpses of a perfect Love — breaking through our hearts like shafts of sunlight from above. A sudden glory fills the sky. An unseen Presence passes by.

January 22nd

"HE who hath done a good turn, should so forget it, as not to speak of it : but he that boasts it or upbraids it, hath paid himself, and lost the nobleness of the charity".

—*Jeremy Taylor*

January 23rd

"GIVE not much to whom you should give little, nor little to whom much, nor something to whom nothing, nor nothing to whom something".

January 24th
POOR MAN'S BEQUEST

HE had no worldly treasures. No fortune he possessed — to leave unto his children, but this was his bequest. He left them all the beauties of earth and skies and seas — the marvels of creation; the birds, the brooks, the trees . . . The salt wind on the marshes, the primrose in the lane. The green and golden meadows — the sun, the stars, the rain. The heather on the moorlands. The swallows on the wing. The snowdrops in the winter — the lilacs in the Spring.

January 25th
PLANT A TREE

THOUGH your little garden patch be smoky, small and bare, Let some green and living thing proclaim God's glory there. It will give you joy. And when you've gone, in years to be, Someone will behold it and be grateful. Plant a tree.

January 26th
A COUNTRY WALK

THERE is nothing more exhilarating than a country walk on a cold bright afternoon in late January. The eye can travel farther in winter than in summer, for open hedges and naked trees reveal much that will soon be hidden by curtains of leaves and blossoms. It is good to lean over a gate and look at a field of fallow earth and to contemplate the beautiful bough structures of oaks and beeches. And when the pale gold of the sinking sun fades out into the smoky grey of the winter dusk, oh how good it is to anticipate tea and crumpets by a cottage fire.

January 27th
A SENSE OF HUMOUR

IF you see the funny side, you'll stroll along the sunny side while other folk are walking in the shade. Things will never harass you, embitter or embarrass you. A sense of humour is the finest aid — to wisdom and philosophy. In trouble and adversity it brings you smiling through the stress and strife. So cultivate the power to see — the little touch of comedy behind the trials and tragedies of life.

January 28th
ONE DAY NEARER

THE Winter is a stillness and a darkness and a sleep But not a death, for in the earth the roots of life go deep. A rest . . . then re-creation and a glad new burgeoning. Every day in Wintertime is one day nearer Spring.

January 29th

EARLY last month I placed four hyacinth bulbs into a bowl of mould and popped them away into a dark cupboard under the stairs. Occasionally I gave them a little water, but for the three weeks of the Christmas excitements they were, I fear, entirely neglected. It was only this morning that I remembered them, and the impossible had happened. I am always sceptical when planting indoor bulbs, they look such dry unpromising looking things when you put them into the soil and it is hard to imagine them bursting out into a blaze of coloured blooms. It's always a surprise when it happens, and this morning I experienced the old astonishment. The mould in the blue china bowl had been pierced by four green tips. Here was a holy mystery. I took the bowl out of the cupboard and placed it reverently on the sunny window-sill. Miracles inspire reverence, and this, truly, was a miracle.

January 30th

"WHITHER shall I go from Thy spirit? or whither shall I flee from Thy presence? If I ascend up into heaven, Thou art there ; if I make my bed in hell, behold, Thou art there. If I take the wings of the morning, and dwell in the uttermost parts of the sea; Even there shall Thy hand lead me, and Thy right hand shall hold me".

—*Psalm 139. 7-10*

January 31st

THE TREE

I AM your friend, your needs I meet.
I am the floor beneath your feet.
I am the beam that takes the strain,
I am the door against the rain.

I am the peg, the post, the tub,
I am the oar, the bat, the club.
I am the stick for summer days,
I am the log for winter's blaze.

I am the altar of the Lord,
I am the sacramental board.
And at the last on earth's brown breast
I hold you in your place of rest.

HINTS AND GLIMPSES

THIS is the soul's month, the month of whispered hopes, the month when we feel that at last we can turn our faces towards the glad promise of Spring. The beds and borders are peppered with green tips and a few snowdrops have swung their fairy bells in the teeth of a raw wet wind. but these are mere intimations. The days between Candlemas and St. Valentine are days in which we must be content with hints and glimpses. Winter has not done with us yet, but the listening heart has caught a far-away sound on the wind and Hope will no longer be denied.

〜 〜 〜 〜 〜

YEAST

FAITH is not a holy thing to keep for special days. It is something to be used, our hearts and hopes to raise. Something to be added to the joy and pain and strife — stirred into the mixture of the common stuff of life.

It's the secret yeast that makes the bread of life to rise, the power of God at work in us, the thing that glorifies — homely tasks and daily duties making dull lives glow. Without this leaven we are only lumps of human dough.

Do not keep religion in a nicely painted tin — marked FOR SUNDAYS ONLY. Tip it out and work it in . . . Work it into everything you think and do and say — Use it for all purposes and live it day by day.

〜 〜 〜 〜 〜

MY FRIENDS

FATE has often led my footsteps
To a place of destiny,
Where I found a kindred spirit,
Someone waiting there for me.

For all other precious things
I've searched and struggled, worked and fought,
But my friends, the best and dearest,
These have come to me unsought.

THE OLD STICK

YOU'VE kept pace with me old friend, along the road of Time. All these years I've leaned on you upon the upward climb. Often you have helped me do that last long weary mile, swinging into step with me by meadow stream and stile.

We, together, we have jogged along a Surrey lane — and have measured many miles across the Shropshire plain. Memories you hold for me of forest, heath and field : the Cumbrian fells, the Sussex downlands and the Kentish Weald.

Many new and sturdy sticks stand waiting in the hall. But it's you I love the best, the very best of all. It is you I like to grip as down the road I wend. You I'll keep until I come to where all journeys end.

February 5th

THE BLUE LIGHT

THERE are certain moments that come with the twilights of February when the colour of the dusk deepens to a blue haze and you are disturbed by an awareness of beauty that is half an ecstasy and half a sadness. Such moments are more noticeable in the towns than in the country where the light is more widely diffused, and it is in the streets of London that one is most conscious of the strange loveliness of a February twilight. Outlines of familiar places soften into the gauzy mist and everything is touched with unreality. It seldom lasts for more than a quarter of an hour. Imperceptibly the blue light thins out into a greyness, and the magic is gone.

February 6th

QUESTION AND ANSWER

WHERE did he fall, that lad of yours ? In what far country did he die ? Did he make the sacrifice on land, at sea, or in the sky ?

It was in the course of duty. As he would have wished to go. It was on the field of service. That is all I need to know.

DREAMING

GREY and cheerless is the garden in the wintry gloom. But I dream of daffodils and appletrees in bloom. Frozen fields lie hard as iron beneath the bitter rain. But I dream of new green wheat and lilacs in the lane.

In the deep and silent woods there is a death-like hush. Yet I seem to hear the singing of an April thrush. Many of our foolish dreams just fade into the blue. But when you dream a dream of Spring, you *know* it's coming true.

～ ～ ～ ～ ～

WELLS OF SALVATION

THERE is no need to die of thirst in the desert of secular life. God has given us His word to revive and refresh us, the living water of the living Christ.

"Therefore with joy shall ye draw
water out of the wells of salvation".

—*Isaiah 12. 3*

～ ～ ～ ～ ～

SNOWDROPS

APTLY named : a drop of snow. Sweet flowers that come when cold winds blow — and in the depths of Winter bring, the whispered tidings of the Spring. You'd think such fairy things would die — beneath the bleak and bitter sky. You'd wonder how the buds uncurled in such a grim and hostile world. . . . Just little frozen drops of snow. How daintily the small bells grow — upon their slender stalks that thrust so bravely through the earth's hard crust ! No sunshine warms their icy bed. No birds make music overhead — when like strangers they appear — at the gateway of the year.

THIS is a month of uncertainties. One day the sun may be shining like the smile of God, and the next a ferocious wind will come roaring up out of the north and the sky will be heavy with the presage of snow. So has it been with us this week. Two days ago I stood in a patch of sunlight looking down at one of Tennyson's "solitary firstlings", and this morning the little fairy bell has disappeared under a drift of snowflakes. The window frames a bleak and bitter scene. The cedar stands clotted with snow, its branches straining under the weight. The thorn hedge is like a pattern of wrought iron, stark against the whiteness of the bank beyond. Hope has been halted in her tracks. It was foolish to have let her get so far. We might have guessed that Winter was only biding its time for a fresh assault.

February 11th

THE GREAT THOUGHT

LEAN upon the thought of God,
A great thought let it be,
Large enough and deep enough to rest in utterly.
Finding consolation, hope, refreshment and release
In the quiet comfort of His presence and His peace.

Lean on this, for this alone
Will take your whole full weight.
And will make you strong to face whatever be your fate.
Every other staff and stay will be of no avail.
Lean upon the word of God for this will never fail.

February 12th

THE OLD LADY

THERE is a beauty on her wrinkled face. Bright as a candle in a holy place. There is a light behind the smiling eyes — merry and humorous, and yet so wise.

There is a strength about her stooping form. A strength that has carried her through every storm. Frail though she seems, her spirit tough and gay — faces the challenge of each passing day.

February 13th

MEMORY'S HOUR

STRANGE are the thoughts that come to mind
When winter dusks fall chill and grey
And firelight flickers red and golden
    At the ending of the day.

Dear is the hour when work is done,
    When lamps are lit and I am free,
For Memory then like some old friend
    Steals in to keep me company.

February 14th

"ST. VALENTINE. A priest of Rome who was imprisoned
for succouring persecuted Christians. He became a
convert himself, and although he restored the sight of his
gaoler's blind daughter he was martyred by being clubbed
to death (February 14th, 269)".

—Brewer's Dictionary

February 15th

ACCORDING to ancient tradition St. Valentine's is the
wedding day of the birds, the day on which they choose
their mates for the year. Chaucer refers to it in "The Parlia-
ment of Foules" and in "A Midsummer Night's Dream"
Shakespeare says,
  "Good morrow, friends ! St. Valentine is past ;
   Begin these wood-birds but to couple now ?"
  Whether accurate or not it is certainly true that with the
ending of February's second week we become aware of a new
song in the air, new yet sweetly familiar. Up to now the
morning wind has been full of the confused sounds of chirrup-
ings and twitterings, but today the confusion has resolved
itself into measured phrases. Deliberate and distinct the
song of a blackbird rises from the thicket, and from somewhere down in the flooded shaw there comes the unmistakable
throbbing of a thrush's note.

THE GREEN PASTURES

"THE Lord is my shepherd ; I shall not want. He maketh me to lie down in green pastures : he leadeth me beside the still waters. He restoreth my soul : he leadeth me in the paths of righteousness for his name's sake. Yea, though I walk through the valley of the shadow of death, I will fear no evil : for thou art with me ; thy rod and thy staff they comfort me. Thou preparest a table before me in the presence of mine enemies : thou anointest my head with oil ; my cup runneth over. Surely goodness and mercy shall follow me all the days of my life : and I will dwell in the house of the Lord for ever".

—The 23rd Psalm

SEWING

IN and out the needle goes along the folded seam — while your heart is following some lost and lovely dream. In between the stitches you can go a long, long way — when you're sitting sewing at the quiet end of the day.

O the things that you remember as you draw the thread ! Odds and ends of memory come back into your head. Names and faces, times and places. Round the world you go. Many miles you travel as you watch the stitches grow.

MAKING FRIENDS WITH THE TREES

IT is possible to strike up a lasting friendship with a tree for it is something more than a piece of wood. It gives off an individual emanation that can attract or repel. A loved tree can become responsive to your moods, sentient and intimate. Many are the trees that have afforded me comfort and companionship. There was a certain alder in the Darenth valley ; there was a lonely pine on a wild bit of heathland in Dorset ; there was a larch on a Shropshire hillside, an oak in a Sussex glade. There was a lovely mulberry tree in the walled garden of a beautiful old house in Winchelsea, and long, long ago when the world was new, there was a twisted little hawthorn in a London park, beloved by a child and never forgotten.

THE LAMP

THE Word of God is like a lamp. It shines upon the unknown way — and sends into the darkest place, a steady glow, a guiding ray.

Light Eternal burning ever as towards the Truth men grope — Leading them by hidden ways along the paths of faith and hope.

> "Thy word is a lamp
> unto my feet".

—Psalm 119

February 20th

WE often need to be reminded why Christ came and for whom. He came for the delinquent, the degenerate, the dispossessed, the riffraff, the hopeless, the ragtag and bobtail of humanity, the black sheep, the bad lot. He came to seek out these lost souls and put them into a right relationship with God, and the continuing of that work should be the prime function of His Church. When a Church goes all out after saving souls it is a living, transforming, dynamic power within society. When it ceases to save souls it becomes a mere institution.

February 21st

THE DAILY SACRAMENT

LOVE is not the dazzling dream that lights up youth's
    bright day,
Love is the sharing of the load along the common way.
Love is not the April rapture of the untried heart,
Love is what is left of joy when golden days depart.

Love is not the flicker of desires that come and go,
Love is the lighting of the lamp that gives a steady glow,
The self-denying impulse and the generous intent,
The holy thing that makes of life a daily sacrament.

WHILE YOU'RE WAITING

WHILE you're waiting for tomorrow, get the best out of today. While you're waiting for the sunshine don't complain at skies of grey. While you wait for future pleasures don't forget the ones you've had. Call to mind the things enjoyed, the happy times and not the sad.

While you're waiting for the granting of the wish you hold most dear, don't lose sight of all the joys that life can offer now and here. Times of waiting can be fruitful and to you much good can bring. Make the winter yield a blessing while you're waiting for the Spring.

February 23rd

NEVER IDLE

IF you have a garden there is always work to do,
  Beds to hoe and grass to mow and things to plan anew,
Shrubs and bushes to be pruned, dead wood to cut away,
  Fresh young shoots to tie and train and apple trees to spray.

Plots to dig and leaves to sweep and compost heap to make.
  Tubs and benches to be painted, leaning trees to stake.
Edges of the lawn to trim, a broken fence to mend,
  The shed to put in order and the rockery to tend.

Ragged hedges to be clipped. The kitchen patch to weed.
  Pots and boxes to be sorted ready for the seed.
Borders to be planted out with next year's show in view,
  In a garden you can always find a job to do.

February 24th

HISTORY

GUARD and cherish jealously places steeped in history. Sites where famous deeds were done, causes lost and battles won. Ground that sets the heart aglow — with great thoughts of long ago. Soil that hides a sacred dust. Earth that we must hold in trust. Never let historic land fall into the vandal's hand. Treasure it and hold it fast. It's the story of the past.

INCREDULITY

I HAVE come to doubt this prophecy of Spring,
　Watching the trees stretch naked arms
　Sapless and stark
　Against a sullen sky.
　Spring !
　I have grown weary in the hope of it.
　Too long root bulb and seed have lain
　Still and unquickened
　In the earth's full womb.
　So long, so long,
　The heart grows sceptical with too much waiting.

＞　＞　＞　＞　＞

DIVIDENDS

MAKE Life pay dividends. You can if you choose — for it's a business, you gain or you lose. Though you have problems and troubles to meet — Don't accept failure and loss and defeat.

Profit by everything. Wrest good from ill. Double your assets of wisdom and skill. Turn to advantage whatever Fate sends. Increase your happiness. Add to your friends.

＞　＞　＞　＞　＞

SHOWING THE WORLD

If you've a song,
Try it.
If you've a tear,
Dry it.
If you've a cross,
Bear it.
If you've a joy,
Share it.
When hope grows faint,
Brace it.
When trouble comes,
Face it.

Where there's a wrong,
Right it.
When life is grim,
Fight it.
If you've a hand,
Give it.
If you've a creed,
Live it.
If you've a faith,
Show it,
And let the world know it.

LINES FOUND IN EXETER CATHEDRAL

"OF all that in the past has witnessed to the Glory of God rather than ministered to the comfort of man a Cathedral Church is perhaps the last survivor. In men's minds the Broken Box of Alabaster has yielded place to the useful drinking trough of stone. Many ears are deaf to the witness of this House of God : but to such as listen for it, it will speak.

The long stretch of Nave and of Quire : the distant aisle and the retired transept : the vaulted roof where the sunbeams linger : each says to us "How wide is the loving Mercy of God ! "

Mark then the massive strength of an arch : the slender grace of a column : the intricate fret of a tracery : the splendour of colour : the wonder of music : the dreams and desires of the artist : the hushed devotion of adoring souls.

O Man, leave the noise and the strife : cast thy burden upon the Eternal : come and worship the Lord in the Beauty of Holiness ".

THE HOYDEN

MARCH has come blustering into the year like a hoyden bursting boisterously into a quiet room. Yesterday everything seemed to be waiting passively for the Spring. Gleams of sunlight stole about the garden, and the blue dusk that clung about the day's end was full of the blessedness of an unutterable peace, but this morning has brought a dramatic change. The new March wind is rampaging lion-like about the garden, roaring down the cottage chimney, tearing at the tiles, shaking the saplings and whirling papers about the lawn from the overturned bins. But it's a good drying wind, and one of the compensations for the commotion it is causing is that it will dry up the pools and puddles which have been lying about since last week's thaw. Rough, ill-mannered, strident March, we forgive you much; for it is you who bring the daffodils, the chiffchaff and the crocuses.

March 2nd

THE HOUSE OF MEMORIES

ONCE the carpet had a pattern, beautiful and gay. Now it's old and faded and the colours worn away. New when Granny was a bride, now threadbare, thin and frayed — like the shabby draperies of blue and gold brocade. . . . The drawing-room is as it was. Victorian maybe. But elegant and restful with a quiet dignity. Lofty ceilings, marble fireplace, woodwork painted white. One can picture ghostly figures in the fading light — conjuring out of the past the scenes of yesterday : lovely ladies dressed in gowns of lavender and grey — moving up and down the room. Is that what Granny sees — sitting there at twilight in her house of memories ?

~ ~ ~ ~ ~

March 3rd

DOORS

THERE are many kinds of doors. Some look inviting to the eye. Some speak a welcome. Some repel the glances of the passer by.

There are friendly cottage doors that have a cosy homely air. Doors where tangled roses cling as if they loved to linger there. Doors of churches, hallowed doors through which upon the Sabbath days — countless worshippers have passed to sing their songs of prayer and praise. Prison doors that men pass through bereft of hope, no longer free. Doors of hospitals that stand for mercy and humanity.

At the doorway of my heart may no one ever fail to find — a swift response of sympathy, a word of welcome warm and kind.

~ ~ ~ ~ ~

"BE civil to all ; sociable to many ; familiar with few ; friend to one ; enemy to none".
—*Benjamin Franklin,*
Poor Richard's Almanac, 1747

March 4th

MUSIC IN YOUR HEART

IF on lonely roadways distant music you can hear — the music must be in your heart and nothing need you fear. Up the hills and down the valleys you will swing along — marching to the secret rhythm of an inward song.

When the way grows dreary and your dearest friends depart — you will never weary if there's music in your heart. You will hear a note of joy beyond the rugged slope — and catch upon the bitter wind the golden voice of hope.

— — — — —

March 5th

SURPRISES

THE first crocuses always take you by surprise. You never seem to see them coming. They spring up overnight. Quite suddenly you become aware of patches of yellow under the trees and flecks of gold along the edges of the path. Soon the whole garden will be fairy-lit with little crocus-candles of ivory and lavender, but it is the bold yellow firstlings that take your breath away. Every year it happens and every year you feel the same old astonishment.

— — — — —

March 6th

THE BEATITUDES

BLESSED are the poor in spirit : for theirs is the kingdom of heaven.

Blessed are they that mourn : for they shall be comforted.

Blessed are the meek : for they shall inherit the earth.

Blessed are they which do hunger and thirst after righteousness : for they shall be filled.

Blessed are the merciful : for they shall obtain mercy.

Blessed are the pure in heart : for they shall see God.

Blessed are the peacemakers : for they shall be called the children of God.

Blessed are they which are persecuted for righteousness' sake : for theirs is the kingdom of heaven.

March 7th

WE WHO HAVE MOURNED

WE who have mourned a soul departed, we who have known the grief of loss. We who have groped for God and found Him in the shadow of the Cross. . . . We have received a secret blessing, having come close to unseen things. We have been shown a glimpse of glory under the gloom of Death's dark wings.

We have been granted consolations ; knowledge too subtle to impart. Sorrow, a gaunt grim guest has come and made his lodging in the heart, but following on with silent footsteps Faith has entered secretly. We who have mourned have looked on Death and seen Love's immortality.

~ ~ ~ ~ ~

March 8th

TO THANK YOU

HOW can I prove my gratitude for all that you have given me,
Happiness and fond affection, comfort in adversity.
Peace of mind and joy of living, help and hope and friendship true,
Richly has my life been blessed with all that I have found in you.

Thank you for your understanding, for your trust and sympathy.
For the gift of your devotion, for your love and loyalty.
Ever I'll remember this no matter what the years may bring.
I'll remember and be grateful. Thank you, dear, for everything.

~ ~ ~ ~ ~

March 9th

THE ALMOND TREE

ONCE again the almond tree is bursting into flower. Early in the year she has her best and perfect hour. Crowned with beauty, wreathed in glory, holding every eye — startling with her loveliness the people passing by. Gay against the sombre tones of laurel and of yew. There she stands triumphant, like a dream of Spring come true.

NOISE

NOISE is the curse of modern life. The sound of a machine seems to raise a jarring voice on every quiet scene. Radio and television, traffic roaring by. The tractor on the plough-land and the jet-plane in the sky.

These things wear upon the nerves, destroying peace and poise. It seems we can't progress unless we make a lot of noise. How different from the work of God that goes on silently, in womb and cell, in seed and shell, in pod and plant and tree.

~ ~ ~ ~ ~

MOTHER TO DAUGHTER

I GIVE you to the man you love upon your wedding day. No tear of mine must mar your joy. I send you on your way — grateful for the golden years when you belonged to me — treasuring within my heart each precious memory.

I'm losing you, my dear, but I am more than glad to know — that you have found your love, as I found mine, long, long ago. . . . And so goodbye, my little girl, God keep you and God bless — granting you your heart's desire and every happiness.

~ ~ ~ ~ ~

SINCERITY

IT'S the little things that count, the way a thing is said. The faint suspicion of a frown, the turning of a head. The tone of voice that's kind or cold, the smile that's real or fake. The wording of a letter — oh the difference it can make ! If the heart is wholly filled with love and charity — All you do will bear the imprint of sincerity.

24

March 13th

THE YELLOW CROCUS

THE first to come: The yellow crocus thrusting boldly up — as if to catch and hold the sunlight in its painted cup. The first one out to shout a salutation of good cheer, making haste to show itself before the rest appear. . . . For soon will come the other members of the family — robed in deepest purple, palest mauve and ivory — and dazzled by their beauty we'll forget to say goodbye — to the first that took the risk and braved the wintry sky.

March 14th

TOGETHER

TROUBLE would be twice as hard with nobody to share it . . . no good companion at your side to help you grin and bear it. Grief would last much longer if you bore it all alone. Few are strong enough to stand entirely on their own.

Human hearts need sympathy and that is why God sends — consolation through the understanding of our friends . . . for a friend can banish clouds like sun in stormy weather. Nothing is so bad if you can talk it out together.

March 15th

COTTAGE WINDOWS

FORTUNATE are they who greet the day through cottage panes — looking out on distant hills, green fields and winding lanes. . . . Fortunate are they who from their lattices can see, the ever-changing beauty of some old and lovely tree.

Lucky is the one whose casements frame an open view — of an unspoilt landscape fading out into the blue. What could be more perfect than to wake and to behold — the country scene through cottage windows flushed with morning gold?

March 16th

THE VIRTUOUS WOMAN

"WHO can find a virtuous woman ? for her price is far above rubies. The heart of her husband doth safely trust in her. . . . She will do him good and not evil all the days of her life. She seeketh wool and flax, and worketh willingly with her hands. She openeth her mouth with wisdom ; and in her tongue is the law of kindness. She looketh well to the ways of her household, and eateth not the bread of idleness. Her children arise up and call her blessed".

—Proverbs, chapter 31

March 17th

THERE is so much happening in the garden these days that you cannot keep pace with what is going on. The crocuses are swarming over the banks and borders. The quince under the window is peppered with rosy buds. The damson blossom is on the point of breaking. The old Dutch honeysuckle is flecked with new green leaves. Hyacinths are pushing up out of the frosted beds and primula wanda makes velvety violet mats of bloom along the edges of the path. The forsythias in the shrubbery are like golden fountains arching gracefully over clumps of jonquils and early primroses. The birds are building. It is a time when you want to slow down the passing of the hours to prolong the delights of anticipation.

March 18th

THE CHINA CABINET

A LITTLE Dresden shepherdess, a figure pink and gold. A dainty bowl of gilt and roses, beautiful and old. A bit of Spode, a Wedgwood jar, a piece of pottery. The Rockingham. The prized possession of the family.

Beauty cherished throughout the years. What happiness it brings — to those who know and understand the worth of precious things. . . . They must be preserved and must be treasured carefully. Thus does loveliness live on for other eyes to see.

ALL THAT'S NEEDED

SOMETIMES all that's needed is a touch of sympathy — to warm a hardened heart and make it glow. . . . Sometimes all that's wanted is a little bit of praise. It often acts like sunshine on the snow.

When a quarrel casts its shadow on a happy pair—when silence separates and love grows chill. Sometimes all that's needed is for one of them to make — a gesture of good nature and goodwill.

~ ~ ~ ~ ~

ASLEEP

DEEP down in the cosy cot a wisp of hair you'll see. A small face lovely as a rose and eyes closed peacefully. A wee thing in a big dark world, a tiny helpless mite, lying in the golden circle of the candlelight. . . . Somewhere in the quiet house there's someone listening — to catch the very slightest cry, the faintest whimpering. And though she may be busy with a mother's load of care — all her thoughts will hover round the little one up there. . . . There's a hushed and sacred silence brooding everywhere. You must ease the squeaking door and mind the creaking stair. Nobody must make a sound. On tiptoe they must creep—when the word has gone around that BABY IS ASLEEP.

~ ~ ~ ~ ~

THE FIRST DAY

THEY say that if the wind is in the north-east on the first day of Spring it remains in that quarter until the first day of Summer, so it was with some trepidation that I went out into the garden this morning to feel what sort of a wind it was that was ruffling the thuya outside the window. My fears were unfounded. It was only a little ripple of air blowing softly up out of the south. The ground was sugared with a light frost but it was melting rapidly under the warmth of the sun. The hope that hung precariously on the edge of the mind for so long now stands firmly as a fact, official and authentic. The calendar confirms what the blackbird has been telling me for the past three weeks. Truly Spring is come.

March 22nd

"JUDGE not, that ye be not judged".
—*Matthew 7. 1*

〜 〜 〜 〜 〜

March 23rd

BEREAVEMENT

IT'S hard to face an empty chair. A bitter thing it is to bear — when one is called and one is left, to face the years . . . of love bereft. But this is Life. God wills it so. And soon or late we all must go — the homeward way ; to find at last — the dear companions of the past.

〜 〜 〜 〜 〜

March 24th

OUT FOR A WALK

DOWN the winding lane you go beneath the elms where black rooks crowd. Gold light filters through the branches as the pale sun breaks a cloud. Past the lychgate of the church — across the bridge beside the mill — lingering a moment here to see the stream slip down the hill. . . . Past the cottage on the corner in its garden snug and neat. Through the gate into the field now striped with green of growing wheat. Pausing, poised against the wind to watch the hills grow grey with rain. On along the wood's dark edge — Then up the road and home again.

〜 〜 〜 〜 〜

March 25th

THE GRANDFATHER CLOCK

PEOPLE come and go, he says, but I go ticking on. Since the day they put me here a century has gone — and still I stand as strong as ever marking out the time — measuring its passing with my deep and solemn chime.

Nothing ruffles or disturbs my equanimity. I dominate the room, for every eye must look to me. . . . I'm the centre. Life revolves around the thing I say. Mine the tongue that speaks by night, the voice that rules the day.

SILVER WEDDING DAY

FIVE and twenty years ago ! It seems like yesterday — that we joined hands and vowed to walk together all the way. It hasn't been an easy path. We've had the hills to climb. We haven't had fair weather and good fortune all the time.

But we've had lots of happiness and blessings manifold. Youth has gone, but we have all its memories to hold. And Life still has its richest gifts to give abundantly — for we can say on this great day : "The best is yet to be".

March 27th

THE OLD BRIDGE

LOVELY is the old grey bridge that takes the burden of the road — Rhythmic arches, gently flowing, bear with grace their daily load. Anglers in the deep recesses, rod in hand, stand patiently. Silent figures in a scene of undisturbed tranquillity.

Time has touched with mellowed beauty every stone of span and pier. Ploughman, pedlar, lord and lady, Roundhead, King and Cavalier. All have crossed this ancient bridge upon the road of history — and stood where now I watch the river going down to meet the sea.

March 28th

THE oak tree proud and ancient and the sapling thin and frail — sway beneath the driving winds and bow before the gale. Bending but not breaking as the storm goes raving past — resisting not the force and fury of the roaring blast.

The winds of God blow round the world and sorrows come to all — but if we bow to Providence we shall not fail or fall — knowing that there is a final purpose to fulfil — finding strength in yielding to His good and perfect will.

March 29th

A SHROPSHIRE LANE

DEAR friend, I long to walk again — along that little Shropshire lane — deep-set in banks of ferns and flowers — where once we spent such happy hours. . . . Each twist and turn of it I know. And oftentimes in thought I go to seek and find those old delights : the summer days, the autumn nights, retracing every step we took — across the bridge that spans the brook — then past the cottage round the bend. Do you remember, dearest friend ?

March 30th

THE LITTLE GRAVE

SO small it is,
The little grave,
Unnoticed you could pass it by.
The narrow mound, the tiny cross
Would never draw the stranger's eye.
Walk quietly, you who come this way
And let this peace be undefiled
By clumsy foot or strident voice
For here they laid our little child.
The babe whose spirit God called home
Is sleeping here, so softly tread.
Where blooms for us the sweetest flower
In the garden of the dead.

March 31st

GOODBYE March. Often you have been rough and un-mannerly. Many times your mischievous winds have whisked off my hat at an inconvenient moment and blown smoke down the chimney when I was expecting guests, but I am ready to forgive your wild ways, for in your footprints the damson blooms and the daffodils dance.

THE TIDES OF SPRING

A WAVE of green has broken on the April countryside —
sweeping round the woods and hedges like a rising tide. . . .
A mounting wave of living green goes rolling round the
world — as on twig and branch and bough the new leaves are
uncurled.

Lovely at this season is the flowering cherry tree — like
a white-sailed galleon upon a restless sea : a ship adrift
before the wind, a fair and graceful thing — riding on the
full green waters of the tides of Spring.

━ ━ ━ ━ ━

April 2nd

"A FRIEND is one to whom we may pour out the contents
of our hearts, chaff and grain together, knowing that the
gentlest of hands will sift it, keep what is worth keeping, and
with a breath of kindness blow the rest away".

—Author unknown

━ ━ ━ ━ ━

April 3rd

TOO LONG

TOO long my heart has grieved, too long. I knew it when
I heard the song that rippled from the blackbird's throat —
for with the rapture of that note there came a sudden sweet
release, and an inner sense of peace on my wounded spirit
stole — bringing healing to my soul. . . . Instead of bitterness and pain — my heart remembered once again — the
things that I had thrust away : the memories of yesterday.
I found again my lost belief. I had forgotten in my grief —
that the world was beautiful and that God was merciful.

April 4th
KNOWING ALL THE ANSWERS

IT is possible to know the ethics of Christianity from A to Z, and yet miss the point of the whole thing. You may know all the answers intellectually and theologically, but unless those answers have been worked out in terms of personal experience such knowledge is superficial and your religion a sham. Nothing is true until you have lived it.

From "The Kingdom Within"

～ ～ ～ ～ ～

April 5th
THE WOODCARVER

IN these days of mass production, cheap and shoddy fake — it is good to come upon a craftsman who can make — lovely things that grow in beauty as the years pass by — satisfying to the mind and pleasing to the eye.

～ ～ ～ ～ ～

April 6th
THE OLD FARMHOUSE

TIME has weathered tile and timber, bricks and beams and stones — tinting gables, roofs and walls in rich warm mellow tones of rosy pink and russet brown, of red and gold and grey. Beautiful, yet solid in a stolid English way.

More than just a quaint old farmhouse pleasing to the eye — for it serves its generation as in days gone by. Through the passing centuries in bad times and in good — strong and comely, in its own green acres it has stood.

People come across the world these English homes to see — cottage, farm and manor rooted deep in history. May we prize this heritage and let no vandal hand — mar the scene and spoil the beauty of our lovely land.

April 7th

DO not fix your gaze upon the things that worry you. Lift your eyes and let them rest upon the wider view. Difficulties loom so large when looked at constantly — filling up the foreground of your life till you can see, nothing but these mountains growing bigger day by day. Solid they appear, but at a touch they melt away.

Do not let your mountains overwhelm you with their size. You will find they're only shadows if you let your eyes — range beyond the trials and tribulations that annoy — seeing only that which makes for hope and peace and joy. Look above the petty things that vex and trouble you. Have a brighter broader vision. Take the wider view.

- - - - -

April 8th

GREAT things hang upon small chances. If the wind had not been blowing so violently in the woods above Gowbarrow Park on a particular Thursday afternoon in April at the beginning of the last century, the daffodils by the lake would not have been swaying about so wildly and it is possible that one of the loveliest poems in the English language would never have been written. Had he been alone, Wordsworth would probably have wandered by in a dreamy abstraction and missed the moment, but luckily for us his sister was with him, and no beauty however fleeting ever escaped the quick-eyed Dorothy. It was Dorothy who made those daffodils dance for William and it was William who made them dance for the world. Over one hundred and fifty years have passed since the writing of that poem, but its magic still works, evoking that April scene by the windy lake. No matter where you are or what the season you can always read it and see the Ullswater daffodils.

> "They flash upon that inward eye
> Which is the bliss of solitude".

SPRING BRIDE

SPRING bride, young and beautiful as blossom on the spray. Live each golden moment of this good and happy day. Make it the beginning of a life that's well worth while — keeping through the future years your radiant wedding smile. . . . Keep unbroken unto death the vows that you have made. Keep the bloom upon your dreams and never let them fade. Let this be your resolution as the glad bells peal. Keep the vision of this hour. Hold fast the high ideal. . . . Then your marriage will be blessed with all felicity. Love will weave a thread of gold through all adversity. Keep your faith forever bright, your heart forever gay — and you'll never lose the glory of this glorious day.

- - - - -

THERE is, indeed, a virginal quality about "the pale primroses, that die unmarried". There is a green tinge in the yellowness that gives them an ethereal look. The crinkled leaves are cool to the touch, and the clumps, like shy maids, are to be found, not in the full glare of the sun, but huddled together in quiet and secluded places. The scent of the primrose is something that cannot be put into words. It is as fresh as wet earth, but faint and elusive. It does not assail the nostrils like a whiff of Parisian perfume, but is an indefinable exhalation from the very soul of the flower, reminiscent of childhood and the faraway woods of memory.

From "The Glory Of The Garden"

April 11th

IT is said that the swallows do about thirty miles a day and take about two and a half months to reach Southern England from the Cape. It is an amazing thought that even while the snow still lay on our gardens the swallows were winging their way up out of the far South, following the old migration routes along the western coasts of Africa, Spain and France. Any day now we may expect the first arrivals, but because the migrants arrive every year without fail we are apt to forget the wonder of it. What strange and irresistible impulse drives the swallows north to pair and nest ? How do those tiny wings beat their way across such vast distances ? How do they know the date to start and the way to come ? It is useless to ask for we shall never know. It is just another one of the great mysteries which are beyond the ranges of scientific explanation.

April 12th

BEAUTY FOR ASHES

"TO give unto them beauty for ashes, the oil of joy for mourning, the garment of praise for the spirit of heaviness ; that they might be called trees of righteousness, the planting of the Lord, that He might be glorified".

—*Isaiah 61. 3*

April 13th

BLOSSOMTIDE

IT is blossomtide again.
In the sunshine and the rain
Thrushes sing a madrigal
For this vernal festival.
From the bare bough there has come
Milk-white bloom on pear and plum,
And upon the apple tree
Pink buds cluster daintily.
Spring's green banners are unfurled.
Joy comes back into the world.
Man may weep, but with one voice
Nature says,
"Rejoice, rejoice ! "

THE MILL STREAM

BY the mill the little stream goes peacefully upon its way. Willows stoop upon the bank where swallows skim and children play. Through the cool dusk of the leaves the dappled gold of sunlight falls — where the swan glides in the shadow of the ivy-covered walls.

Once the stream rushed loud and busy past this lattice window pane — full of froth and self-importance, turning wheels and grinding grain. . . . Now unhurriedly it flows where green boughs trail amongst the reeds — softly slowly slipping out into the quiet water-meads.

THE FOREST GIANT

PLANTED when the Norman hunted in this fair and verdant glade. While you grew in strength and beauty history was being made. Half as old as England's story, undefeated there you stand. Proud with age, a living symbol of our dear and ancient land.

Strange it seems that though so old, so venerable and serene — you deck yourself with every Spring in fresh new leaves of tender green. . . . England too is old in years, and yet her vigour she retains. Though wide her boughs and deep her roots, the sap of youth flows in her veins.

THE GARDEN AGAIN

EVERY year the same old jobs, the digging and the hoeing. The path to weed, the beds to plan, the planting and the sowing. The same routine to follow, but the joy is ever new — when the winter's over and the garden calls to you. . . . The kitchen plot to clear and rake, the seedlings to be tended. The lawn to mow, the edge to trim and fences to be mended. Put that book back on the shelf and shun the fireside chair. The garden is demanding every moment you can spare.

ILL WIND

EVERY wind that blows brings something good to some-body. Even ill winds of mischance and of calamity — often carry as they go the seeds of Providence, so that out of trouble comes some happy consequence.

Damage may be done, but in the pathway of the gale — somebody may find it's left a blessing in its trail. When an ill wind blows your way and everything goes wrong . . . someone somewhere may be glad of what it brings along.

THE AIRMAN TO THE BIRD

WE have a kinship, you and I,
We know the secrets of the sky.
We know the thrill of sheer delight
That comes from cleaving air, in flight.
We two, detached from mortal things
Can rise upon untrammelled wings
And thread our way through stars and clouds
Above the world of streets and crowds.
God gave the freedom of the sky
To you.   But now I too can fly.
I too can skim the tops of trees,
Can sail the billows of the breeze,
Can race the wind, can dip and soar
And span the sea from shore to shore.
Sing on, sweet songster of the air,
I too know what it's like up there.

LIFE AND DEATH

WHEN blossom breaks on bush and spray. God speaks to all who grieve. There is no death, He seems to say. Look up, have faith, believe.

Our loved ones pass beyond our sight. We say that they have gone. But they are somewhere in the light where life and love go on.

So when you see the flowering hedge — and green leaves on the tree. Remember it is Nature's pledge of immortality.

A MOTHER'S DAY

WORK from dawn till bedtime. That's a mother's busy day. Washing, cleaning, cooking. Never time for rest or play. Looking after home and baby and of others too. Every day the same routine to tackle and get through. . . . That's a mother's day. But when the family has grown — When her life is not so rushed and she is left alone — Looking back across the years those days she will recall —And tell you that they were the best and happiest of all.

❧ ❧ ❧ ❧ ❧

FRESH AIR

THE finest tonic in the world,
The cheapest and the best,
Put the pills and drugs aside
And put this to the test.
Take a walk and fill your lungs
With air that's fresh and clean.
Even in a city you can find a patch of green.

When you feel run down
And out of tune with everyone,
Get out in the open
In the rain or in the sun.
Breathe the air that blows from heaven
Deeply, thankfully.
It is Nature's medicine.
It's wonderful.   It's free.

❧ ❧ ❧ ❧ ❧

"THEY that wait upon the Lord shall renew their strength ; they shall mount up with wings as eagles ; they shall run, and not be weary ; and they shall walk, and not faint".
—Isaiah 40. 31

April 23rd

SHAKESPEARE

FROM the corners of the globe all creeds and colours meet
In the humble cottage of a little Stratford street.
And pilgrims walk the meadows where the Avon winds its way
The fields where Shakespeare must have dreamed on many an
April day.

Sacred are the trees that cast their shade about his head.
Hallowed are the cobblestones that echoed to his tread,
The boy who won a poet's crown of immortality
And carved a matchless name upon the scroll of history.

— — — — —

April 24th

THE SILENCE OF A WOOD

THE silence of a wood is a living silence. It is full of breath
and rustlings and movement. The wind stirs, a mere sigh
in the sentient trees. A sudden flutter of wings rips at the
quiet air and is lost in the muffled whisperings of startled
leaves. The crack of a distant shot emphasises the peace which
it disturbs. The trill of a bird sets up a soft ripple along the
surface of the stillness and the sob of doves beats like a hidden
pulse at the heart of the silence.

—From "Every Common Bush"

— — — — —

April 25th

THE PRUNING

DEATH came this way,
Sharp as a knife
Cutting through all our love and laughter.
Death came a-pruning
Leaving bare my life,
But blossom came after.

"THE law of the Lord is perfect, converting the soul : the testimony of the Lord is sure, making wise the simple".
—*Psalm 19. 7*

⌐ ⌐ ⌐ ⌐ ⌐

BUT THAT WAS YESTERDAY

THE outlook was a gloomy one,
And I had lost my way.
I saw no hope, no sign, no sun,
But that was yesterday.

⌐ ⌐ ⌐ ⌐ ⌐

THE GARDEN OF ENGLAND

KENT has everything : the Thames, the sea, an enchanting countryside, a long and ancient history, hops and strawberries, Canterbury, Knole and Penshurst, but the glory of Kent is the glory of her orchards when April passes over the little hills and valleys and the clowns' caps of the oast houses peep out from between great foaming masses of apple and cherry blossom. Spring touches every county with a fairy wand, but nowhere with such a magical effect as down in this old, old corner of the Island that in spite of the vandalism of the planners can still be called the Garden of England.

⌐ ⌐ ⌐ ⌐ ⌐

LILACTIDE

WHICH is the fairest month of all ? How hard it is to say — Once the Winter turns to Spring it's beauty all the way. From the time of daffodils until the woodlands blaze with the fiery splendour of the lovely autumn days. . . . Primrosetide and tuliptide and rich rose-scented June. Lammastide, the time of golden sheaf and harvest moon. All seem dearest in their turn, but when an April shower glitters through the lilacs, is this not the sweetest hour ? Lilactide. . . . Could anything be lovelier than this : rain-wet blossom opening beneath the sun's warm kiss. Through the dripping branches fragrance drifts and thrushes call — as God paints the glory of a rainbow over all.

GOODBYE APRIL

YOU can never say goodbye to April without a pang. All through the long dark months of Winter you dream of Spring, but when it comes all sorts of lovely things crowd in upon you at once and there is no time to stand still with your thoughts, gazing at the wonders and marvelling at the miracles. Rainbows, primroses, daffodils, bluebells, the return of the swallows and the blooming of the old apple tree. It all seems to happen in a rush. You can't keep pace with it. As soon as you realise that the daffodils are fading you see hawthorn in the hedges and buttercups in the meadows. But there is no time for shedding the tear that is in your heart as April disappears over the hills, for you are being rushed headlong full into the arms of Summer.

May 1st

MAY DAY

MAY Day conjures up the picture of a merry scene. Children dancing round the maypole on the village green. May Day was a day for play and long awaited joys, for dairy maids and shepherd lads and laughing girls and boys. . . . May Day takes us back to that great age in history — when poets sang with silver tongues and Drake was on the sea. For when we see our lovely land bedecked in May's gay dress — we think of Merrie England and the days of good Queen Bess.

May 2nd

LESSONS AND MEANINGS

AT the heart of every situation there is a lesson for you if you care to look for it and to learn it. No matter how baffling outward appearances may be, try and think your way quietly through to the meaning. Be still and listen to what God is saying to you in the language of circumstances.

May 3rd

THE BIRD OF DREAMS

WHEN the house is quiet with the coming of the night — wrapped about in rosy veils of softly fading light. The Bird of Dreams on silent wings comes to my windowsill. The clock chimes out the sunset hour, but Time itself stands still. Years are moments. In a flash I live the past again. I hear a voice, I see a face. I feel the joy and pain, as if it were but yesterday. What is this magic power — that calls up ghosts out of the shadows of the evening hour? . . . I light the lamp, and in the dazzle of the sudden glare — the vision goes. I look around, and there is no one there. But through the window in the dark, beyond the lamp's bright ray — I see the Bird of Dreams spread out its wings and fly away.

— — — — —

May 4th

OFF SONG

WHEN things go all wrong
And you're feeling off song
Do not think that you won't sing again.
Skies may frown, but they'll brighten,
Cares press, but they'll lighten
And sunshine come after the rain.
The songbirds can't sing
Summer, Winter and Spring.
Everything seems to swing to and fro,
First its music and gladness
Then silence and sadness.
No doubt Life was meant to be so.
You may feel subdued,
But it's only a mood,
It will pass, the dark cloud will depart.
Things will change without warning.
You'll wake up one morning
And find there's a song in your heart.

May 5th

OILING THE HINGES

DO not bolt the door of your mind and then wonder why nothing lovely ever happens to you. You must give free access into the house of your life if you want to receive God's blessings. You must live in a state of happy expectancy of good. Optimism is not just a cheery frame of mind ; it is a spiritual attitude towards life and it is essentially Christian. See that the hinges on the doors of your mind do not get rusty through lack of use. Oil them with prayer and keep them swinging, so that they offer no resistance to angels passing by in the traffic of daily experience.

—From "The Kingdom Within"

* * *

May 6th

A DREAM COME TRUE

THIS is what I dreamed about beside the fire's warm glow — in the bleak and bitter days of fog and frost and snow. This is what I pictured through the streaming window-pane, when it seemed that sunny days would never come again: lupins rainbow-tinted all along the border bed. Tulips massed in blazing groups of gold and rose and red.

This is what I longed for when the clouds hung dark and grey : the glory of the garden in the lovely month of May. Peonies and irises and wallflowers by the path. This is what I thought about beside the firelit hearth. This is what I have imagined all the winter through. This the golden dream I dreamed . . . and now it has come true.

* * *

May 7th

"ROUGH winds do shake the darling buds of May,
And summer's lease hath all too short a date".

—Shakespeare

May 8th

PHILOSOPHY

WE boast of our philosophy when things are going well.
It's not until Life puts it to the test that we can tell —
what it's worth and whether it is false or genuine. Basking in
the golden glow of Fortune's smile we spin — the threads of
fancy and of fact, of thought and theory — into pretty patterns
that we call philosophy. . . . A puff of wind — away it
goes — the work of many years. A sudden storm, and what
becomes of all our grand ideas ! We stand alone exposed to
every bleak and bitter gust — having no protection and no
truth that we can trust. . . . We must weave into our webs
a faith that's real and strong — something that will help us
stand the test when things go wrong. Not until Fate turns
against us do we really see — the strength, the weakness and
the worth of our philosophy.

— — — — —

May 9th

HOMING PIGEONS

ACROSS the vast and trackless distance of the boundless
sky — over meadow, moor and sea the homing pigeons
fly. By what mystic knowledge do they make their homeward
flight, guided by a sure unerring instinct day and night ? In
a measure we possess this homing instinct too. Fo no matter
how our thoughts wing out into the blue, they turn towards
the homes we've loved when lost in reverie : the childhood
homes of long ago, so dear in memory. And though we have
the wanderlust and venture far afield — we have the instinct
to return, and to this urge we yield. It is stronger than the
passing whims that make us roam — and in time it gets us
all . . . the longing to come home.

THINK IT OVER

WHEN the tides of anger rise,
Think it over.
Don't be hasty,
Wait, be wise,
Think it over.
Don't fly off into a rage
Your hurt feelings to assuage,
Keep your temper,
Be your age,
Think it over.
You may lose more than you gain,
Think it over.
Just go slowly.
Pull the rein,
Think it over.
Think before you bark or bite,
When tomorrow comes you might,
See things in a different light
Think it over.

FATHER'S PIPE

HIS forehead may be lined with care, but when he settles in his chair — and lights his pipe. . . . Peace reigns supreme. He sinks into a silent dream — and one by one the wrinkles clear as trials and troubles disappear.

O magic pipe ! You must contain the anodyne for all life's pain. What other joy could ever smoothe — the furrowed brow ? What else could soothe with pleasure that could so beguile — and turn a frown into a smile ?

The outlook may be bleak and grim. The world go mad. What's that to him ? as he sits beside the fire, puffing at his favourite briar—meditating dreamily in a secret reverie. All is well and worries cease — when Father smokes the pipe of peace.

May 12th

SQUARE DEALER

BE a square dealer,
You'll find it will pay,
Always be honest and just.
Be a fair dealer
And never betray
Those who accept you on trust.
Someone may play you a trick that is mean
But cling to your own high ideal,
See to it that your own record is clean
And give every man a square deal.

~ ~ ~ ~ ~

May 13th

"THE fear of the Lord tendeth to life : and he that hath it shall abide satisfied ; he shall not be visited with evil".

—*Proverbs 19. 23*

~ ~ ~ ~ ~

May 14th

HUMOUR

HUMOUR is the spice of life. Without it we should be — dull and solemn, working out our problems gloomily. We'd be at the mercy of each bitter pen or tongue. Humour makes us tolerant, and keeps us gay and young. . . . If you have a sense of humour you will always find — something to amuse you when the world has proved unkind. Humour saves your sanity when you are taxed and tried — helping you to see the comic touch, the funny side.

May 15th

IN A HURRY

EVERYONE seems in a hurry, running here and there.
Speeding blindly down the roads and flying through the
air. Record-breaking liners throb their way from port to
port — and communications flash like lightning, quick as
thought. Everybody in a hurry, dashing to and fro. What
it's all about nobody really seems to know. Time alone
remains the same. You can't speed up the clock. It goes on at
the same old pace : tick-tock, tick-tock, tick-tock.

May 16th

AN ENGLISHMAN IN EXILE

BY the light of memory he wanders once again
Following the pilgrims down a Canterbury lane.
And through a golden mist of dreams the spires of Oxford rise
Beautiful against the cloudy blue of summer skies.
In the freedom of his thought he ranges far and wide
From Somerset to Windermere, from Thames to Severnside.
Birdsong in a Surrey wood and boom of Devon foam
Mingle in a single voice to call the exile home.

May 17th

THE BUNDLE

THE stork called round one morning at Number Forty
Eight — and left a little bundle outside the garden gate.
A funny crinkled wrinkled scrap enveloped in a shawl : two
eyes, ten toes, a button nose and fingers pink and small.

It caused a great commotion. The news went round the
town. The house was in a ferment, the place turned upside
down. The peace was rudely shattered. The wee mite in the
shawl — had become the most important personage of all.

Through the strange adventure that we call a human
birth — God had sent another pilgrim out upon the earth.
Another soul had entered on the mystery of life : the rapture
and the agony, the glory and the strife.

May 18th

HAPPY TOMORROW

SOME people never find joy in the present,
They cling to their woe and their sorrow,
Missing the blessings right under their noses
While dreaming of good things tomorrow.

Some folk don't notice the sun when it's shining
Or hear when the songbirds are singing,
They're so busy looking across the horizon
To see what the future is bringing.

Some never think Life is good at the moment.
To them it is futile and hollow.
So with a shrug and a sigh of self-pity
They sit down and wait for tomorrow.

May 19th

THE SWEETEST SONG OF ALL

IN the woods the choirs have massed, and through the arches of the trees — Golden throated music breaks in waves of joy upon the breeze. Thrush and blackbird, lark and linnet, willow-warbler, finch and wren — sing the day out to its close. But when the last has sung Amen — Darkness falls, and from the thickets where the white moon sails — Comes the sweetest song of all . . . the song of nightingales.

May 20th

YOUNG AGAIN

LOVELY are the lanes of England when the hedges are in flower. Fragrant is the scent of may that drifts from every cottage bower. Charming are the little gardens where the wayside orchards grow, when the lupins line the borders and the lilac tassels blow. . . . Everything is fresh and sparkling, warmed by sun and washed with rain. May has waved her magic wand and all the world is young again.

DERWENTWATER

I KNOW a place where silver waters lap the shores where mountains rise — lifting up their misty ranges to the wide cloud-haunted skies. . . . I know a place of fairy islands, verdant vale and tumbling stream — where Nature speaks through lakes and hills the language of a poet's dream.

⸺　⸺　⸺　⸺　⸺

THE GARDEN PATH

WHERE does it lead, the garden path?
To the lily pond where the blackbirds bath?
Or the rustic seat where the old trees lean
To make a bower of gold and green?

It does not lead to the pool at all,
Or the wicket gate in the orchard wall.
It leads you into a world apart,
To the garden of dreams that is in your heart.

⸺　⸺　⸺　⸺　⸺

THE TRAVELLER

WHEN he comes to the end of the road of life his hands are scarred and worn. His feet are sore and weary and his garments stained and torn. . . . But if he reached the Sunset Gate unsoiled, untouched, unscarred — It may be that the traveller would find the gateway barred. His rags and wounds are proof that he has borne a heavy load — Has fought with giants along the way and come by the hardest road.

May 24th

BEFORE YOU'VE TRIED

NEVER say you cannot reach that peak beyond the blue. Never say you've failed to do the thing you meant to do. Never say that anything on earth has beaten you. . . . Before you've tried.

Never drop out of the race until the course is run. Don't admit of failure or defeat to anyone. And if a thing looks difficult — don't say it can't be done. . . . Before you've tried.

— — — — —

May 25th

WEATHERCOCK

TURNING this way, turning that way, as the breezes blow. Pointing to whichever way the winds of heaven go. Having no direction and no spirit of its own — No will to move or to resist, except as it is blown. . . . All too often we behave just like the weathercock — fickle, feckless, veering round with every passing shock. Facing sunwards for a time, then gloomy dull and sad — according to our mood and to the kind of day we've had. . . . But if we live according to a true philosophy — we are not at the mercy of the winds of destiny.

— — — — —

May 26th

FAITH WITHOUT WORKS

FAITH without works brings no glittering prize. Hope without effort is hope that soon dies. Life without service is futile and vain. Love without labour no glory can gain. . . . Creeds high and lofty in fine terms expressed — are worthless until they've been put to the test. Prayer without practice will meet no man's needs. Talk without sacrifice, words without deeds.

May 27th

" AND the Lord God formed man of the dust of the ground,
and breathed into his nostrils the breath of life ; and man
became a living soul".

—Genesis 2. 7

- - - - -

May 28th

LOVE LAUGHS AT DEATH

LOVE is enough. We do not ask to hear
The well loved voice, nor do we seek to see
The angel form. Sufficient for the heart
  Faith, and the peace that heals its agony.
Love waits unchanged through all the changing years
  Fed by the streams of living memory.
Love laughs at death. For death is but a dream
  From which we wake to immortality.

- - - - -

May 29th

FRIENDS IN ADVERSITY

FRIENDS in adversity ! . . . These are the real friends.
These are the true friends, the finest, the best — Those who
come forward your burdens to share with you — proving
their love for you. . . . This is the test.

Fair weather pals you'll find, sharing your pleasures —
when fortune is smiling and everything's grand. . . . But
give me the friend who will weather the storm with you — give
you encouragement, lend you a hand.

Friends in adversity ! Have we not found them ? Time
teaches many things, changing our view. Tearing the mask
from the false and the trivial — making us value the real and
the true.

LIVING THE BIG WAY

LIVE in the big way, the way that Christ taught. Big in your judgments, your outlook, your thought. . . . Generous, tolerant, thinking no ill. Lavish in charity, rich in good will. Stoop not to pettiness, things mean and small. Live in a big world — there's room for us all. Cast off your grievances, start out anew. Live life the big way, and take the broad view.

〜 〜 〜 〜 〜

May 31st

MAY has been as fitful as April, capricious and unpredictable, but the past few days have been warm and lovely. Another May passes into memory. Not for another year shall we see again the azure haze of the bluebell woods, the gold of the buttercup meadows and the fresh tender green of the Maytime hedges. The roses, impatient of the calendar, are already peeping at the lattices and opening their folded buds against the sun-warmed brickwork on the south wall. June is at the gate with her finger on the latch.

〜 〜 〜 〜 〜

June 1st

THE GIFT OF JUNE

JUNE comes again to place on earth's warm breast — her sweetest gift, the fairest and the best. Roses their velvet-hearted blooms unfold — crimson and apricot, ivory and gold. . . . In stately grounds and in the cottage beds. In park and plot they lift their lovely heads. Yet when they come my heart remembers Time. Is not the year already near its prime?

June 2nd
SHOW A LITTLE GRATITUDE

SHOW a little gratitude when someone's helping you. Go out of your way to say a little word or two. No reward is sweeter than a thank you and a smile. Compensates for trouble taken ; makes it seem worth while. . . . Oftentimes we take for granted all the kindliness — of people near and dear to us. By deed, word or caress — we can show we know and notice and appreciate. There's nothing half so sad as to remember this . . . too late.

⌐ ⌐ ⌐ ⌐ ⌐

June 3rd

"CREATE in me a clean heart, O God ; and renew a right spirit within me. Cast me not away from thy presence ; and take not thy holy spirit from me. Restore unto me the joy of thy salvation."

—Psalm 51. 10-12

⌐ ⌐ ⌐ ⌐ ⌐

June 4th

ROUND the arbours of remembrance
 Youth's unfading roses climb,
And the hidden seeds of friendship
 Grow between the stones of Time.

⌐ ⌐ ⌐ ⌐ ⌐

June 5th
AT THE STILE

THERE'S nothing half so lovely as to lean against a stile. Lost in thoughts of sweet contentment, resting for awhile. Breathing in the country air and listening to the birds — conscious of a peace of mind too deep for spoken words . . . thinking of the people who have sat on those same bars — lovers who have lingered there beneath the evening stars — sun-tanned workers from the fields upon their homeward way — young folks strolling back from church upon the Sabbath day.

June 6th

THE NEW DAY

TO be given a new day is to be given a new lease of life. Don't snatch at God's gifts without a thank you as if your mere existence entitled you to expect a fresh supply of blessings every morning. Accept the gift of the new day with reverence, grace and gratitude.

—From "The Morning Watch"

~ ~ ~ ~ ~

June 7th

SWEET PEAS

DELICATE and beautiful and vivid as the sunset skies — a mass of sweetness, like a cloud of pink and crimson butterflies. Are they flowers, these moth-like things with brightly tinted wings of flame ? Sweet peas . . . that is what they're called — but can such beauty have a name ?

~ ~ ~ ~ ~

June 8th

NO GOING BACK

THE path of daily life is strewn with opportunities passed by — with beauty trodden underfoot and flowers of friendship left to die. Good intentions, lofty aims and high resolves that faded out — in the dust of disappointment, fear, frustration, failure, doubt. . . . Oh, if we could only turn and go back just a mile or two — To say the things we should have said, and do the things we meant to do !

~ ~ ~ ~ ~

June 9th

THE SONG OF THE STREAM

WHAT is it saying, that gay little stream as it goes babbling along ? Year in and year out repeating itself with its monotonous song. It never gets weary or changes its tone, or tries out some other refrain. It just goes on singing the same little phrase, over and over again. . . . And yet it comes fresh to my ears every time. I never grow bored with that theme. All day I could listen and never get tired of hearing the song of the stream.

TO A BABE

POOR little pilgrim starting out upon your journey through this life ! Little do you know of all the pain, the peril and the strife. You've come into a mad bad world. Well might we wonder why you came, to travel on so rough a road. You look so sweet — it seems a shame. The times are grim. One almost feels it was a sin to give you birth. And yet, who knows ? Your eyes may see God's kingdom come upon the earth.

~ ~ ~ ~ ~

June 11th
THE WINDOWS OF THE HEART

SHUT not your mind against the joys of life. Songbirds still call and sunlight gleams. Send forth your questing thoughts on wings of hope. Open the casement of your dreams. . . . Live not in shuttered gloom of vain regrets — in mental darkness set apart. Happiness beckons you and new life calls. Open the windows of your heart.

~ ~ ~ ~ ~

June 12th

AN OLD STREET

I LOVE an old street in an old fashioned town — a street that goes wandering uphill and down. A street that wakes echoes wherever you tread, and quaint timbered gables lean over your head. Where sunlight and shadow make patches of gold — on bricks, tiles and cobblestones centuries old. . . . I love an old street where you see at a glance — glimpses of history, beauty, romance.

YOUR JOB IN LIFE

WHATEVER you do, do the best that you can — and do it with joy and good cheer. For each individual God has a plan. A mission, a job to do here. . . . So find out the purpose intended for you — that nobody else could fulfil — and bend every effort that aim to pursue, with all of your heart and your will. . . . All other paths are but byways that lead — to failure, frustration, unrest. Find your own niche if you want to succeed — and richly your work will be blessed.

- - - - -

BREAD IN THE MAKING

BREAD in the making . . . the green turns to gold — and over far vistas the eye can behold — the wheatfields spread wide over valleys and hills — Grain for the granaries, grist for the mills. In these broad acres good promise we see — rich and abundant the harvest will be. . . . Nature beneficent ; here is no dearth. . . . Bread in the making — God's gift to the earth.

- - - - -

A RIVERSIDE HOLIDAY

IF you're weary, longing for a restful holiday — shun the crowds and spend your leisure in a quiet way. Find some little river where the shady willows lean — a river that goes wandering by meadows cool and green. . . . It may not be as thrilling as the music of the sea — But listen to the gentle water flowing dreamily. No golden sands, no wheeling gulls, no waves, no rolling tide — But you'll find rest and peace and beauty by the riverside.

June 16th

THE BORDERLANDS

LOVELY are the borderlands where Wales and England meet — the secret lands of hidden vale and mountainous retreat. A chain of noble castles marks the ancient boundary — from Chepstow to the old walled town of Chester on the Dee.

Blood and tongue are mingled here where once were feud and strife — loyalties and cultures merged into a common life. . . . And here is beauty unsurpassed, unspoiled by vandal hands : the wild romantic beauty of the lonely borderlands.

June 17th

WHAT WE NEED

A LITTLE more laughter, a little more song. A little more music to help us along. A little less talk and a little more "do". That's what is needed to carry us through. . . . A little more faith and a little more fire — would give us the kind of a world we desire. A little more bread and a little less cake. A little more give and a little less take.

June 18th

AT THE OTHER END OF NOWHERE

AT the other end of nowhere off the track of road and rail — there's a lost and lonely cottage in a lost and lovely vale. . . . In a deep forgotten corner of a far forgotten place — in a land of mist and shadow at the edge of time and space.

If I looked in at the window would there be strange faces there ? Should I find a sleeping beauty or a witch with night-black hair ? . . . I shall never know the answer for I'll never find the trail — to that lost and lonely cottage in the lost and lovely vale.

STRANGE SOIL

FAITH blossoms in the strangest soil,
   Where once was doubt and unbelief,
A seed of faith takes root and grows
   Out of an old and bitter grief.
And flowers of faith are loveliest
   Where there has fallen dew of tears.
God raises up his sweetest blooms
   Out of the sorrows of the years.

— — — — —

ON THE CREDIT SIDE

BENEFITS and blessings, compensations big and small.
Check them up. You'll find life's not so hopeless after
all. . . . Difficulties may increase and trials be multiplied —
but don't forget to count the entries on the credit side.

— — — — —

LIGHT IN DARKNESS

LET your love so shine about the world in which you live —
that others may be warmed and gladdened by the light you
give. Trim the lamps of faith and keep them burning constantly — serving man and praising God wherever you may
be.

> "Let your light so shine before men that they
> may see your good works . . ."
>
> —*Matthew 5. 16*

June 22nd

THE NEW FOREST

HERE grew the oaks, the mighty oaks from whose stout hearts our fathers made — the wooden walls of Nelson's day : the little English ships that laid — the first foundations of our strength upon the waters of the sea ; the glory of our naval power, the greatness of our history.

Here grew the yews, the noble yews, from which the archer's bow was made. Here in this Hampshire wilderness of rambling wood and cloistered glade. . . . Here where the immemorial trees about your path their shadows cast — the wind blows through the boughs and brings a haunting echo from the past.

June 23rd

HARD TO BELIEVE

IT'S hard to believe that every cloud has got a silver lining — although we know that behind the grey the sun is always shining. . . . It's hard to believe in happiness and in a bright Tomorrow — when under the shadow of some great grief, anxiety or sorrow. . . . It's hard to believe that clouds will pass and sorrow have an ending — but no wound's too deep for God to heal, no broken heart past mending.

June 24th

WORDS OF ENCOURAGEMENT

A WORD of encouragement means a lot to those who are trying to do their best. It helps them put in that extra bit with a lighter heart and a greater zest. . . . A word of praise where there's credit due — is never wasted or out of place. It will put a song in a weary heart and bring a smile to a frowning face.

"TAKE therefore no thought for the morrow : for the morrow shall take thought for the things of itself. Sufficient unto the day is the evil thereof."

—Matthew 6. 34

June 26th

HURDLES

THERE are many hurdles on the course that you must run. No race for any worth while prize could be an easy one. Difficulties have to be surmounted every day. Obstacles rise up across your path to bar the way. . . . If there were no hurdles tame and dull the race would be. You'd never have to brace yourself to act courageously. You have to learn to make a jump although the hurdle's high — perhaps to take a tumble, and to have another try.

June 27th

KEEP YOUR PROMISES

ALWAYS keep your promises if you would keep your friends. Keep your word no matter what the cost. Confidence is not restored by making swift amends. It's hard to win back trust when once it's lost. . . . Don't make idle promises. Make sure that you can see — just how you're going to do the thing you say. Once you give your word you are committed morally — and having started must go all the way.

June 28th

THE MYSTERY

WHY one and one alone in all the world should mean so much — and cause the heart to miss a beat by glance or word or touch. Why one and not another has the power to cast a spell — of magic over everything is something none can tell. Nobody can guess the answer, clever though they be. For no mere man has yet unravelled Love's sweet mystery.

VAIN REGRETS

DO not waste regrets upon the things you meant to do : fallen castles, broken dreams and friends that proved untrue. The effort that you failed to make, the prize you might have gained — the hopes that crashed all unfulfilled, successes unattained.

Profit from your past mistakes. Draw wisdom from your pain. Look beneath the surface for the meaning. Start again. Deepened by experiences that have come your way — building your tomorrow on the ruins of today.

June 27th

EASY TO SMILE

IT'S easy to smile when you haven't a care and there isn't a cloud in the blue — When you're happily sitting on top of the world and enjoying the beautiful view. . . . It's easy to smile when it's bright all the while, facing life with a jest and a song — but the time to be cheery is when you feel weary and everything's going all wrong.

June 28th

"TIME wastes us, our bodies and our wits
And we waste time : so time and we are quits."

—*From an old sundial*

June 29th

WAIT TILL THEY ARRIVE

DON'T go out to look for troubles, meeting them halfway.
Don't anticipate disaster. Live from day to day. When
they're really on your step and knocking at the door. That's
the time to start to worry. Then and not before.

Life's made up of trials and troubles, problems big and
small — but half the things we dread don't come to anything
at all. If fears could kill there wouldn't be a lot of us alive.
Troubles you are bound to meet, but wait till they arrive.

June 30

OVER in Punchbowl Meadow the grass has been mown
and stacked and the evening air is sweet with the heavy
scent of new hay, but the field beyond the gate is still uncut
and you wander thigh-deep through a wavy sea of sorrel,
moon daisies, faded buttercups and feathery grasses. The
banks along the lane are gay with meadowsweet, agrimony
and ragged robin ; the hedges are garlanded with honeysuckle and wild roses ; the old elder tree spreads its creamy
corymbs by the cottage gate and the lily buds are bursting on
the pool in the shaw. Lovely beyond all telling are the quiet
fields in the evening hour at June's end, a picture to hang in
the galleries of memory, to come back to and gaze at when
the glory is vanished and the winter nigh.

July 1st

THE PRESENCE

IN a quiet garden where birds and flowers abound
   Speak gently and tread softly,
   You walk on holy ground.
For unto every garden God cometh secretly
   His presence there disclosing
   To all with eyes to see.

—

"And they heard the voice of the Lord God
   walking in the garden in the cool of the day."
                                        —*Genesis 3. 8*

62

LIVING AND LEARNING

THINGS that would have made us angry in our younger days — cease to rile. We learn to smile, and go from phase to phase, gathering experience with every twist and turn — profiting from failures and mistakes . . . We live and learn.

We were given powers of reason, ears and tongues and eyes — not for mere enjoyment but to make us strong and wise. Many lessons we must master, some are hard and stern — but that's how we progress, for only thus we live and learn.

If your troubles have not taught you to philosophise — then you've missed the point of Life. You've failed to realise— that happiness is not a gift, but something you must earn. To live is not enough. We're put on earth to live . . . and learn.

July 3rd

GOD'S OWN GARDEN

IN God's garden you will find no formal paths for you to tread — No ornaments of lifeless stone, no plan, no trim and tidy bed. It has no fence to close it in ; no privet hedges and no wall. No bolted gates to keep you out. The countryside is free to all. . . . Flowers of every kind and colour here grow wild beneath your feet : clover, poppy, honeysuckle, pimpernel and meadowsweet.

July 4th

THE year is half gone. For a few more weeks we shall keep the sweet illusion of high summer, but gradually now the songs of the birds will fade into muted twitterings. There will be a feeling of heaviness in the thick woods, the deep drowsiness that follows upon fulfilment. There is still much to anticipate : the pageantry of the mid-summer garden and the harvesting of corn and fruit, but he who is in tune with the moods of the earth will experience a sense of impending change. The blaze of noon has passed, and imperceptibly we have turned our faces towards the sunset of the year.

THE WAY, THE TRUTH AND THE LIFE

" JESUS saith unto him, I am the way, the truth and the life : no man cometh unto the Father, but by me."

—John 14. 6

~ ~ ~ ~ ~

NOT AFRAID

DO not be afraid of Life, the pain, the peril and the strife. Do not shrink with fear and dread from the things that lie ahead. Do not be afraid to try — for no goal can be too high. You may fail, but don't complain. You can always try again.

Do not be afraid to speak. To adventure and to seek. Do not be afraid to live. Fortune has rich gifts to give — to the one who does not shirk, knowing how to wait and work. Do not be afraid to be — master of your destiny.

~ ~ ~ ~ ~

ALWAYS A HOPE

THERE'S always a hope though it may be quite small There's always a star, though the darkness may fall. There's always a glimmer of gold in the grey and always a flower growing wild by the way. . . . There's always a song floating out on the air. There's always a dawn to the night of despair. There's always a path for the faithful to tread and always a bend in the roadway ahead. . . . There's always a chance, but you've got to believe. You've got to be ready to see and receive, the hints and the signs although faint they appear — to wait and to trust till the meaning grows clear. . . . And when through the murk of the shadows you grope — You've got to remember — there's always a hope.

July 8th

THE AQUARIUM

WE wonder at the Mind behind such vast variety — when we're looking at the things that live down in the sea. Fish : the monstrous and minute, of every kind and size — wonderful creations that have gills and fins and eyes. Through the water we can see the flash of silver scales, the glint and gleam of gliding shapes, the flickering of tails — the opalescent shells, the floating weeds, the rocks, the sand — Every tank reveals the marvels of a wonderland.

July 9th

WEAR A SMILE

A LITTLE smile works wonders, enhancing charm and looks. And though you may not see it in the beauty books — It's a tip worth having. You'll take it if you're wise. It banishes the wrinkles and lights the tired eyes. You may make every effort to dress in perfect style — but it will all be wasted unless you wear a smile.

July 10th

FORGIVING

LET us forgive and try to cast old hurts out of our hearts — the thorn that presses on a nerve, the wound that throbs and smarts — ingratitude, inconstancy, injustice and foul play — Forgive it and forget it. Fling the memory away — and start again, free from the pain of grudges held too long. Every question has two sides, and maybe YOU were wrong.

July 11th

CODE OF THE ROAD

I VOW today to go my way, determined not to speed.
This day right now I take the vow that I will always heed
The regulations of the road ; the signals and the lights
Keeping in my mind the thought of other people's rights.
Selfishness and recklessness may lead me to a smash
Causing death or even worse all in a moment's flash.
Is it worth the risk to gain a minute or a mile
Thinking in my folly that I'm driving in fine style ?
Lack of thought for other drivers might well prove to be
A perilous and most expensive business for *me*.
So on this and every day I vow to keep the code
And do my own small bit towards the safety of the road.

⌐ ⌐ ⌐ ⌐ ⌐

July 12th

DAILY TASKS

DO not make a hardship of the things you have to do.
Don't regard them as a bore, it all depends on you —
whether you enjoy your work or whether it's a strain. You
make your own conditions by the thoughts inside your
brain. . . . It's your mental attitude. Yourself. Your frame
of mind. Some folk let things weigh them down, and others
are inclined — to take a different point of view, and do with
willing hands — all the little things that go to make up life's
demands. . . . Do not frown or make a fuss or grumble at
your lot. If there's something to be done then do it on the
spot. Welcoming the chance to do a service great or small.
Isn't that just what you're put on earth for, after all ?

⌐ ⌐ ⌐ ⌐ ⌐

July 13th

"MY soul is detached
From everything created,
And raised above itself
Into a life delicious,
Of God alone supported."
—St. John of the Cross

July 14th

RIPPLING WATER

THIS is peace . . . sublime, profound. To lie and listen to the sound — of seas that flow melodiously — in tides of rhythmic harmony. The lilt of rippling water has the power to calm the mind — on the shore or in the woods where hidden streamlets wind.

— — — — —

July 15th

THE THIMBLE

A THIMBLE . . . just a little thing, but a little thing can bring — memories that come with tears, conjuring out of the years, a dear sweet ghost that stirs again — forgotten scenes of joy and pain. . . . Are you there ? I can't believe — that my own eyes would deceive. In your old accustomed chair, I can see you sitting there — stitching in the lamplight's glow — just as in the long ago. . . . So you've cheated Death, my dear ! And you've found your way back here, taking up your work again : silver thimble, silken skein. . . . Many times I dreamed you came. Many times I've called your name, but you chose to stay away. Strange it is that now today — this small thimble in my hand — brings you from that Other Land.

— — — — —

July 16th

MOTHER-IN-LAW

THE loveliest words that have ever passed between one woman and another were spoken by Ruth to her mother-in-law Naomi when her husband had died and Naomi was preparing to return to her own country. These words were not spoken in the first happy flush of getting to know each other, but after ten years of the mother-in-law daughter-in-law relationship. It is a pity that they cannot be read at every marriage service.

"And Ruth said, Intreat me not to leave thee, or to return from following after thee : for whither thou goest, I will go ; and where thou lodgest, I will lodge : thy people shall be my people, and thy God my God. Where thou diest, will I die, and there will I be buried : the Lord do so to me, and more also, if ought but death part thee and me."

—Ruth 1. 16

FOXGLOVES

OF all the lovely things that grow in summer's golden hours — the foxglove is the loveliest. She lifts her purple towers — above the wildflowers at her feet. She needs no gardener's hands — to tend her. Proud and dignified in regal pride she stands. . . . And every time there comes a sudden rush of wind or wing — the stately steeples rock and all the fairy clappers swing. If mortal ear could hear the chiming of the foxglove bell — would it be a joyous pealing or a solemn knell ?

July 18th

"THOSE who wish to forget painful thoughts, do well to absent themselves for awhile from the ties and objects that recall them : but we can be said only to fulfil our destiny in the place that gave us birth. I should on this account like well enough to spend the whole of my life in travelling abroad, if I could anywhere borrow another life to spend afterwards at home ! "

—Hazlitt

July 19th

THE WHEATFIELD

THE ripening wheat is like a rolling sea of green and gold — and when the vagrant wind goes by how lovely to behold, the gentle heaving of the wheat beneath the summer sky — swept with moving shadows as the clouds go drifting by.

Here and there a scarlet poppy flares out vividly — like a red sail on the waters of a restless sea — dipping with the passing breeze upon the waves they ride — borne upon the golden billows of the rising tide.

July 20th

APPLES OF GOLD

" A WORD fitly spoken is like apples of gold
in pictures of silver".

—*Proverbs 25. 11*

〜　〜　〜　〜　〜

July 21st

STOP THE CLOCK!

THE Summer's zenith has been passed,
The longest day has come and gone,
The fields are mown, the hay is stacked,
Oh, why must Time go rolling on ?
The corn has ripened in the sun
The fruit turns red upon the spray.
If only I could stop the clock
And hold this fair and lovely day !

〜　〜　〜　〜　〜

July 22nd

ONCE YOU'RE ROUND THE BEND

SOMETHING unexpected may be around the bend.
Something to encourage you, a lift, a gift, a friend. . . .
Something that will strengthen you to face the road ahead —
spurring you along upon the pathway that you tread.

Do not halt or waver. Go forward. Keep straight on.
Even if the reason for confidence has gone — Just go on
believing that things are on the mend. Life may look quite
different, once you're round the bend.

〜　〜　〜　〜　〜

July 23rd

LOVE'S PHILOSOPHY

IF we have each other, nothing matters, come what may.
Life to us will bring new hope with every passing day. . . .
Alone I halt and falter, but together we go far. Love shall be
our guide, our sunset lamp, our morning star.

EBB AND FLOW

WHEN you watch the ebbing tide you know without a doubt — that it will come back again. You see it going out — but at its own appointed moment it will rise once more — flowing in to reach again its mark upon the shore.

So it is in life. The tides of fortune ebb and flow. Joys recede and troubles come — but this we surely know . . . that God is good. And if in hope and patience we abide — happiness will come again upon the turning tide.

INTO THE NIGHT

WHEN I go out into the night beyond this world of ours, I dare not hope to find at once the shining heavenly bowers,
No saintly halo have I won, no crown, no angel wings
For I've been busy all my life just doing little things.

It may be I shall have to go a long and toilsome way,
It may be cold and dark and lonely. That is why I pray
That when God calls me home at last unto that far abode
I'll meet some dear familiar face upon the unknown road.

TRUE FRIENDSHIP

THOUGH meetings may be far apart and years roll in between. Time can never change true friendship. It is evergreen. Affection that has stood the test of life's experience — the love of one who never doubts and never takes offence. . . . This is God's most precious gift, and as our way we wend — we find the greatest thing of all if we can find a friend.

CONVALESCENCE

NATURE does the healing work and slowly strength returns again. Secretly she makes and mends : a marvel no one can explain. But the process can't be hurried ; hour by hour and day by day. God restores to health and wholeness in His own mysterious way. Surgeons do their skilful job, but Nature does the miracle. She performs the healing work, the part that's strange and wonderful.

~ ~ ~ ~ ~

July 28th

CHANGES

WHEN upheavals shake your world and bring a sudden change — Do not be afraid of what is new to you and strange. Adapt yourself to fresh conditions. Make another start. Accept the role that life assigns you. Play a different part. . . . Someday you'll be glad that you were jolted from your groove. Out into an unknown future be prepared to move — looking forward, pushing onward, boldly, hopefully. Changes often force the door of opportunity.

~ ~ ~ ~ ~

July 29th

TIMING

YOU cannot master the art of happy and successful living until you have mastered the technique of timing, knowing when to do a certain thing, and knowing the psychological moment when it is finished. There is always a right time to say the right thing, and there are times when any word will be the wrong word. Ecclesiastes, the old religious philosopher writing over six hundred years before the birth of Christ understood the importance of timing. "There is a season and a time to every purpose under the heaven" he says. . . . "A time to rend, and a time to sew ; a time to keep silence and a time to speak."

July 30th

SEA MOODS

YOU cannot look out at the sea and not be moved at all —
by the endless wonder of the waves that rise and fall. The
restless tides that ebb and flow in darkness and in light —
swing to an eternal rhythm, morning, noon and night. . . .
Gold and azure, green and silver, different every day. Blue
and tranquil in the sun, then stormy wild and grey. Breaking
in an angry roar, then sighing peacefully. There's a fascin-
ation in the ever-changing sea.

July 31st

JULY slips off the calendar. The farmer looks anxiously at
his ripening corn and weighs the chances of a good harvest.
School holidays have begun and crowds of holidaymakers are
flocking to the seaside. The verges of woods and meadows are
embroidered with the lovely rosebay willowherb, the hedges
garlanded with traveller's joy and the banks of the stream
down in the shaw are gay with meadow-rue and purple
loosestrife. In the garden, the first of the chrysanthemums
keep company with the last of the delphiniums in the crowded
borders where the lemon and cherry-coloured spikes of the
gladioli are thrusting up between tangled masses of gaillardias,
coreopsis, gypsophila, clarkia and marigolds. In the rosebed
Madame Butterfly looks a little weary. Lady Forteviot and
The Doctor seem to be taking a rest. Caroline Testout and
Ophelia are still putting up a show, but it is the Poulsen poly-
anthas that are holding the stage at the moment with their
gorgeous trusses of pink and crimson blooms. Every day now
we shall move a little nearer to Summer's ending, but there is
no time for regrets. There's always some new thing waiting
round the corner, some new loveliness to be perceived, some
new joy to be experienced.

THE PASSING OF SUMMER

IF it were always summertime how weary we should grow —
of the changeless weather and the sun's unfading glow ! If
there were always roses blooming down the garden ways —
they would not call forth from the heart such words of joy
and praise.

It is the expectation of the sunshine and the flowers —
that makes us welcome with delight the summer's golden
hours. . . . The waiting in the winter and the hoping in the
Spring. It's twice as sweet because we know that Time is on
the wing.

⌣ ⌣ ⌣ ⌣ ⌣

THERE'S ALWAYS AN ANSWER

THERE'S always a solution when a problem you've been
set. There always is a way in which the challenge can be
met. There always is a means of getting over every fence —
with just a little patience and a bit of common sense.

There's an answer to the question. Never have a doubt.
You will get it if you are resolved to work it out. A way round
every difficulty you can always find — if you really tackle it,
determined in your mind.

⌣ ⌣ ⌣ ⌣ ⌣

MAKE SOMEBODY HAPPY

MAKE somebody happy every day of every week.
    Write a letter, give a treat or word of kindness speak.
Make things better for another, something do or say
    To lighten someone else's load or brighten someone's day.
Go out of your way to warm a heart that's hard and cold.
    Give out love and you will find it comes back sevenfold.
Every day make someone glad, or someone's faith sustain,
    And in the evening you will know you have not lived in vain.

"AND they shall beat their swords into plowshares, and their spears into pruning hooks : nation shall not lift up sword against nation, neither shall they learn war any more."
—Isaiah 2. 4

CHILDREN BY THE SEA

COULD there be a happier sight than youngsters by the sea — with their boats and balls and buckets playing merrily? Lovely are their small brown limbs by air and sunshine tanned — paddling at the water's edge and romping on the sand. . . . Busy building castles with their spades and pails they go — up and down the crowded beaches, running to and fro. If you've lost your joy in life, don't hug your misery. Go and look at little children playing by the sea.

WAIT BEFORE YOU WONDER

WAIT before you wonder what Tomorrow may unfold. Wait before you worry as to what it's going to hold. Do not peer in fear along the road that lies ahead. Many things may happen to prevent the thing you dread. . . . Do you really think that only evil things can be ? Do you not believe in God ? Then trust Him utterly. Live in hope and confidence, by nothing be depressed — then you'll draw unto yourself the good things and the best.

YOU'LL WIN

HIDE your tears, but show your smiles ; the world needs happiness. Keep your fears but share your joys, and don't let others guess, the secret sorrows of the heart for these things are your own. All have burdens they must learn to bear, and bear alone. . . . Try to walk with head held high, unbowed by grief or loss — never seeking sympathy, but carrying your cross — leaning not on others but upon the Power within. Then no matter what you have to battle through — You'll win.

KEEP ON DREAMING

KEEP on dreaming. . . . That's the way to make a dream come true. Keep on building all the while your castles in the blue. Never think you're wasting time in planning lovely things. Dare to reach out for the rainbow. Let your thoughts take wings. Fix your eyes upon the stars and follow where they guide. Every day's a new adventure and the world is wide. Hold on to your heart's desire though folly it may seem. Do not be afraid to pray, to hope, to wish, to dream.

∽　∽　∽　∽　∽

GRAIN

GRAIN is bread, and every single grain a miracle. In the field the wheat has ripened brown and beautiful. Dust of gold to pour into the empty granary. Food of man, the strength and stay God gives abundantly. . . . Grain is life, the magic seed within the ear concealed. Is it not a marvel what a slender stalk will yield? A loaf may be a common sight — but pause and think again. Meditate a moment on the mystery of grain.

∽　∽　∽　∽　∽

THE CROWNING OF THE YEAR

"THOU crownest the year with thy goodness . . . and the little hills rejoice on every side. The folds shall be full of sheep : the valleys also shall stand so thick with corn that they shall laugh and sing."

—Psalm 65. 11-13

MY HOLIDAY

FREE to spend the precious days exactly as I choose. Lying on the golden sand or gazing at the views. Roaming round the little town or sailing in the bay. Free to do just as I please each moment of the day. . . . No trains or buses to be caught, no strict routine to keep — from the minute I awake until I fall asleep. Free to live my life, to read, to dream, to swim or walk. To steal away in solitude or find a friend and talk. . . . That's my mood, so please don't make a single plan for me. Let me taste the sheer delight of feeling really free. Next week I'll be back at work and have no time to play — but till then I'll make the most of this . . . my holiday.

~ ~ ~ ~ ~

THE HARBOUR

LIKE two mighty arms of stone stretched out into the sea — the harbour holds the little ships in snug security. . . . Here the tides are gentle and the water flows and falls — lapping in a lazy wash against the jetty walls. . . . And in the evening when the sunset stains the rocking hulls — and the spars point upwards through a cloud of wheeling gulls — men with sun-brown faces stand in groups about the quay — talking of eternal things, the weather and the sea.

~ ~ ~ ~ ~

UNDERSTANDING

THE gift of understanding springs from love and sympathy. Those who look beneath the surface can discern and see — the anxious thought behind the smile, the tear behind the eye — secrets that are hidden from the casual passer by. They can catch the note of sorrow in a laughing jest — can sense the fears that haunt the heart though dumb and unexpressed — can see the other side of things : the real, the human side — underneath indifference or bitterness or pride. . . . Let us try to cultivate the power to understand, knowing when to stand apart and when to lend a hand — knowing just the thing to say in every circumstance ; seeing to the heart of every problem — at a glance.

COMPLACENCY

WHEN you're feeling satisfied with what you've said and done — That's the time to call to mind your failings, one by one. . . . When you rest complacently, contented with your score — that's the time to buckle to and do a little more !

August 15th
THE WEB OF FRIENDSHIP

WE have made a web of words and thoughts, my friend and I. Of rainbow-coloured recollections from the days gone by. Every thread a memory, some bright, some dewed with tears. Wider grows the web of friendship with the passing years. Sorrows shared and joys remembered touch and inter-twine — worked into the weaving of the intricate design. Hopes confided, griefs divided, these things go to make — the lovely pattern of the web that time can never break.

August 16th

"AND the work of righteousness shall be peace ; and the effect of righteousness quietness and assurance forever."
—*Isaiah 32. 17*

August 17th
THE GOOD INTENTION

GOOD intentions often take us far out of our way — and lead us into trouble, for the hand of fate will play — against us through an action or a word misunderstood — resulting in disaster, though the thought was kind and good. Maybe when we're judged God will look down into the mind — and see the motive and the inward wish that lay behind — the folly and the failure, the mistakes that we have made — when we've hurt and harmed the very ones we'd hoped to aid.

So when you yourself feel injured, think before you judge. Do not let your wounded feelings grow into a grudge. If there is a doubt then let them have the benefit — Maybe there's a good intention at the back of it.

CHINESE IDOL

LITTLE Chinese idol made of jade and ivory — What a story you could tell if you could speak to me ! Such exquisite craftsmanship, such subtlety and skill ! When I see you there upon my cottage window-sill — I thrill to think that long before Christ walked the Holy Land — you were carved and fashioned by some little yellow hand — and still you stand, a thing of beauty and of mystery. It's odd that you will still exist when I have ceased to be !

～ ～ ～ ～ ～

THUNDERCLAP

FATE will sometimes deal a blow and hurl a bolt at you — like a sudden clap of thunder bursting in the blue. Then how silly seem the things that riled you yesterday — and you wonder why you fussed in such a foolish way. . . . Any time a thunderclap may smash your world apart — so if things are going well be grateful in your heart. When some trifling thing annoys you do not carp or whine. Make the most of sunny days. Be happy while it's fine.

～ ～ ～ ～ ～

DEEP WATERS

WHILE we're in the shallows we're content to drift and dream — on the smooth sun-dappled waters of the windless stream. Far from Life's realities we float unheedingly — till the moment when the river runs into the sea. . . . We cannot drift forever in the shallows. Soon or late — we're drawn by the compelling motion of the tides of fate — out into deep waters, swept along by sudden force — lashed by winds of circumstances, driven from our course. . . . It's then we need to take on board the Pilot of the soul — to steer us through the hidden channels and to take control. By rocks and reefs of shocks and griefs our fragile craft to guide — and bring us safely into harbour on the evening tide.

OUR ANNIVERSARY

THIS is the happy day that means so much to you and me. The milestone of our memories, our anniversary. The day on which we two set out towards our promised land — pledged to take the winding road together hand in hand.

Time has brought its changes, many storms have rolled above — but all the clouds have never dimmed the sunshine of our love. So may we continue till the last hill we ascend — Good companions on life's journey ; sweethearts to the end.

EVENING IN THE HARVEST FIELD

THE last man passes through the gate ; the long day's work is done. The golden stubbles catch the glory of the setting sun. Brighter glows the gleam of lamps behind the cottage panes. Fainter grows the distant sound of voices in the lanes. . . . Tomorrow they will come again their labours to complete. But tonight how strangely lovely is this field of wheat ! On the gathered sheaves a holy silence seems to brood — like the hush that falls upon a praying multitude.

"BE not overcome of evil, but overcome evil with good."

—Romans 12. 21

August 23rd

THE FELLOWSHIP OF THE FIELDS

HARVEST-TIME is a time of friendliness, helpfulness and co-operation. Farmers give each other a hand ; men expect to work overtime ; even the children do their bit in the common effort ; feuds are forgotten ; the only thing that matters is getting in the crop. What a different world it would be if this sort of spirit existed in industry, but it would be asking too much of human nature. A man who has worked all weathers in a particular field will feel a sense of personal responsibility in getting results, but no such devotion could be inspired by a machine. You can love a field but not a factory. And even if it were possible, the Trade Unions would soon discourage any enthusiasm for work which went beyond the rules and regulations. Thank God that in spite of the many inventions of science the earth still demands of man an uncompromising devotion, and an obedience not to State-made laws but to the laws of Nature. Thank God for the fellowship of the harvest fields.

August 24th

WHY WORRY ?

CARES like storm-clouds pass away,
If you wait and trust and pray
God will send another day,
Why worry ?

August 25th

KENTISH HOPS

DOWN in England's garden the hops in long straight lines — hang in ripe profusion on the climbing bines — making aisles of shadow, cool and deep and green, soon to be the setting of a lively scene. . . . Crowds of happy hoppers will descend on Kent. In the rain or sunshine long hours will be spent — by the busy pickers in a carefree way — making work a pleasure, and toil a holiday. . . . When the days are ended with the fall of night — darkness will be broken by fire and lanternlight ; and from farm and chalet, caravan and tent — Wealden winds will carry songs of merriment.

THE EXPLORER

ON his tiny feet he staggers, pail and spade in hand — making for the sea that shines beyond the crowded sand. Mother's fallen fast asleep ; a chance it seems to be — for a great and grand adventure of discovery. . . . Many things he sees upon his journey to the waves : Punch and Judy, crabs and pebbles, shells and rocks and caves. What a thrill to go exploring. It's just glorious — with nobody to spoil the fun and make a silly fuss. . . . Now and then he wobbles over, but he doesn't care. Up he gets and on he goes with a determined air — pressing forward to that blue horizon far away — where the silver water sparkles and the mermaids play.

~ ~ ~ ~ ~

THE COUNTRY

WHEREVER you may picnic
By stile or stream or tree,
Remember where you're sitting
Belongs to somebody.
The corner of the cornfield,
The path beside the brook,
The gap between the hedges,
The bank, the shady nook.
It all belongs to someone,
It's someone's special care,
So leave it clean and tidy
That others passing there,
Might rest where you have rested
And see no telltale trace
That someone's had a picnic
And spoilt a lovely place.

SOMEONE NEEDS THE RAIN

RAIN upsets a holiday and spoils a lot of fun, but we cannot always have the glory of the sun. Somewhere someone prays for rain to bless the thirsting earth—someone dreads the days of drought, for drought means death and dearth. . . . Someone needs the rain to fill the well and swell the spring. Somebody in field or garden hopes the day will bring — water for the wilting flowers or for the pasture grass — looking up and praying that the storm cloud will not pass. . . . So when weather spoils the show, the party or the fair. Remember that for someone it's the answer to a prayer. Some folks long to see a shower and others want the sun. Whichever way it goes, it can't be right for everyone.

⌐ ⌐ ⌐ ⌐ ⌐

HOLIDAY MEMORIES

A MORNING swim, a warm blue sea. A stroll along the cobbled quay. A drive by cornfields brown and gold. A cottage tea-room snug and old. A hazy, lazy afternoon. The Pier, the band, a catchy tune. A crimson sail against the sky and clouds of white wings whirling by. . . . The little cake shop on the square. The smell of seaweed in the air. The sound of waves, the taste of spray. A full moon lighting up the bay. A conversation at a dance. A lovely friendship made by chance. The happy memories remain. And you can live it all again.

⌐ ⌐ ⌐ ⌐ ⌐

APPLES

APRIL'S promise has come true.
　　Now against a sky of blue,
Thickly fruited boughs are spread,
　　Green and russet, gold and red.

IT is the quiet time for the birds. It is silent down in the wood where the shadows lie darkly under the heavy foliage of late summer. Where now are the blackcap, the whitethroat and the warbler? The lark too holds his peace. How lonely it seems up on the Downs without the lark. The old plum tree is hung with fruit, and the wasps cluster thickly over the cracked plums. The apples turn their cheeks to the sun. The pears hang ripe and juicy on the overladen branches. The corn stands ready for the threshers, cut and stacked; the stubbles lie ready for the plough. The moors and commons are carpeted with heathers in beautiful shades of mauve, pink and purple. In the garden the roses are budding for a second blooming. It is the hour of maturity, the season of fruit and fulfilment, of gathering and garnering.

September 1st

A GARDEN IN A BOX

I GROW no tall delphiniums, I have no hollyhocks. My estate's a small one: just a wooden window box. Seven inches deep and two feet six across the sill. It doesn't take a lot of work this tiny space to fill.

It is just a pocket plot, a Lilliput affair. Yet from March till Summer's ending colour blazes there. First come yellow crocuses, then hyacinths unclose, in a richly blended mass of purple, white and rose.

Next the fiery splendour of the red geraniums — edged with blue lobelia and fragrant alyssums. I don't envy anyone their lilies or their phlox. I am quite contented with a garden in a box.

"THE FOOL HATH SAID"

'THERE is no God' the speaker cries,
　'Don't let your thoughts be chained ;
This Universe evolved itself,
　The world is self-contained.'

Just then an urchin in the crowd
　A skilful pebble throws
Which accurately lands upon
　The atheistic nose.
'Who threw that stone ? ' the speaker roars ;
　At which the cockney elf,
Intuitively keen, retorts,
　'No one ! It frew itself'.

So a pathetic casualty,
　Discomfited and worse,
Goes home to meditate upon
　This causeless Universe.

—Author Unknown

＿　＿　＿　＿　＿

THIS LOVELY DAY

DEAR, let us remember this when we are tired and old —
When we sit beside the fire and days are drear and cold.
Let us warm our hearts against this golden memory — keeping
it forever bright through all the years to be. . . . Say you
never will forget these good and happy hours — The gay
September garden with the sunshine and the flowers. Say you
will remember when the gold has turned to grey. Let us keep
unto the end this lovely, lovely day.

September 4th

TO shoot or not to shoot. That is the question when the squirrels are making predatory excursions into the vegetable patch and helping themselves to anything that takes their fancy. They say that one pest keeps down another and that to destroy one is to upset the balance of Nature. Is that the real reason why one hesitates to lift the gun? It is easy to persuade oneself that a squirrel is only a sort of rat, so swiftly and silently does it move; one has no compunction about exterminating rats, but when the fascinating little nuisance squats a few yards away from you examining a nut in its forepaws you forget about the rats. You see an engaging little creature absorbed innocently in its own problem looking like a cross between a baby with a toy and a short-sighted old gentleman reading *The Times*. To shoot or not to shoot; that is a question which can be answered only by the true countryman. It is too profound for a mere gardener.

September 5th

HOLLYHOCKS

UP and down the garden path the coloured steeples rise — all astir with questing bees and wings of butterflies. Stately stems, thickset with blooms that soar above the hedge. Towers of flowers — a blaze of glory down the border edge. Rosy red and butter-yellow, pink and snowy white. Hollyhocks, just hollyhocks . . . an ordinary sight. But surely there's a question here for those with eyes to read. How did all this beauty spring from one small pinch of seed?

September 6th

LIFE'S LITTLE WORRIES

SOMETIMES it's the little things that put you to the test. Petty irritations bring the worst out — or the best. Small frustrations fray the nerves destroying peace of mind — and you're apt to grow impatient, fretful and unkind. . . . Most of us can stand up to the big things when they come. It's the little vexing things that make life burdensome. It's the tiny worries piling up from day to day — that take the spirit out of you and make you old and grey.

CONSIDER THE LILIES

"CONSIDER the lilies how they grow : they toil not, they spin not ; and yet I say unto you, that Solomon in all his glory was not arrayed like one of these." In other words, Jesus was saying, don't fuss over yourself or worry about the future. Be content to grow where God has planted you.

— — — — —

September 8th
THE SEVENTH DAY PAUSE

THE mind needs its Sabbath as well as the body. A day of rest is a necessity for overworked brains and overstrained nerves. It is a good thing to pause every seventh day and rest your mind in quietness, contemplating those things which lie beyond the fret and fever of the workaday world.

"Six days shalt thou labour".

—Exodus 20

— — — — —

September 9th
SEPTEMBER TAPESTRY

ROSES pink and crimson where the yellow sunflowers nod. Rows of blazing dahlias and spires of golden rod. Bronze and white chrysanthemums along the border bed. Fading leaves of vine and creeper, amber, flame and red. . . . Glorious and lovely is the scene at summer's end — fruits and flowers and berries into glowing colours blend. This I shall remember when the days turn grey and cold : this gay September tapestry of beauty rich and bold.

A SUSSEX LANE

I KNOW a lane in Sussex, a twisty, crooked track — that straggles up and down and round, then loops and turns right back. A feckless, crazy sort of lane that can't make up its mind — where it really wants to go. You know . . . the Sussex kind. It starts off at the duckpond. You think you're going straight — then suddenly you find that you are at the parson's gate, heading east, or so it seems ; a bend, then west you go. Where exactly you are going you would like to know. . . . No use asking anyone. It's rather hard to say. There's no knowing when you're going down the zigzag way. . . . If you take this turning, will it get you home again ? Does it really matter when you're in a Sussex lane ?

THE CLIMAX

IN Spring I thought my garden was a paradise sublime. In June I said the time of roses was the sweetest time. Now as I go strolling past the border by the wall — I declare my autumn garden is the best of all. . . . Shaggy-headed dahlias in every tint and tone — flaunt their gay and gaudy blooms against the old grey stone. Glorious chrysanthemums in copper, pink and white — weave about the berried shrubs a pattern rich and bright. . . . Daisies, mauve for Michaelmas — the sunflowers' wild display — the fountains of the golden rod . . . No wonder that I say — my September garden with its colours bold and clear — is the loveliest of all : the climax of the year.

THE UNFORGETTABLE THING

YOU soon forget the things that happen on a holiday. Once you're back at home again it seems to fade away — but always there's one memory that lingers strangely on : something that remains with you when all the rest has gone.

A sunset, or a picnic or a white sail in the breeze. The moonlight on the water or the sunshine through the trees. A heathered moor, a golden shore, a garden or a glade. A picture painted on the mind that Time can never fade.

WINDOWS

TELL me what you see, my friend,
From the windows of your house ;
    I see green meadows flecked with flowers
    And silver trees in sunlit bowers,
    I see bright birds, the sky's wide dome
    And happy children running home.

Tell me what you see, my friend,
From the windows of your soul.
    I see tired creatures, weak and blind,
    The agonies of all mankind,
    The stranger's need, my brother's loss
    And Jesus hanging on a cross.

⌇ ⌇ ⌇ ⌇ ⌇

THE DAY IS ALWAYS NEW

EVERY day we rise and do the same old things once more. Every day we lift the latch upon the same front door — and step out on the very pavement that we walked upon — when we went out yesterday. . . . But yesterday has gone.

The road may be the same one, but the day is always new. Though your eyes are looking at the same familiar view — You're a different person, for we change from day to day — shaped by what we do and what we think and what we say.

Every day's a new adventure, never lived before. Fresh experience awaits you. New things lie in store. You can start your life again, for you can be reborn. Every time unto the world God sends another dawn.

SAVE THE TREES

WHO will save the trees of England? Save them from the woodman's hand? Who will save the glorious trees that grace our green and lovely land? "Timber, timber" cries the builder. But we too have needs and rights — we who love the shady glade, the stately park, the wooded heights.

We who love the oaks and beeches, we who weep to hear the axe — echoing in lane and copse and ringing down the forest tracks. We whose joy it is to wander where the dappled pathways wind — mark the scars and watch with grief the swift destruction, mad and blind.

Speak! All you who would preserve the beauty of our native scene — you who love the sylvan groves of ancient woodlands, cool and green. Raise a cry that will be heard from Berwick to the Channel seas. Call a halt to the despoilers. Speak and save our English trees.

— — — — —

NO TIME TO SPARE

OUR time belongs to those who need us. It is not our own — for we were not meant to live for self and self alone. The passing days are precious gold to use and not to waste. There's not much time for others when we live our lives in haste.

We make excuses for ourselves when faced with hard demands — something that requires a willing heart and ready hands. We say that we are weary with the burdens of the day — yet we seem to find the time for pleasure and for play.

We talk as if our lives belong to us exclusively. But our lives belong to God. Though busy we may be — the world is full of folks in need of comfort, help and care. This remember when you say you have no time to spare.

"WHEN thou shalt besiege a city a long time, in making war against it to take it, thou shalt not destroy the trees thereof by forcing an axe against them : for thou mayest eat, and thou shalt not cut them down — for the tree of the field is man's life."

—*Deuteronomy 20. 19*

"And the leaves of the tree were for the healing of the nations."

—*Revelation 22. 2*

September 18th

"And all discover, late or soon,
Their golden Oxford afternoon."

GERALD GOULD'S Oxford afternoon was "spring-coloured". Mine was touched with the tints of autumn for I came to Oxford when the creepers flamed against the weathered stone of church and college and "the dreaming spires" of the old, old city lay steeped in the soft gold light of a warm September sun. This, surely, is the time to have your "golden Oxford afternoon", when the leaves are beginning to flutter about the old grey walls and there is an autumn stillness in the air. This, surely, is the time to stand and listen to the chimes of Merton echoing along the corridors of history and to look through lovely old gateways at the quiet beauty of noble buildings and cloistered lawns. The mood of September is the mood of the Oxford that lies behind the ancient walls, tranquil, mellow, mature.

September 19th

SILVER AND GOLD

WHEN the woods grow silent and the summer's tale is told — the silver birches wrap themselves in cloaks of fairy gold, as if the final hour demanded that they look their best — going to their winter rest in robes of glory dressed. . . . Slim and graceful, leaning on the wind they stoop and sway — the loveliest things in all the world upon this lovely day. A memory to take into the bitter days and dark : the shimmer of the sun on golden leaves and silver bark.

RED SHAWLS

THE little old-world cottages along the village street—look so warm and snug beneath their thatches, thick and neat. And when the Autumn creepers drape the windows and the walls — they look like dear old grannies muffled up in crimson shawls.

WHEN Kipling wrote of one spot on earth being "beloved over all" there is no doubt that he was thinking of Bateman's, the beautiful Jacobean house where he lived for over thirty years. There it stands in its little Sussex valley with its beautifully weathered walls of local dressed stone surmounted by a great central stack of six brick chimneys. When you pass through the stone piers of the gateway you see something more than a converted farmhouse in a setting of green lawns and clipped yews. You see something that is typically English, pleasing to the eye and satisfying to the mind, for you are looking upon the creation of a poet to whom this particular bit of God's earth was the spot "beloved over all".

TOO YOUNG FOR SLEEP

IT cannot be that you are sleeping in this quiet resting place — you whose hands were never still, whose feet moved at an eager pace. . . . You who loved the throb of life, the crowded street, the stir of things. You who loved the busy world, the whirr of wheels, the rush of wings. . . . Too young you were to fall asleep. Too young to rest in Death's embrace. I know you must be striding out towards some strange and lovely place. The grave could never hold your spirit nor your quick and questing mind. You walk ahead with bolder step, new paths to seek, new tasks to find.

September 23rd

HARVEST HOME

FROM sowing-time to harvest home, the farmer watches, works and prays — that fruitfulness and rich reward will bless the labour of his days. . . . Men work in wood and coal and steel — At loom and lathe and bench they stand — and some must feel a glow of pride at work well done by head and hand. . . . But only those who spend their lives at work beneath the sky's wide dome — can share with God this golden hour and know the joy of Harvest Home.

‿ ‿ ‿ ‿ ‿

September 24th

"AND he said unto them, Take heed, and beware of covetousness : for a man's life consisteth not in the abundance of the things which he possesseth."

—*Luke 12. 15*

‿ ‿ ‿ ‿ ‿

September 25th

LITTLE COUNTRY TOWNS

WHEN sunlight glows on cobbled streets by houses quaint and old — a spell is laid upon the heart, a spell that seems to hold — the magic of enchantment as the golden glory falls — on weathered wood and mellowed tile of windows, roofs and walls.

This is England's greatest charm : her little country towns — set by roads and rivers, hills and valleys, dales and downs. . . . Let us guard these precious jewels of our lovely land. Keep the planner from the gates and never let his hand — touch the things that Time has hallowed, things of style and grace — things that tell in brick and stone the story of our race.

LOVE

WHAT is the meaning of life and of living?
  The joy and the torment, the taking, the giving?
Love is the answer, the power and the glory.
  Life without love is a meaningless story.
Love is the light on the untrodden road,
  Our hope and salvation, the heart's true abode.

———

"Beloved, let us love one another :
    for love is of God".

I John 4. 7

~ ~ ~ ~ ~

UPS AND DOWNS

EVERYBODY knows life can't be pleasant all the time —
yet we grumble at the hills when we are forced to climb.
We seem to think the roadway should be smooth and flat and
bright. We do not like it when an awkward corner comes in
sight.
  Dull this life would soon become and flabby we should
grow — if we did not have to strive and struggle as we go.
Do not be surprised when roads turn rough and Fortune
frowns. That's the way it has to be : storms, sunshine, ups
and downs.

~ ~ ~ ~ ~

ON WINGS OF FAITH

IF the migrant bird could see the way it had to fly —
It might not risk the long hard flight across the unmapped sky,
But God gives it sufficient strength to launch out into space
Setting forth on wings of faith for some far distant place.

BLESSINGS IN DISGUISE

DOES your burden seem too heavy for your back to bear ? Do you ever think that life is cruel and unfair ? Do not yield to bitterness for that way lies defeat. Things will take a turn someday and life be good and sweet. . . . You will find that all the trials that put you to the test — spurred you on and made you stronger, bringing out the best. The troubles of the present you will view with different eyes — and someday you will see that they were blessings in disguise.

— — — — —

September 30th

THE last day of September is a milestone. Once it has been passed you can no longer hang on to your illusions of Summer. The swallows have gone and the fieldfares and the redwings have arrived. Ladders stand against the trees in the orchard where the pickers are still busy with the apple-harvest and the wind is full of leaves whirling about the lanes and streets, but it is not through any particular observations that you know that the Autumn is come. To those who are in tune with the moods of Nature the change in the season is sensed rather than observed ; it is something felt in the blood. The mist in the valley and the sharp tang in the morning air confirm what has already been discovered and acknowledged.

— — — — —

October 1st
THE GOLDEN DAYS

CRIMSON vine and fading roses on the cottage wall. One is half inclined to say, This is the best of all : this time of fruit and falling leaf, blue smoke and pearly haze. Time of peace and of fulfilment : Autumn's golden days.

October 2nd

LOVELY are the grey-blue twilights of October when you sit at the window looking out at the first stars pricking through the dusk, but all too soon the darkness drops down over the quiet fields and it is time to draw the curtains and light the lamps. It is now that one rediscovers the joy of living in an old country cottage for the low rooms are warm and cosy and there is always plenty of wood to be had for the hearth. And how good it is to hear again the crackle of blazing logs and to see the soft golden glow of the lamplight reflected in the gleam of old oak and polished copper. In such a place one can catch the mood of the season, the tranquillity of spirit that comes with the twilight of the year.

– – – – –

October 3rd

"PEACE I leave with you, my peace I give unto you".

— *John 14. 27*

– – – – –

October 4th
CHRYSANTHEMUMS

CHRYSANTHEMUMS are Nature's consolation to the heart — that grieves to see the splendour of the golden days depart. The roses fade, the dahlias droop, the leaves are blown away — all around are desolation, ruin and decay — save where the chrysanthemums display their vivid blooms — setting garden paths ablaze and lighting chilly rooms with their bold array of colours, brilliant, rich and bright : amber, lemon, bronze and copper, gold, maroon and white.

October 5th

LIFE WITHOUT COLOUR

LIFE without colour. . . . How drab it would be. God, the great artist of earth, sky and sea — makes the world lovely with shadow and light — painting His pictures in tones rich and bright.

So with our thoughts . . . some are sombre and grey — others are vivid, inspiring and gay. Some lift the spirit and some bring it low. Some are like rainbows that glisten and glow.

Don't let your life become dull, dim and drear — a colourless scene framed in worry and fear. Take from Hope's palette a thought big and bold — and splash at the canvas with crimson and gold.

October 6th

BLIND me not with too much light, I do not ask to see
Over the horizon where Thy hand is leading me.
Give me a candle to hold, O Lord, sufficient to illume
Every dark and secret corner of the inner room.

October 7th

"I SEE the winter approaching without much concern, though a passionate lover of fine weather and the pleasant scenes of summer. But the long evenings have their comforts too ; and there is hardly to be found upon earth, I suppose, so snug a creature as an Englishman by his fireside, in the winter. I mean, however, an Englishman that lives in the country".

—*Wm. Cowper, Oct. 7th, 1783*

IF YOU ARE LOVED

IF you are loved by someone, be grateful and be glad. Fling off every mood that tends to make you glum or sad. You are Fortune's darling and richer than a king — having the greatest blessing that life can ever bring. . . . Love is a tender flower, so keep it fresh and fair — Water it with kindness and cherish it with care. Hold it if you have it, for it's God's own gift to you. A wonderful possession is a love that's warm and true. . . . If you are loved, speak softly. Let gentle things be said. No bitter word be spoken, to spoil the years ahead.

October 9th

WITHIN YOURSELF

WITHIN yourself you have the power to be what you desire. Within your soul there is the goal to which your thoughts aspire. Not in the outside world, but in yourself potentially — You are the kind of person that you really wish to be.

October 10th

ISN'T IT A PITY

WHEN people die we praise them in all sincerity,
But it's when they're living that folks need sympathy.
We send them lovely flowers, affection to express
Too late for it to bring them a bit of happiness.
Their good points we remember, their failings we ignore,
We wish that we'd been nicer, and done a little more.
We speak of them with kindness, and loving things are said,
But isn't it a pity we wait until they're dead!

October 11th

THE garden-lover has no time to lament the passing of the summer for there is so much to do and so little daylight now in which to do it. Old flower heads must be snipped off and put on the compost heap, dead leaves must be swept up tidily into piles, the garden seats must be put away for the winter, the old bulbs must be labelled and stored and the new ones planted out. And the Spring display must be planned, so that the beds can be prepared and orders despatched. The maker of a garden never lives in the present. He is always a season ahead, always dreaming some new dream of the future, making good his past mistakes and planning to do better next time.

October 12th

OPPORTUNITIES

TRY to turn calamities into opportunities by twisting them to something good and fine. Wring joy from failure, gain from loss. Thus make a blessing of your cross — and shape it to a beautiful design.

Turn your trials and tragedies into opportunities, and seize a boon from each experience. Resolve to snatch some happy chance from every adverse circumstance — and make it serve the ends of Providence.

October 13th

MONEY

IT'S certainly true that we can't do without it — and yet when we've got it we're troubled about it. Poor folk seem happy, they laugh quite a lot, making the most of the little they've got. Rich ones look bored, for a life that's all leisure — seems to lack something that makes for real pleasure. . . . Men risk their lives for this thing we call money. Steal for it, kill for it — Isn't it funny? No matter how much we've got in our store — Everyone wants just that little bit more.

THE QUIET DAYS

WHEN troubles come we look back on the uneventful days — and wish that we were back again along the humdrum ways. We wonder why we ever grumbled at monotony — and said that life was dull and slow when things went quietly.

When worries come and break the rhythm of the old routine — we think about the times when all was peaceful and serene. Quickly luck can change and weather turn from gold to grey — so welcome as a blessing every good and quiet day.

"AND grieve not the holy Spirit of God, whereby ye are sealed unto the day of redemption. Let all bitterness, and wrath, and anger, and clamour, and evil speaking, be put away from you, with all malice : And be ye kind one to another, tenderhearted, forgiving one another, even as God for Christ's sake hath forgiven you."

—Ephesians 4. 30-32

TIME TO THINK

GIVE yourself a little time to let your thoughts take wing. For a moment now and then let go of everything. And think of things that lie outside your day-to-day affairs — beyond the little circle of your problems and your cares.

Do not fill each passing minute of the busy day — taken up with food and clothing, pleasure, work and play. Make a quiet pause before the shadows start to fall — and think about the things that really matter most of all.

THE DREAMERS

DREAMERS can't keep up with those who walk the quickest pace. They like to stroll while others rush to win life's hectic race. Those who push the rest aside, the hustling bustling kind — forge ahead and seem to leave the dreamers far behind.

But the dreamer sees a lot the other fellows miss. He has time to look around and feel the sun's warm kiss. Time to watch and time to wonder, pausing here and there. Time to pray and time to ponder. Time to stand and stare.

Oftentimes the hustlers flag before they reach their goal — having no resources left of body, brain or soul. . . . And the dreamers overtake them, ambling gaily past — having come the long slow way, they get there at the last.

— — — — —

LOVE AT FIRST SIGHT

LOVE at first sight is a strange mystery, for life starts anew at a glance. Joy thrills the heart as it wakes and breaks free — into a world of Romance. . . . Once in a lifetime this drama takes place. It seems that the stage has been set. A stranger, a meeting, a voice and a face — a moment we never forget. This the most beautiful memory of all, recalling that old sweet delight. Happy the heart that has known what it means : the rapture of love at first sight.

— — — — —

THE LONDON DUSK

LOVELY is the London dusk when autumn twilight falls — cloaking in a gauzy mist the blitzed and blackened walls. Golden buds of light unfold along the crowded ways. Grey and silver flows the river in the pearly haze. Down the streets and round the squares the tattered leaves are blown. Beauty veils the hard and haggard face of brick and stone — Homeward stream the crowds into the softly fading light — caught up for a moment in the magic of the night.

THERE is a sameness about the summer trees when the forms of bole and bough are covered in heavy green foliage, but in the autumn when the leaves begin to fall one sees the individual outlines of the trees and marks their different colourings. In the garden there is a glorious blaze of sumach, liquidambar, maple and cherry, with the beautiful parrotia persica outglowing all, a burning dome of gold and crimson leaves. In the wood, the oaks are still green above the brown bracken, but the birches toss their yellow leaves into the wind, slim and graceful amongst the solid masses of the fruited thorns. But if you want to see a sight to take your breath away, seek out a lane that is lined with beeches. Wait for the sun and watch it drawing the fire out of the bronze and coppery leaves that burn above your head and smoulder beneath your feet.

— — — — —

NELSON'S PRAYER

before the Battle of Trafalgar, October 21st, 1805

MAY the great God Whom I worship grant to my country, and for the benefit of Europe in general, a great and glorious victory ; and may no misconduct in any one tarnish it ; and may humanity after victory be the predominant feature in the British Fleet. For myself individually I commit my life to Him that made me, and may His blessing alight on my endeavours for serving my country faithfully. To Him I resign myself, and the just cause which it is entrusted to me to defend. *Amen.*

THE HOUSE OF MEMORY

LOFTY windows, draughty hall,
Stain of damp upon the wall.
Place too big for present day,
Out of date is what they say.
Musty, dingy, dark and cold
For a lady tired and old.
Why then does she love it so?
That is what they want to know.
I have guessed.   It's plain to see
It's her House of Memory.
Someone's laughter echoes there,
Through the rooms so big and bare.
Footsteps on the stairs she hears,
And a smiling ghost appears
As she dreams by firelight glow
Of the days of long ago.
Once again she's young and fair,
A happy bride with golden hair.
Sell the place, they all advise.
But she'll be there until she dies.

THE THOUGHT OF YOU

THE thought of you runs through my days — a thread of
gold that glints and gleams. The thought of you is never
absent when I weave my webs of dreams. The thought of you
brings out the sun when shadows fall around my path. It is
the road that leads me homeward and the flame that warms
my hearth.

WHEN ALL IS WELL

WHEN all is well we soon forget the worry and the pain. Quickly then do we respond to happiness again. Swiftly do the shadows flee when sunshine fills the mind — when wishes have been granted and our sorrows left behind.

When we reap a harvest where the seed of hope was cast. When faith has had its rich reward and dreams come true at last. Gratitude to joy be added. Let the heart declare— its thankfulness by offering a glad and grateful prayer.

October 25th

GROWING OLD AND KEEPING YOUNG

GATHER wisdom as you go and have a grown-up mind, But always keep a childlike heart and you will always find Wonderful surprises ; new adventures every day.
Strange and lovely things will happen all along the way.
Do not let the flight of Time depress you or alarm,
Don't resist the passing years. Grow old with grace and charm.
Keep the simple faith of childhood if you would possess
The secret joy which is the source of all true happiness.

October 26th

"AND they brought young children to him, that he should touch them : and his disciples rebuked those that brought them. But when Jesus saw it he was much displeased, and said unto them, Suffer the little children to come unto me, and forbid them not : for of such is the kingdom of God. Verily I say unto you, Whosoever shall not receive the kingdom of God as a little child, he shall not enter therein. And he took them up in his arms, put his hands upon them, and blessed them."

—Mark 10. 13-16

GRATITUDE

BE grateful for the things you have — for grateful thoughts can mend — a broken life, a broken heart. A grateful mind will lend — a splendour to the darkest day. Too often do we brood — on losses and forget the gains. Lord, give us gratitude.

AUTUMN

MAY the final phase of life
Be like the earth in autumn mood,
Rich with blessing and contentment
    Full of peace and quietude.
For all mercies glad and grateful,
    Having neither doubts nor fears,
May I walk with my beloved
    In the autumn of the years.

THE STILE AT BY-PATH MEADOW

"**N**OW when they were gone over the stile, they began to contrive with themselves what they should do at that stile, to prevent those that should come after from falling into the hands of Giant Despair. So they consented to erect there a Pillar, and to engrave upon the side thereof this sentence : 'Over this stile is the way to Doubting Castle, which is kept by Giant Despair, who despiseth the King of the Celestial Country, and seeks to destroy his holy Pilgrims.' Many, therefore, that followed after read what was written and escaped the danger."

—John Bunyan

October 30th

GIANT DESPAIR

DON'T give way to Giant Despair. He may look strong to you — but fight him as you'd fight a deadly foe. Do not let him get you down whatever he may do. Face him out and give back blow for blow.

Giant Despair will try to crush out all that's good and gay — once he gets a grip upon your soul. Do not give him half a chance, for if he has his way — he will have you under his control.

Giant Despair's a coward at heart. He slinks off out of sight — if you show that you too can be tough. . . . He is seen for what he is when Faith turns on the light — and Hope comes on the scene to call his bluff.

➥ ➥ ➥ ➥ ➥

October 31st

THE trees, at this season, are giving us demonstrations in the science of composting. The falling leaves appear to be dead, but nothing is wasted in Nature's economic system. The leaves, rotting down into the earth, will change their form, structure and substance and eventually become a rich mould, nourishing the soil about the parent tree and forming a fertile bed for the germination of new seed. What seems like decay is only a phase in the eternal processes of transmutation and renewal.

The good gardener, like Nature, wastes nothing. Ash, soot, grass cuttings, decayed vegetable matter, kitchen waste, all must go back into the earth. If he is wise, he will not dose his soil with chemical cocktails to stimulate an artificial fertility, but will be content to get results the hard way, the slow way, Nature's way.

November 1st

ALL SAINTS' DAY

THIS is the day for saluting the memory of the saints, the great saints and the little saints, past and present, known and unknown. In the times of the early Church a saint was just another name for a Christian. "Called to be saints" says St. Paul. It may seem that there is no room for sainthood in the modern world, but every age is saved by its saints. "God has never left Himself without a witness". We must take the idea of sainthood out of its niche of piety and try to see it as something to be worked out in terms of daily living. The canonized saints might have been other-worldly in their spiritual lives, but they were also tough, practical and capable. They weren't saints because they did tremendous things ; they were able to do those tremendous things because they were saints.

November 2nd

ALL SOULS' DAY

YESTERDAY we saluted the saints. Today we think of all souls that have passed over into the unknown, especially of those whom we have loved and lost. And remembering, we take comfort from the words, "The gift of God is eternal life through Jesus Christ our Lord". Immortality is not something that can be achieved through merit. It is the gift of God, something to be asked for and bestowed. This is the Christian hope that puts a quiet confidence into the heart of the sorrowing and the bereaved.

November 3rd

FAR AWAY

FAR away the Winter seemed when blossom hung about the pane — and the garden gay with colour shimmered in the summer rain. . . . Far away the Winter seemed when thrushes in the eves of June — sang on through the golden sunsets to the rising of the moon.

Far away the Winter seemed, a thought I could not entertain — while the roses threaded garlands through the hedges in the lane. . . . But now it's come, I'm well content, for knowing that it must be so — I seek again the quiet joys of home and hearth and firelight glow.

THE OLD UMBRELLA

HOW sad it looks, my old umbrella in the garbage bin ! The broken cord, the battered frame, the cover torn and thin. How smart it was when it was new, bright silk and pattern gay. The sight of it has brought to me old thoughts of yesterday. That April morning in the park — the daffodils in flower — and lovely London at its best, with rainbow, sun and shower. And someone very sweet and dear was walking with me there — sharing my umbrella. . . . Happy days ! without a care.

THE OPEN DOOR

KEEP the doorway of your heart open to the passer-by. Many folks are on the road, trudging 'neath a starless sky. Hungry for a bit of love, a friendly and a helping hand — looking out for someone who will comfort, cheer and understand.

Keep the door unlatched, who knows ? — One may come some day and bring — some new joy into your life, some unlooked-for lovely thing. . . . Do not bolt and bar the door on the world that waits outside. An angel in disguise may come, may knock and enter and abide.

APPLE WOOD

I LOVE to burn an apple log upon a chilly day — when all the world outside seems cold, disconsolate and grey. I love to watch the flicker of the flames on polished oak, and catch about the house the teasing fragrance of the smoke. . . . For when I'm burning apple wood I always seem to see — a vision of the strength and beauty of the fruited tree. And in the rustle of the flames I hear the thrushes call. I catch the whisper of the wind and hear the apples fall.

November 7th

"A MERRY heart doeth good like a medicine : but a broken spirit drieth the bones."

—Proverbs 17. 22

~ ~ ~ ~ ~

November 8th
AT THE ENDING OF THE ROAD
THERE'S a meaning in life's mystery, its raptures and despairs. There's a reason for our sorrows, for our losses and our cares. There's a purpose in life's journey if with faith we bear our load — and the hope of God's forgiveness at the ending of the road.

~ ~ ~ ~ ~

November 9th
THE THREAD OF FRIENDSHIP
NOTHING dims the brightness of a friendship tried and true. The colours may be faded, but the gold comes gleaming through. We were meant to share the lovely things the good God sends. Joy is doubled, sorrows halved, when we are with our friends. and fortunate are they who looking back with smiles and tears — can trace the thread of friendship through the pattern of the years.

WRINKLES

WRINKLES tell the tale of life upon a human face. As the years roll over us a finger seems to trace, their story for the world to see, our weakness and our strength. Time's hand may be gentle but the marks will show at length.

Corrugated foreheads, tell-tale lines and puckered flesh. Yet if we could always keep our faces smooth and fresh — they would look like marble statues without warmth and breath, lacking in expression like a mask, a mask of death.

Life has made our faces and we cannot long conceal — what we are and what we think and what we truly feel. That's what makes them interesting, laughter, worry, strife — draw the wrinkles that declare the story of a life.

November 11th

THAT OTHERS MIGHT LIVE

HE gave the greatest gift of all, the gift of his unfinished life. That was the measure of his faith. He did not flinch from fire and strife, but plunged into the heat of battle, giving all he had to give. Offering his sacrifice that others might be free to live.

He was young and tender-hearted, loving peace and peaceful ways — wanting only fun and friendship, laughter, life and happy days. But he knew the price of freedom, wise beyond his meagre years — knowing what the cost would be in blood and sorrow, toil and tears.

One of England's best and bravest, we salute his memory. To him and to his kind we owe our hope, our life, our liberty.

November 12th

THE HEALING POWER WITHIN

IS it not a miracle how Nature works a cure? Slow her methods may appear, but they are wise and sure. Strength and confidence return in a mysterious way — gaining just a little hour by hour and day by day. . . . There's a healing power within. On this we can rely — to refresh our minds and bodies as the years go by. It is thus that we renew the springs of health and youth. Cast out fear and rest your faith on this eternal truth.

RYE

IF you wander for long enough around the quaint old cobbled streets of Rye there is bound to come a moment when you ask yourself if you are dreaming. You walk along the Strand with boats on one side and the town on the other with houses at all levels perched on the terraced cliffs. You come to the Mermaid Inn and you wonder if it's really true or merely a figment of your imagination. You make your way by Henry James' Lamb House into a narrow passage which leads into Church Square. You enter the beautiful old Norman church and stand gazing up at the great pendulum which has been swinging from the clock for more than 400 years. You gaze up at the glorious blue window blazing like a huge sapphire in the grey twilight of the transept. You look at the Burne-Jones window of the Magi and at a carved altar front of Spanish mahogany, believed to be part of a ship of the Armada. You come out dazed and dazzled into the quiet little Square with its fairy-tale cottages and beautiful timbered houses. You walk along Watchbell Street and look out across the marshes trying to imagine what it was like when the sea washed up against the cliffs. At any time of the year Rye is romantic but, to my way of thinking, you have to see it in the dusk of a November afternoon to catch the essence of its magic, for it is then that the cottage casements glow with lamplight and the mist coming up from the marshes seems to add to the sense of dreamlike enchantment that hangs like a spell over the quaintest little town in all Sussex.

～ ～ ～ ～ ～

A BEAUTIFUL DAY

WHAT if Time's finger has wrinkled the face
  And there is grey in the gold?
When youth is ended and age takes its place
  We should not mind growing old,
If we can say as the shadows depart
  And the last light dies away,
"Thank you" to God from the depth of the heart,
  "It's been a beautiful day".

TRANQUILLITY

GIVE me tranquillity of mind,
  A heart content,
With all at peace.
  Lead me, O Lord, down quiet ways
My soul sustain,
  My faith increase.
Give me a calm and steadfast will
  To meet whatever is to be.
Facing the future unafraid,
  With courage and serenity.

— — — — —

WORST OR BEST?

IT'S the little things of life that make it all worth while,
  The gracious gesture quietly made, the unexpected smile.
The courteous act, the loving thought,
The kindliness that can't be bought.
It's the little things that prove the sort of folks we are,
What we say can charm or please, or it can hurt and jar.
It's the little things that test, and show us at our worst or best.

— — — — —

WITH GRATEFUL HEART

MAKE the most of every moment. Seize life in its flight.
Take the best from every season whether grim or bright.
Be it winter, spring, or summer let each day you live — yield
some joy, for every day has some good thing to give.

  It is useless to lament the passing of the years. Time
goes by and will not stop to heed our foolish tears. Round and
round the clock will go whatever you may say — so take with
grateful heart what Life is offering today.

COLOUR SCHEMES

IMAGINE what this world would be without the varying hues, the purples and the yellows and the crimsons and the blues. How dull and drab the earth would seem without its colour tones. Nature paints the flowers, the shells, the rainbows and the stones — the brown of soil, the green of leaves, the grey of evening mist — rocks and gems, the pearl, the sapphire and the amethyst. Even we have different skins according to our race — black and white and dusky brown. And so in every place — God carries out His colour schemes down to the smallest thing — not forgetting to tint the feathers of a finch's wing.

November 19th

DAWN

EVERY dawn is a miracle,
    God makes the world anew.
The grey light breaks and brings another day.
    Every morning is wonderful,
The black skies turn to blue
    As moon and stars grow faint and fade away.
Every day is a mystery.
    Our portion of the earth
Swings once more across the sun's bright track.
    Every dawn we are born again.
Each day a strange rebirth
    As consciousness returns and life comes back.

RECONCILIATION

SWEET is reconciliation, casting out all doubts and fears.
Life is short, too short for quarrels. Yet we spoil the golden
years, clinging to a sense of grievance, standing upon dignity.
Oh, the precious time we waste in self-inflicted misery ! . . .
If you feel you have been wronged, be generous — wipe off
the debt. Do not try to wound or punish, but forgive and then
forget. Rise above the petty wish to hurt and to humiliate.
Take the opportunity. Tomorrow it may be too late. Let no
bitterness remain. No grudges rankle in the mind. Let for-
giveness be complete ; resolve to leave the past behind.
Love is all that really matters, so why suffer needless pain ?
Sweet is reconciliation. Say the word, and start again.

THESE THINGS REMEMBER . . .

DAYS that were sunny and dreams that came true. Years
that were happy and skies that were blue. The good
things, the bright things, the best things of all. These things
remember when life's shadows fall. . . . Hold to the thoughts
that are dearest to you. Keep the high hope of the future in
view. Friends that were faithful and hearts that were kind.
Keep the sweet memories stored in the mind—cherished with
gratitude, treasured in love. Forget not these things when the
storms break above. In the remembrance of all that was
best — You will be comforted, strengthened and blessed.

MOST of the trees in the garden are bare now. Only the oaks cling tenaciously to their leaves, so that although many have fallen, the trees still make great gold and russet domes against the November sky. It is as if the oaks, having weathered so many storms and survived so many winters, are determined to hold on to the last. The east end of the cottage garden is bounded by a glade of ancient oaks, and when one remembers the rapacity of man and his dependence upon wood, it is surprising that they have stood for over two centuries. How many narrow escapes they must have had ! And how many millions of acorns they must have scattered on the floor of the wood. Every time the wind rushes at them they drop a potential forest. You seem to draw strength from oaks, especially when the leaves thin out and you begin to see the majesty of their forms and the structural strength in the upward and outward thrust of branch and bough.

— — — — —

TIDES OF FORTUNE

WHEN Fortune's tide is ebbing, leaving driftwood on the sand — That's the time to plan new ventures, not the time to stand — gazing at the floating wreckage of your ship of dreams, brooding on your loss and the frustration of your schemes.

Far beyond the broad horizon hidden from your view — Isles of treasure and of fortune are awaiting you. There they lie for those who have the courage to explore, setting out on stormy waters for a distant shore.

Waste no time in watching at the white edge of the foam — waiting for the waves to bring the ruined cargo home. Dare to dream your dream again. The sea is deep and wide. Launch another lovely ship upon the morning tide.

EVENING REFLECTIONS

WHAT have I sacrificed? What have I done?
What have I lost? And what have I won?
What have I given and what have I got?
How have I helped, just a bit or a lot?
Have I kept back what I might have bestowed?
Have I made easier somebody's load?
Have I been honest at work and at play?
What kind of show have I put up today?

〜　〜　〜　〜　〜

ECHOES

LOVELY are the common shells that lie upon the sand —
beautiful in shape and colour. Take one in your hand.
Mark the inner lining, smooth as china, pearly bright. Note
the grey-blue outer surface, veined with rose and white. Place
it to your ear and listen. You will hear the waves—echoing
like fairy music in enchanted caves. The soul of the eternal
deep is in that secret sound. Peace and tempest, grief and
rapture, mystery profound. . . . The heart is like a shell in
which we hear the distant sea — voices calling from beyond
the Isles of Memory. When upon the lonely shores of sorrow
we are cast. In the silence we can catch the echoes of the past.

〜　〜　〜　〜　〜

THE MEANING OF THE CROSS

LIFE is not an easy stroll along a peaceful path — Nor is it a
pleasant dream beside a quiet hearth. Life is not a bed of
roses. It's an uphill climb ; and we have to fight and suffer,
struggling all the time. . . . That's God's way of making us
courageous, brave and strong — Not by smoothing out the
road when things are going wrong. If we never had to meet
with adverse circumstance — Soft and weak we'd soon
become — unable to advance. Some go under, broken by
the first stroke of the rod. Others see in every lash the hidden
hand of God. Trouble, sorrow, difficulty, pain, disaster, loss.
That is how we live and learn the meaning of the Cross.

HAPPY HOME

KEEP your home a happy home and guard it carefully. Let no ugly chord be struck to spoil the harmony. Make of it a place of peace where voice is never heard — raised in anger or complaint with hard and unkind word. Try to make it beautiful though small your means may be. Spare no pains to keep it lovely, shining spotlessly. Give your home a cheery look, a gay and smiling face — so that all who come may feel it is a well loved place. Let it be a quiet haven of tranquillity ; a centre of affection for your friends and family. Far away for very long you'll never wish to roam — once you've got that precious thing : a good and happy home.

YOUR JOB

THERE'S a special piece of work that you were meant to do. That is why you're where you are. God set that task for you — Not along some other road but where your ways now lie — is the niche that you and you alone can occupy.

Don't complain if you dislike the place where now you stand. That's the place of your appointment. Do the job in hand. Do your duties faithfully though trifling they appear — if you want to qualify to reach a higher sphere.

No one else can do the special task that you've been set. When this one is finished other orders you will get. When you've proved your worth and you have shown yourself to be — ready for the next step forward in your destiny.

MISJUDGMENT

IF you have an enemy, a grievance or a grudge. Think before you cast a stone. It's easy to misjudge. You may be mistaken in the view that you have had. Folks are queer, but oftentimes you find they're not so bad . . . when you get to understand what's hidden underneath, something hurting inwardly that makes them show their teeth : bitter disappointments, fear, remorse and secret pain : loneliness, a broken heart, fatigue and nervous strain.

Try to get at this and make them smile instead of frown. Get behind the barriers and try to break them down. Many people hide their better selves behind a wall. Don't judge them in haste . . . or better still, don't judge at all.

∼ ∼ ∼ ∼ ∼ ∼

IT has been a month of dramatic sunsets. Yesterday at dusk the hills were a deep violet colour, and behind them the clouds massed in fantastic formations, like great rose and golden bubbles lit by a fiery glow that seemed to strike up from under the horizon. Along the edge of the sky hung a long bar of green light which lingered on until the darkness closed in.

November air is exhilarating when there's no fog about. It is full of the sharp smell of burning wood, wet earth and rotting leaves. There's a tang in the wind that sets the blood moving to a quicker rhythm. One steps out briskly into the morning conscious of a new vitality, braced for the threat of winter.

As the sun's arc grows smaller the world too seems to diminish in size. Life centres about the hearth. There is, as always, much to do in the garden, but there is a strange spirit of quietness brooding out there amongst the leafless trees. It is as if Nature is saying, "Let everything lie fallow for a bit. Rest and wait."

December 1st
THE COTTAGE OF CONTENT

THEY called it The Cottage of Content.
I knocked to find out what it meant,
For all my life I'd sought to find
The secret of a quiet mind.
"Come in", the owner said, "come in.
The things you seek are here within.
Love tends the hearth and keeps the blaze
To warm the heart on bitter days.
Hope trims the lamps and makes them bright
To give a good and kindly light.
Faith keeps her watch in every room
To banish doubt and fear and gloom."
I turned away and homeward went
To build my cottage of content.

December 2nd

"THE Old Testament is really the story of God's patience
in waiting for His Mother. In the whole world He
chooses one nation, in that nation one tribe, in that tribe one
family, and in that family He chooses one lily, one little girl,
that she may be His handmaid, that she may have this im-
mense vocation to be the Mother of the great God, and that
she may be such a mother that she could see and share His
pain".

FATHER ANDREW,
From *The Melody of Life.*

December 3rd

BREAD AND STONES

"OR what man is there of you, whom if his son ask bread, will he give him a stone? Or if he ask a fish, will he give him a serpent? If ye then, being evil, know how to give good gifts unto your children, how much more shall your Father which is in heaven give good things to them that ask him?"

Matthew 7.9-11

Prayer is always answered, but we fail to understand the answer when it is given. How often we pray for stones because we mistake them for bread, and when God gives us bread we think we are getting a stone.

December 4th

THE EMBER-HOUR

THERE'S something in the ember-hour that seems to set us thinking — of the things that might have been. We watch the red coals sinking — as silence settles round the house. It's time to go to bed — and yet we stay there dreaming till the fire is all but dead.

It's strange how far into the past the questing mind can go — when the heart is quiet and the flames are burning low. We live again Love's golden Aprils and Life's grey Decembers — when, surrounded with our ghosts, we dream beside the embers.

December 5th

"HOW may he long abide in peace that meddleth himself with other men's cares, that seeketh occasions outward and seldom gathereth himself within himself".

Thomas à Kempis

December 6th

GREY DAYS

GREY are the days when drear December veils the world
in fog and gloom. Dusk brings the sweet and welcome
thought of lamp and book and firelit room.

Short is the journey of the sun. No shaft of glory cleaves
the skies. Brief is the light and long the night as hour by hour
the old year dies.

Dreams must await their resurrection, buried in Winter's
frozen tomb. Dreams of the gold of crocus cup and orchards
white with April bloom.

— — — — —

December 7th

GLOOM AND GLORY

MONTH of mingled gloom and glory,
　　Sun and shadow, fog and rain,
Weeping woods and silent gardens,
　　Glowing hearth and frosted pane
Time of endings and beginnings,
　　Bringing to a weary earth
Tidings strange and wonderful,
　　The tidings of a Saviour's birth.
Welcome, welcome grey December
　　With your message of good cheer,
Light your lamp at Winter's gate
　　And crown with joy the passing year.

December 8th

YOU wouldn't think it possible that you could go out into the December garden and pick something gay for the house, but it is surprising what you can find when you look for it. This morning I searched amongst the melancholy ruins of bed and border and gathered a winter bouquet, and very lovely it looks in its great earthenware jug, making a splash of colour against the white walls of the parlour. It is made up of laurustinus, now breaking into creamy bloom, a dozen or so twigs of willow and scarlet dogwood, a spray of winter jasmine, some late chrysanthemums that had somehow escaped the frost, a sprig of holly and a few Christmas roses. And wanting something to place in a shallow bowl as a centre piece for the hall table, I went to the heath corner where the erica carneas are now flowering in glorious shades of rose, and carmine.

December 9th

THE GOLDEN BOY

THE skin of his face was warm and fair,
The light of the sun was in his hair,
The soul shone pure and undefiled,
In the wide clear eyes of that golden child.
I turned away, for I could see
The Christ child looking out at me.
Before that frank unflinching gaze
I stood condemned in all my ways.
And that is why I could not bear
The stare of the golden boy.

December 10th

"I AM not at all sure that immortality will not turn out to be a conditional thing, the conditions being in no way theoretical, but natural, almost mechanical. A soul that has got weight and momentum will naturally tend to go on. A light-textured paper-bag sort of a soul will be blown by 'a violent cross-wind, transverse, into the devious air.'"

Thos. Ed. Brown

THE LITTLE THINGS OF LIFE

DO the thing you have to do and do it faithfully. Consecrate the commonplace wherever you may be. Someone may be influenced by what you say and do. Somebody may learn a lesson, just from watching you. . . . Nothing's insignificant in day-to-day affairs : the trifling incidents of life, the small domestic cares. Dull and unimportant though the humdrum tasks may seem. All have part and place within the universal scheme.

IT IS ENOUGH

IF it were given us to know the whole of life's unfolding plan — If we could see what waits for us out there beyond our little span — There'd be no lovely mystery, no wonder at the heart of things — for we with open eyes would see the answer to our questionings. . . . It is well God keeps His secrets, for if everything we knew — Where would be the need of faith to strive for ends beyond our view ? It is enough to know that He is there and here, below, above. That all the boundless universe is in his Hand. . . . And He is Love.

BOOKS

THE books we love grow dearer as the years go rolling on.
They are there to comfort us when other joys have gone.
Life is changing all the while and people come and go,
But books remain the same, come grief or gladness, sun
    or snow.
Often would the heart grow sad and lonely we should be
But for these, our silent friends, who keep us company,
Drawing us away from self by paths that twist and wind,
Opening the gateways to the country of the mind.

A S the winter deepens the advantages of living in an old cottage become more and more felt and appreciated. The old Tudor builders knew what they were about. Wide hearths, small windows and low ceilings make for a cosiness that can never be enjoyed in a modern house. The old cottage that has been brought up to date by the electrician and the plumber represents the perfect marriage between the functional and the æsthetic. It is a tragedy that in the past fifty years so many lovely old places have been allowed to fall into ruin, condemned by the authorities and demolished. With a little foresight and imagination they could have been saved. And had this been done there would have been no post-war housing problem in rural areas. Let us always be grateful to the builders of the past and to all who have preserved our beautiful old churches and cathedrals, our stately houses and sturdy cottages. All that is worth looking at in the English countryside today comes to us from the past. This is the England that people cross the world to see. Let us cherish and preserve it.

December 15th
CHRISTMAS CHARITY

I T is good that once a year we have to think of giving.
Christmas turns our thoughts away from mere self-centred
living,
It makes us think of other people and of what they need
And offers us a golden chance to do a kindly deed.
To think of those outside the circle of the family.
All God's children have a claim upon our charity.
Let your Christmas giving go beyond your own small fold,
Remembering the lonely ones, the sick, the poor, the old.

EVERYTHING MATTERS

EVERYTHING matters : the trivial act that hardly seems
worth while. The word that sends the stranger on his
journey with a smile. The tiny gift that gives such pleasure to
a lonely heart. The thought that helps an erring soul to
play a nobler part.

Everything matters : the little blunder and the big
mistake. The way you do your daily job ; the trouble that
you take. In the crucial things of life and in the small things
too — You leave your mark for good or ill in all you say
and do.

━ ━ ━ ━ ━

ALWAYS

THERE'S always something to live for if you only look
around. An old friend to be visited, a new one to be found.
A job of work to tackle, something really well worth while,
and lots of folk who need a hand to help them at a stile. . . .
There's always something to live for though the best in life has
gone. There's always a reason for being grateful and for
keeping on. Someone is treading a lonely path whose heart
is breaking too — someone looking along the road for somebody like you.

━ ━ ━ ━ ━

PRAYERS IN STONE

LOVELY are our great cathedrals, prayers in stone they
seem to be. Raised up for the love of God, they stand in
quiet majesty, witness to eternal truths and to the faith of
righteous men, symbol of the mysteries that lie beyond our
mortal ken.

Look upon their grace and splendour, gaze upon their
towers and spires — set like rich and precious jewels in the
cities and the shires. Round their old and hallowed walls
the gales of history have blown. Still we worship at their
altars. England's glory : prayers in stone.

WAYS HOME

HOMEWARD we are often led along the strangest ways.
Unexpected turnings take us back to bygone days.
Suddenly we go astray though straight the track appears —
and we find we've struck the road of the forgotten years.

A snatch of song heard on the wind when passing down a
street. A poem, some remembered lines, a foolish thing, but
sweet. Bells on Sunday mornings, Toby jugs and willow
plates. Shining knockers, hollyhocks and little wicket gates. . . .
These awaken memories and back our thoughts will fly —
down the long, long lane of all the dreams that never die.
Ways home for the weary heart. Ways home to peace and
rest — finding at the journey's end the good things and the
best.

〜　〜　〜　〜　〜

December 20th

THE TREE IN THE WINDOW

IN the little window stands a tinselled Christmas tree,
Gay with candles, red and gold, a lovely thing to see.
Lighting up the grim surroundings for the passer-by
With a glow that warms the spirit and delights the eye.
To the ugly street there comes the hint of holy things,
A flash of glory in the gloom, a rush of angel wings.
The heart is touched by something that is strange and mystical,
And faith returns, the faith of childhood, new and wonderful.
This is what we need today, so shine out little tree !
Give us back what we have lost : faith, hope, simplicity.

〜　〜　〜　〜　〜

December 21st

LOOKING BACK

LOOKING back we see it was the hardship, not the ease —
that taught us most of life's philosophy. The hurts in
things, the stabs and stings that brought us to our knees, to
learn new wisdom from calamity. Looking back, we see that
it was failure, not success — that goaded us to fight against
despair. Looking back we see that it was pain, not happiness—
that led us, groping, to the place of prayer.

THE real message of Christmas is that we do not have to worry overmuch about the mystery of life and the magnitude of the cosmos. For all thinking men life forms itself into a gigantic question mark. Philosophers, scholars, theologians, believers and non-believers try to puzzle out the enigma of existence, but the great question has been answered for all time and for all men by what happened in a stable nearly two thousand years ago. Here is something definite to cling to amidst the shifting sands of speculation. Here is something that can be pinned down in history. All other facts about life are charged with the significance of the supreme fact of the Incarnation. The whole truth about man and God has been reduced to something simple enough and small enough to be put into a cattle trough.

～ ～ ～ ～ ～

THE STABLE DOOR

THEY came that night to Bethlehem,
  The simple and the wise,
The shepherds and the magi saw
  The glory in the skies,
And sought the holy manger bed,
  That place of mystery
Where God Himself had broken in upon humanity.
  The greatest men who walk the earth
Can offer us today,
  No diviner revelation,
This, then, is The Way.
  Though to knowledge high and vast
The human mind may soar,
    Every man must come at last unto the
      stable door.

December 24th

MOONLIGHT lay white over the frosted fields as I passed the lighted windows of "The Plough." They were doing good business. Several cars were parked outside the saloon and the locals were having a sing-song in the public bar. Like most country innkeepers, Jim Orford farmed a few acres and kept horses and cows, and I could see the light of his lantern moving about in the stableyard. Suddenly I lost my foothold in Time. Was not this the eternal Bethlehem? And with this question came the warming thought of the homeliness and the simplicity of everything that had to do with the Incarnation : the sheep in the fields, the cattle at the mangers, and the crowded inn. Strange things can happen to you when you are out under the stars on Christmas Eve, for as I stood there looking at Jim's lantern it was as if everything was poised on the edge of the silence, breathless and expectant. The very beasts seemed to be watching for the glory, waiting to see God.

〜　〜　〜　〜　〜

December 25th

"AND the angel said unto them, Fear not : for, behold I bring you good tidings of great joy, which shall be to all people. For unto you is born this day in the city of David, a Saviour, which is Christ the Lord."

—Luke 2. 10-11

〜　〜　〜　〜　〜

December 26th

"OUR breakfast consisted of what the squire denominated true old English fare. He indulged in some bitter lamentations over modern breakfasts of tea and toast, which he censured as among the causes of modern effeminacy and weak nerves, and the decline of old English heartiness ; and though he admitted them to his table to suit the palates of his guests, yet there was a brave display of cold meats, wine and ale on the sideboard."

Washington Irving
From "Christmas at Bracebridge Hall"

December 27th
ENJOYING THE GOOD THINGS

GOD wants us to enjoy life to the full. "I am come that they might have life" said Jesus, "and have it more abundantly." C. S. Lewis once said, "God never meant man to be a purely spiritual creature, He likes matter. He invented it." Of course He wants you to enjoy the taste of the plum pudding, the flavour of the wine and the warmth of the fire. All these things come from the earth, His earth.

From "The Kingdom Within"

December 28th
NEW LIFE

NEW life is what we all of us desire.
New dreams to set the weary heart afire.
New hopes to take the place of hopes now fled,
New wisdom for the path that lies ahead.

New thoughts to light the eyes and make them shine.
New faith to stiffen up the sagging spine.
Make this your prayer as you the future view,
"Lord, take my bad old self and make it new."

December 29th

"AND be not conformed to this world : but be ye transformed by the renewing of your mind."

—Romans 12. 2

December 30th

WE are waiting for the old year to die. It is a strange interval, this pause between Christmas and New Year. It is good that we do not have to face up to the tremendous moral challenge of a New Year immediately after the excitements of Christmas. We are granted these few days for making a quiet approach to the new beginning, remembering past mercies and marshalling the scattered rabble of our good intentions. Let the cynics say what they will about the futility of making resolutions, the New Year affords an excellent opportunity for stiffening up the will, and oh how much we all need to have a bit of starch put into our flabby spines ! Resolutions are soon routed by the devil unless subjected to a strict discipline. The person who never makes a New Year's resolution must be very self-satisfied or very lazy.

~ ~ ~ ~ ~

December 31st

"RING out the grief that saps the mind,
For those that here we see no more ;
    Ring out the feud of rich and poor,
Ring in redress to all mankind.

Ring out the valiant man and free,
    The larger heart, the kindlier hand ;
    Ring out the darkness of the land,
Ring in the Christ that is to be."

—*Tennyson*
From "In Memoriam"

PATIENCE STRONG'S

BIRTHDAY BOOK

———————

Daily readings in prose and verse

To My Father

He taught me the things that every child should know,
Things about gardens — how to plant and sow.
A love of walking, striding stick in hand
Down the green ways of Nature's wonderland.

January 1st

MAY the way that lies ahead be lit with sunny gleams—and prove to be the road to the fulfilment of your dreams. May it lead you to the place where lost hopes are restored— Where love is true and life is good and faith has its reward.

o   o   o   o   o   o

January 2nd

BIRTHDAYS are the gateways of the future,
  May this one,
Open into pleasant places
  Out into the sun.
Showing you the pathway of Tomorrow bright
  and clear.
God be with you at the gateway of another year.

o   o   o   o   o   o

January 3rd

DO not let the unknown future fill you with dismay. It is in the hands of God, so go upon your way. Trust in Him and have no fear. You do not walk alone. He leads the faithful in the dark and careth for His own.

January 4th

RAISE the edifice of life upon foundations strong and sure. Put the best into your task and build with things that will endure. With the tools of hope and patience fashion something true and fine. Scorning all that would destroy the harmony of your design.

⚬ ⚬ ⚬ ⚬ ⚬ ⚬

January 5th

OPEN the windows of my mind that I may catch the morning light. Grant me, Lord, a wide horizon, and a vision broad and bright. Give me eyes to seek for beauty and a heart to understand. Ears to hear the voice of conscience, feet to run at Love's command.

⚬ ⚬ ⚬ ⚬ ⚬ ⚬

January 6th

ONE year older ; one year wiser may you prove to be. One year nearer to the thing you've worked for faithfully .... Count each a friend who comes with gifts for hand and heart—a friend who leaves you happier when it is time to part.

January 7th

THE world was never meant to be an earthly paradise. We are here to learn the way of love and sacrifice. Here to do the Master's bidding, servants of His will. With a duty to perform, a purpose to fulfil.

o   o   o   o   o   o

January 8th

GOD'S unfailing goodness is a current deep and strong. Trust it and you'll find that it will carry you along. Take the risk and fling yourself on His omnipotence. Leave the shallows. Get into the stream of Providence.

o   o   o   o   o   o

January 9th

MAKE an adventure of all that you do,
      Do it with humour and zest,
Looking at life from the broad point of view,
Giving your utmost and best.

January 10th

THIS is an imperfect world as you will surely find — and if you would be happy in it you must bear in mind — that things are as they are. Life can't go always as you plan. You have to work with broken tools and do the best you can.

∘ ∘ ∘ ∘ ∘ ∘

January 11th

DO not count the years but count the blessings they've bestowed.
And the many friends that you have made along the road.
Do not count the birthdays, let them come and let them go.
Time is not your enemy unless you make it so.

∘ ∘ ∘ ∘ ∘ ∘

January 12th

BELIEVE in the future though dark be the sky. The storm will pass over. The clouds will roll by. Believe in the best though it's hidden from view. For this is the faith that will carry you through.

January 13th

WE are given strength to bear the burdens of
each day,
Grace sufficient for the hour and light to see the
way.
Whether in the vale of shadows or on heights
sublime,
Live your life with hope and courage. One day
at a time.

January 14th

SO long as you can pray when all your world
has gone awry,
So long as you can sing when there are rain clouds
in the sky.
So long as you can cling to hope when luck has
passed you by,
You will come out smiling in the end.

January 15th

LIFE should be a festival of hope and merriment — with everyone in high and happy
mood. Every day that passes should be well and
truly spent — and hearts be lifted up in gratitude.

January 16th

TACKLE something truly great and aim at something high. You don't know what you can achieve until you really try. Do not be content to take life's joys and pull no weight. Man was made for enterprises glorious and great.

January 17th

LIFE is what you make it, bright or gloomy it can be. Your mental outlook colours everything you do and see. Your world may wear a dingy air or have a rosy glow. It all depends on what you think, for " thinking makes it so."

January 18th

THIS may be the very day that you've been praying for,
The day on which Good Luck will come aknocking at your door.
Bringing you that long awaited opportunity,
So greet it in a happy mood of gay expectancy.

January 19th

WISHES will not lead you to the things you
would possess.
Wishes will not bring to you the prizes of success.
But work and faith will surely get you where you
want to be.
Effort and determination spell prosperity.

❀　❀　❀　❀　❀　❀

January 20th

MAKE a resolution as your birthday dawns
once more — To be a nicer sort of person
than you were before. To be a little wiser and
improve upon the past. And make the coming
year a little better than the last.

❀　❀　❀　❀　❀　❀

January 21st

DO not choose the easy task or seek the safest
road. Do not shirk the sharing and the
bearing of the load. Obstacles you will encounter
on the way ahead — but do not shrink from difficulties . . . . Conquer them instead.

January 22nd

WE do not always get the thing we aimed for at the start. The sweet desire of early youth, the dear wish of the heart. But through our disappointments God's own wisdom we can trace. Something is denied — but something better takes its place.

o   o   o   o   o   o

January 23rd

THE best and sweetest things in life are things you cannot buy : the music of the birds at dawn, the rainbow in the sky. The dazzling magic of the stars, the miracle of light. The precious gifts of health and strength, of hearing, speech and sight.

o   o   o   o   o   o

January 24th

WHILE you're waiting for the future, don't forget to keep in view — all the good and all the joy that life today can offer you. Go on dreaming of the harvest and of what the year may bring — But make the winter yield a blessing while you're waiting for the Spring.

January 25th

IT'S the light of happiness when shining in the mind — that makes the day look bright to you and life seem good and kind. It's the inner sunshine gives your world a smiling face — and helps you see the loveliness behind the commonplace.

∘ ∘ ∘ ∘ ∘ ∘

January 26th

DO not be discouraged if you don't seem to advance.
Do not be downhearted in the face of circumstance.
It is not the speed that matters as the road you trace.
Be content to jog on at a good and steady pace.

∘ ∘ ∘ ∘ ∘ ∘

January 27th

WE can't undo what has been done and what was said we can't unsay. We can't go back and live again a single hour of yesterday. We have to take life as it is and learn to face the present scene — never wasting time and thought upon the things that might have been.

January 28*th*

WHEN you feel that your courage is sagging—
It's not easy to work up a smile. There are rough bits of road on all journeys, for it couldn't be smooth all the while. But when tempted to think of misfortunes — think too of how much you've been blessed. Don't brood on the worst life has brought you, and fail to remember the best.

∘ ∘ ∘ ∘ ∘ ∘

January 29*th*

THROUGH the stark limbs of the trees no sap
is rising yet — But soon upon the leafless boughs the blossom will be set. In a way most marvellous that no man can explain. There will be a resurrection. Spring will come again.

∘ ∘ ∘ ∘ ∘ ∘

January 30*th*

THERE'S time for all you have to do,
And time to dream a little too,
But none to spare for sighs and tears
Wishing back the bygone years.

January 31st

IF you do not try to force the pace of Providence,
  Time will work things out and with a happy
    consequence.
Difficult your life may be and hard your present
  plight,
But wait before you grumble. Give Time time to
  put it right.

o o o o o o

February 1st

WE cannot halt the pace of Time, the clocks
  go ticking on. When birthdays come
along we say " Another year has gone." But let
it go without regret whatever it has brought.
Greet the future with a happy and courageous
thought—welcoming another year, believing hopefully—that the worst's behind you and " the best
is yet to be."

o o o o o o

February 2nd

DON'T expect a heaven in a world like this.
  Don't look for perfection or for flawless
    bliss.
Take life as you find it with its joy and pain
Bearing with good humour YOUR part of the
  strain.

February 3rd

BLESSINGS seem to fall upon the joyous and the gay.
Fortune is attracted by a smile.
Lady Luck will join you if you go the sunny way
And will walk beside you all the while.

❀ ❀ ❀ ❀ ❀ ❀

February 4th

REMEMBER that the darkness often veils a mystery—and conceals the shape of all the good that is to be . . . . . Just keep going bravely on and confident remain—until God rolls the shadow back and sends the sun again.

❀ ❀ ❀ ❀ ❀ ❀

February 5th

GREET your birthday morning with a bright and smiling face. Turn your little world into a good and happy place. Ask a blessing. Pray that you'll be strengthened, helped and led. Take a new self out upon the road that lies ahead.

February 6th

WE do not always reap in every field—the sort of crop we hoped that it would yield. But often we have found in time of need—we've gathered where we've never sown a seed.

February 7th

PROFIT by everything. Wrest good from ill. Double your assets of wisdom and skill. Increase your happiness. Add to your friends. Turn to advantage whatever Fate sends.

February 8th

IT'S your thoughts that matter. What you think within your heart—will decide if you're to play a mean or noble part. Lift your thoughts on wings of prayer. There is no better way—of beginning and of ending every passing day.

February 9th

WITHIN yourself you have the power to be what you desire. To reach the shining goal to which your hopes and dreams aspire. Not in realms of fantasy, but in your heart and mind—The magic you'll discover and the secret you will find.

o o o o o o

February 10th

LOOKING back, we see it was the hardship not the ease—that taught us most of life's philosophy. The hurt in things, the stabs and stings that brought us to our knees—To learn new wisdom from calamity.

o o o o o o

February 11th

WE have had to go a-seeking for the treasures we have bought—But our friends, the best and dearest, these have come to us unsought. Life has crossed our paths with theirs when quite by chance we've turned a bend—and God has led us to the place where we have made another friend.

February 12*th*

THE whole world's woes you cannot bear.
But you can halve your neighbour's share,
And on the path that now you tread,
A little sunshine you can shed.

❦ ❦ ❦ ❦ ❦ ❦

February 13*th*

YOU must have a plan and a purpose. Though
swiftly the years may depart—You'll always
have something to live for—if you have a dream
in your heart.

❦ ❦ ❦ ❦ ❦ ❦

February 14*th*

LOOK at life with eyes that see the best things,
not the bad. Cherish in your memory the
good times, not the sad. Choose the bright side
of the road where sunshine lights the way. Walk
in the direction of the blue sky, not the grey.

❦ ❦ ❦ ❦ ❦ ❦

February 15*th*

LET Hope be your companion along life's
winding road. When the skies are stormy
and heavy is the load—She will point you on-
wards to that distant star. Keep Hope close
beside you and you'll travel far.

February 16th

THE happy heart is that which is content with little things. · The heart that loves a simple life, the heart in which there springs—a sense of joy with each fresh day, a prayer of gratitude—for the morning miracle of health and strength renewed.

February 17th

TRUST in God a little more and let Him work things out. When around your path the shadows fall. " Be not anxious for the morrow." Never fear or doubt. It may never happen after all.

February 18th

GLADLY let us face the future knowing all is well—thankful for the good things we've received, for who can tell ? Though with golden happiness the past years have been blessed—The years that lie ahead may be the brightest and the best.

February 19*th*

GAY be your heart and happy be the hours,
     Whether you walk in sunshine or in
     showers.
Bright be your life with friendships fond and true.
Blessings be yours and Time be kind to you.

February 20*th*

WE think we know what's best for us. We
    plan and plot and scheme—to reach the
shining goal we have in view. But oftentimes
we find we have to dream another dream—and
build another castle in the blue.

February 21*st*

ONE by one Time steals away the good and
    golden years—leaving us our recollections
and our souvenirs . . . . so that when the winter
comes wherever we may be—we can always pluck
the wayside flowers of memory.

151

February 22nd

DO not let the flight of Time depress you or alarm. Don't resist the passing years. Grow old with grace and charm. Keep the simple faith of childhood if you would possess—the secret joy which is the source of all true happiness.

o o o o o o

February 23rd

SOMEONE'S got to stitch the golden threads into the grey. Someone's got to make the music on a dreary day. Someone's got to clear the clouds and let the sunlight through. Someone's got to brighten up the world. So why not you ?

o o o o o o

February 24th

DO not be discouraged if the trail is taking you—Far away from all the shining goals you had in view . . . . Fate has something else in store. Press on and you will see. There are many turnings on the road of destiny.

February 25th

WHEN a birthday comes along you turn a clean white page — Another chapter to commence, whatever be your age. Although the story of the past was one of want and woe. This can be a new beginning if you will it so.

February 26th

OUR minds like houses shabby grow.
A sudden flash of truth will show
How much we need to sweep away
The dusty thoughts of yesterday.

February 27th

IF you never lose your sense of joy and gratitude. Day by day within your spirit youth will be renewed. If in " every common bush " God's glory you behold. Let the years roll by ! You'll be a long time growing old.

February 28th

SEASONS pass in Love's green garden and the years their changes bring. But beneath the fallen blossoms hope takes root and new joys spring. Round the arbours of remembrance, flowers of friendship ever climb—and the mosses of affection grow between the stones of Time.

March 1st

BIRTHDAYS seem to bring to mind our childhood memories—and to wake an echo of forgotten melodies. Happy birthdays of the past ! The heart recalls once more—the parties and the presents and the postman at the door. Happy birthdays of the future ! Many may there be—bringing blessings of contentment and felicity.

March 2nd

DWELL not on the things that fill the heart with sad regret. The past has gone, so let it go. Your grievances forget. Remember only this, that Fortune follows in the train—of those who have the pluck and courage to begin again.

March 3rd

OPEN the windows of faith today and pray
that a wind will blow your way — To
scatter all thoughts of doubt and fear—and bring
you a message of hope and cheer.

* * * * * *

March 4th

TIME brings many changes, turning golden
hairs to grey. But if the heart is young
we grow not old. It's always May. The young
in heart look through the clouds and see the
golden gleam—because they never lose the power
to laugh, to hope, to dream.

* * * * * *

March 5th

WE need no other rosary if we can string our
days with beads — of friendliness and
charity, of loving thoughts and kindly deeds.
For everything we do or say to ease the strain
and calm the strife — adds another bead of
beauty to the rosary of life.

March 6th

IF your mood is gloomy — break it. If you want the sunshine — make it. Though the sky be leaden and the thunder loud. Go you singing through the storm. It will turn out fair and warm — If you sew a silver lining in the cloud.

March 7th

WELCOME the new. Let go the old. Mourn not the things now ended. Have you not dreamed a brave new dream and seen the vision splendid ? Great is the goodness of the Lord. Go forth and have no fear — Out into the golden promise of another year.

March 8th

THINK not of the hopes that failed, but of the wishes that came true. The answered prayer, the dream fulfilled, the cloudy sky that turned to blue. Brood not on the disappointments, but remember on this day : how God's love has been around you all the while and all the way.

March 9th

WE were meant to share the lovely things that heaven sends. Joys are doubled, sorrows halved, when we are with our friends .... And fortunate are they who looking back with smiles and tears — can trace the thread of Friendship through the pattern of the years.

March 10th

FRIEND of my soul, leave me not, I pray Thee,
Lost and alone on life's winding way.
In Thy dear Presence I fear no evil,
Walk Thou beside me night and day.

March 11th

FATE is fickle like the vane that turns upon the spire. The winds don't always blow just in the quarter you desire. Learn to take with cheerfulness whatever comes your way — for life is like the weather, sometimes sunny, sometimes grey.

March 12*th*

FIND your joy in simple things, for money cannot buy — the music of a blackbird or the rainbow in the sky — the fragrance of the roses and the stars at eventide. All the green and golden glory of the countryside.

o   o   o   o   o   o

March 13*th*

WE are on a journey and we are not here to stay. That is why we have to make the most of every day. We plot and scheme and plan and dream and build our castles high — But often we forget that we are only passing by.

o   o   o   o   o   o

March 14*th*

NEVER let your trials and troubles fill you with dismay. There's a purpose in them all as you will find one day. Often the calamities are blessings in disguise. The things that make us humble are the things that make us wise.

March 15th

IN life there is no going back. The road lies straight ahead. You can't return along the track to seek out what is dead . . . . Your past mistakes you can't undo and wishing is in vain. But don't forget it's true that you can always try again.

❍   ❍   ❍   ❍   ❍   ❍

March 16th

THERE are windows in the mind and we should keep them clean—so that when we're looking out upon life's changing scene—we see a vision beautiful, a landscape fair and bright— Glorified at every point by the eternal Light.

❍   ❍   ❍   ❍   ❍   ❍

March 17th

HAPPINESS is never found by searching here and there. You've got to take it with you where you go. If you've got it in your heart you'll find it everywhere — and everything will wear a rosy glow.

March 18*th*

MAKE a vow to live for NOW and not the unknown morrow. Make the most of present joys expecting more to follow. Your future lies in God's own hands. Be thankful it is so. Surely there is nothing more you need to ask or know.

o   o   o   o   o   o

March 19*th*

DO not look for easy paths, but see your shoes are strong—so that when the track is stony you can get along. Don't go shod for pleasant ways but for the uphill climb—then you'll be prepared for any road at any time.

o   o   o   o   o   o

March 20*th*

YOU will never grow old if you have a goal and a purpose to achieve. You will never grow old if you have the power to hope and to believe. You will always be young if you take your place in the march of new ideas—for you'll have the zest and the best of youth . . . . with the wisdom of the years.

March 21st

I T is a lovely and wonderful thing — to be born on the very first day of the Spring. To enter the world as the Winter grows old — and the daffodils open their trumpets of gold.

o   o   o   o   o   o

March 22nd

L IFE is double-sided ; there's a wrong side and a right. A sad side and a happy side, a black side and a bright. So if things seem dark to you just change your thoughts about. Life will look quite different if you turn it best side out.

o   o   o   o   o   o

March 23rd

T IME is precious. Do not waste it. Use it carefully. Think before you fritter it away. Time is Life : your little portion of eternity— the part that lies before you now, today.

o   o   o   o   o   o

March 24th

W E all have a share of the woes and the blows. At least, you can't say Life is tame. The building, the breaking—the giving, the taking . . . . It's all a part of the game.

March 25th

WHO would want an easy creed ?
      Heaven would be cheap indeed,
If we did not pay with tears
For the wisdom of the years.

o   o   o   o   o   o

March 26th

WHEN the evening shadows fall — May the
      quiet heart recall — not the troubles of
the day, but small mercies by the way : the unexpected gift bestowed — the friend you met along
the road. Not the things you failed to do — but
the wishes that came true.

o   o   o   o   o   o

March 27th

IF the root is deep enough the tree of life will
    grow — lovelier as the years advance, although
the storms may blow — and shake the blossoms
from the boughs in gusts of wind and rain. God
always sends another Spring. The sap will rise
again.

March 28th

LORD, give me light upon my way — and wisdom for each passing day — that I may prove what I profess — continuing in faithfulness.

o o o o o o

March 29th

DREAM a little, not too much. Just enough to give a touch — of splendour to the darkest day : a bright edge to the cloud of grey. Enough to keep within your heart — as one by one the years depart — the magic of the golden days : the power to see with youth's clear gaze.

o o o o o o

March 30th

FOLLOW your star, the star of fate that leads you know not where. Follow the secret trail of faith, made bold by hope and prayer. Follow the music of your dreams beyond the last ascent. Fear not the hazards of the way for God is provident.

March 31st

HOUR by hour and day by day fresh beauties burst upon our sight. The trees once dark against the sky are caught in webs of golden light. Outlines soften, colours deepen. New songs echo down the lane. A miracle is happening. The world is being born again.

o   o   o   o   o   o

April 1st

THOUGH the years take much away and Time be rapid in its flight — I pray I never fail to find my joy, my peace and my delight — in Nature's sweet companionship, the music of the mountain rills — the fragrant lanes, the furrowed fields, the deep green woods, the windy hills.

o   o   o   o   o   o

April 2nd

SEEN from the shadows through windows shut fast — the future is veiled in the mists of the past. But eyes that can see with a faith big and bold — look through the clouds to horizons of gold.

April 3rd

GIVE me ears to hear Thy voice in every human plea, and through all discords to discern potential harmony. Give me thoughts that bear me up when life would crush me low. Give me eyes to see Thy light wherever I may go.

* * * * * *

April 4th

BENEFITS and boons and blessings, mercies big and small. Add them up. You'll find life's not so hopeless after all. Difficulties may increase and cares be multiplied — but don't forget to count the entries on the credit side.

* * * * * *

April 5th

YOU are not the only pilgrim on this bit of road. Everyone must pass this way and each must bear his load. But faith shall justify itself and lost things be restored — the weary heart be comforted and love have its reward.

April 6th

EVERY dawn is a miracle. We wake to life once more. Every morn is a key that opens yet another door. Every day is a precious gift that God bestows on you — and an opportunity to prove yourself anew.

⋄　⋄　⋄　⋄　⋄　⋄

April 7th

EVERY passing phase of life brings something to remember. April dreams, and Junetide joys to brighten grey December. Every changing season brings its own sweet consolations. Time may fade the flowers, but there are always compensations.

⋄　⋄　⋄　⋄　⋄　⋄

April 8th

MAY you find contentment and tranquillity of mind. May Time's finger touch you lightly and the years be kind. Blessings round your path unfold and happiness increase. God be gracious, granting you prosperity and peace.

April 9th

TAKE the compass of your faith and brave the far unknown. Dare to strike out on the deep adventuring alone. Don't stand waiting on the quay, just weaving idle schemes. Take a boat and row right out to meet your ship of dreams.

o   o   o   o   o   o

April 10th

WHEN you know that round the bend decisions must be made. Pray for guidance. Keep right on and do not be afraid . . . . You won't take the wrong direction or be led astray, if you read the signposts that God sets along the way.

o   o   o   o   o   o

April 11th

DOES it really matter when the first grey hair appears ? No-one's getting younger and we can't hold back the years. Time goes on regardless of our efforts and our tears. We're only here a lifetime after all.

April 12*th*

I T'S fatal to procrastinate and then to put the blame on Fate — because you find it's just too late . . . . Tomorrow never comes.

o   o   o   o   o   o

April 13*th*

I F you see the funny side you'll always walk the sunny side and come out smiling through the stress and strife.   So cultivate the power to see— the little touch of comedy behind the trials and tragedies of life.

o   o   o   o   o   o

April 14*th*

L IFE upon this little globe is just an episode.   A journey : and we pass but once along this bit of road.   So do to others as you would that they should do to you.   You will not come this way again.   You're only passing through.

o   o   o   o   o   o

April 15*th*

I F when you wake you can take the bright view.   You'll always look out on a world fresh and new — And life will hold endless surprises for you — because you will never grow old.

April 16*th*

SCATTER seeds of friendship, thoughts and words and deeds. Though the soil looks stony, scatter wide your seeds. Every kindly action, every word sincere — every good intention meant to help or cheer, is a seed of friendship and somewhere, someday — it will root and blossom in its own sweet way.

April 17*th*

FAITH removes mountains. Faith heals. Faith restores. Faith scoffs at logic, rough paths and locked doors. Faith laughs at obstacles. Faith goes right on — when the last word's been said and the last hope has gone.

April 18*th*

THE riddle of existence is beyond us. Let's admit — that though we're clever we don't really know the half of it. But we know there is a Power behind the mystery. A Mind that knows the answer and a God who holds the key.

April 19*th*

THE love that runs with eager feet to do the thankless tasks — The love that seeks for no reward, the sort of love that asks — the chance to do a little more, but never any less. This is the kind of love that brings the greatest happiness.

*   *   *   *   *   *

April 20*th*

WAIT before you worry. It will all come right. Why be in a hurry, Trouble to invite. Don't get in a flurry, giving way to doubt. Pray before you worry. Let Time work things out.

*   *   *   *   *   *

April 21*st*

LOOK forward with a hopeful mind. Look forward ! Resolve to leave the past behind. Look forward ! You can't afford to let your gaze Turn back to rest on other days, Down brighter better broader ways — Look forward.

April 22nd

O NE life and one alone you have to live upon this little earth. One life in which to learn so much, to seek and find and prove your worth. The gold of Time is yours to squander — or with care to use and spend. Waste it not in fruitless quests that get you nowhere in the end.

❧   ❧   ❧   ❧   ❧   ❧

April 23rd

O HAPPY day that brings to mind the little Stratford Street — where England's greatest bard was born and countless pilgrims meet — To walk the banks of Avon and to feed the sacred flame — that burns around the memory of that immortal name.

❧   ❧   ❧   ❧   ❧   ❧

April 24th

S HINE and shower ! They come together all along the way. Life with all its ups and downs is like an April day. It's easy to go smiling through the bright and sunny hours — but we have to learn to go a-singing through the showers.

April 25th

BE true to the best that is in you. Be upright and fair and sincere. Stoop not to the smallest deception. Have nothing to hide or to fear. And when the last task is completed — the last battle over and won — the voice of the Master will greet you with " Well done, good servant, well done."

o   o   o   o   o   o

April 26th

WHAT are ends but new beginnings ? Journeys end and friends depart . . . . But there is always another chapter in the story of the heart.

o   o   o   o   o   o

April 27th

O MAY the first prayer of my day be always one of thankfulness. Thankful may I always be if Fate sends failure or success. Thankful for the blows and blessings and the mercies shown to me. Thankful for the undertones as well as for the melody.

April 28*th*

STRANGE is life's music. Some is gay and some in minor key. But sad and sweetest tones must blend to make the harmony. That's what makes the song of life into a symphony : mingled notes of rapture, sorrow and felicity.

April 29*th*

ONE kind thought can work great wonders. One small rift can break a cloud. One brave heart can strengthen many. One bright word can cheer a crowd. One good soul can give to others something that will be a stay— when they're toiling up the hill and there are shadows round the way.

April 30*th*

A COVENANT of mercy the Lord has made with man — and when across the heavens we see a rainbow's span — We know that God is making His promises anew. We know the pledge is certain. We know His word is true.

May 1st

THE new-born lamb, the fledgling bird, the buttercup, the honey bee. The pregnant earth, the greening wheat, the flush of bloom on bush and tree. Once again the flowers are blowing and the songbirds call their mates. Spring returns in all its glory. Man destroys and God creates.

o   o   o   o   o   o

May 2nd

YOU can't retrace your steps in life. The road goes winding on. You can't return along the track in search of what has gone. You have to keep right on and use the light that's given you — your own small mission to fulfil, your purpose to pursue.

o   o   o   o   o   o

May 3rd

EVEN in the midst of crowds the heart in silent prayer — can hold a brief communion for God is always there. A moment in His presence is enough to heal and bless — and carry you through many hours of work and weariness.

May 4th

IF you travel your road with a faith in your
heart, it will give you the courage to grope—
up through the valleys of failure and fear, spurred
by a wonderful hope. While you have faith you
will feel every day the urge to go forth with a
smile—believing you'll find when you've climbed
the last hill, the Something that makes all worth
while.

○ ○ ○ ○ ○ ○

May 5th

BUILD your castles, but remember dreams are
not enough. Castles must be underpinned
with sterner stronger stuff. Courage and determination, faith and energy — You will need to
turn your dream into reality.

○ ○ ○ ○ ○ ○

May 6th

IF you have the power to take the bright and
rosy view. It will bring you smiling through
the worst that Fate can do. None can take it
from you if this treasure you possess — for it is
the gift of God : the gift of happiness.

May 7th

THERE'S no meaning in the creed that I repeat each day — unless I try to live it as I go upon my way. There's no meaning in the words unless they strengthen me — and give me faith to face the challenge of adversity.

o   o   o   o   o   o

May 8th

LET us be content, my soul, with what the years have brought. We desired a heaven, but it seems that we were caught—in the net of mundane things. Life did not bring romance. We trod the old prosaic path of humdrum circumstance. And yet it has been good, my soul, for looking back today—I see there was a golden light on the familiar way.

o   o   o   o   o   o

May 9th

WALLFLOWERS in the cottage gardens. Hawthorn in the lane. Bluebells in the dappled woods and buttercups again. Apple-blossom in the orchards. Swallows on the wing. Could Heaven be more beautiful than England in the Spring?

May 10*th*

THERE'S a special job in life that you were meant to do. That is why you're where you are. God set that task for you. Not along some other road, but where your ways now lie — is the place that you and you alone can occupy.

∘ ∘ ∘ ∘ ∘ ∘

May 11*th*

WHEN you look back over the way you've come and start to count the miles — you often find that half the fun was getting over the stiles . . . . It wasn't the smooth and easy bit that brought the greatest thrill. It was clambering over the obstacles and pushing up the hill.

∘ ∘ ∘ ∘ ∘ ∘

May 12*th*

GIVE Fear no lodging in your house, no place in which to dwell. Bar him out of every thought and know that all is well. God giveth strength sufficient for each day and its demands. Trust and fear not for the morrow. Leave it in His hands.

May 13*th*

THERE are ruts in the road on life's stony street. There are dangerous places for stumbling feet, where the strongest have fallen and cowards turned back — to look for a safer and easier track. But remember that under Time's rutted clay — the steps of the Master have marked the way.

o o o o o o

May 14*th*

KEEP the lamp of friendship burning with a sure and steady glow. Feed it with the oil of kindness. Never let the flame get low. Old friends, new friends, welcome them within the warm room of your heart — then lonely you will never be as one by one the years depart.

o o o o o o

May 15*th*

WHEN the day is over may I know within my heart — that I've tried to do my duty and have played my part. Given all I had to give and followed faithfully — on the path where I believed Thy hand was leading me.

May 16*th*

THE world is full of clocks that tick our little lives away. We cannot halt or hold the minutes of the passing day. So make the most of every one, the sunshine and the showers — and fill your heart with memories of good and happy hours.

∘   ∘   ∘   ∘   ∘   ∘

May 17*th*

THE heart is a house of many rooms where things are stored away : the treasures of life's remembered joys, the pearls of yesterday . . . . But there is a corner of the heart, a secret place where we — Cherish above all other things . . . . a Mother's memory.

∘   ∘   ∘   ∘   ∘   ∘

May 18*th*

TOMORROW ! . . . . Would you really wish to see into that unknown land ? Sufficient for the heart to know that everything is in God's hand. It's only in the present moment that your life is yours to live. So take with joy and thankfulness the utmost that it has to give.

May 19*th*

HERE and there upon life's path a broken stone appears. Yet Time is kind — and in the crazy paving of the years — it covers up the jagged cracks and hides them from our sight — with the moss of sweet remembrance ever green and bright.

o   o   o   o   o   o

May 20*th*

EVERY phase of life should teach,
Something new. And so we reach
The point at which the heart can rest
Knowing all is for the best.

o   o   o   o   o   o

May 21*st*

JUST keep going — knowing that you'll get there in the end — Just keep showing you believe there's something round the bend . . . . Many falter when misfortune's icy winds come blowing — but those who live to reach their goals are those who just keep going.

May 22nd

SEE all the beauty the world has to show. Take all the blessings that Life can bestow. Hear all the music and pluck all the flowers — making the most of the wonderful hours. Quickly, too quickly, the years slip away. Walk while you can in the sunshine of May.

⚬ ⚬ ⚬ ⚬ ⚬ ⚬

May 23rd

STRENGTH for the day. That is all that I ask. Light for my guidance and zest for my task. Peace and contentment, a quiet abode And grace for my soul at the end of the road.

⚬ ⚬ ⚬ ⚬ ⚬ ⚬

May 24th

IF we could plan our lives there'd be no trials, no tears, no loss. But then how should we ever learn the meaning of the Cross ? If all went well we'd never need to kneel and close our eyes— and never learn about the things that make us strong and wise.

May 25th

TIDES of Time roll in and bring — Summer, Autumn, Winter, Spring. Tides of Life . . . . they ebb and flow — leaving driftwood as they go. Search the shore and you will find — what the tide has left behind.

May 26th

BLOSSOMTIDE in England, cherry, plum and pear. Flowering apple orchards . . . . What could be more fair ? Yet the bloom must wither and the beauty go. The blossoms must be scattered that the fruit might grow. Nature's ways are perfect. She must work her will. Springtime gives the promise Summer days fulfil.

May 27th

HAVE your schemes all fallen through ? Have you got to start anew ? Maybe it is good for you. Why worry ? . . . . Do your best and do your share. Keep straight on and don't despair. If you've said your daily prayer — Why worry ?

May 28th

GIVE me patience for the humdrum duties. Keep me humble, never ˙seeking praise. Make me conscious of the things of beauty — as I go about my quiet ways . . . . Make me wise for there are problems pressing. Make me calm amidst the storm and strife. Make me worthy to receive Thy blessing — glad and grateful for the boon of life.

❍   ❍   ❍   ❍   ❍   ❍

May 29th

YOU have two hands, so take with one and with the other give. That's the way that life works out and that's the way to live. What you get and what you give must balance up some-day. It's give a little, take a little, all along the way.

❍   ❍   ❍   ❍   ❍   ❍

May 30th

LEAVE the world a little better for your tiny span. The good you do may go unnoticed by your fellow man — but it is recorded, every detail, every phase. An unseen pen is writing out the story of your days.

May 31*st*

GO through the day with a song in your heart. Doing your duty and playing your part. Harness the hours so that none is ill spent— wherever you are being glad and content . . . . Keep a wise check on the unruly tongue—ready to learn from the old and the young. Taking what comes with a smile and a jest—facing life squarely and giving your best.

June 1*st*

THIS is what we dream about all through the winter gloom. The good and golden season when the roses are in bloom. When ramblers cover fence and wall and bushes in the bed— glow in lovely tones of yellow, white and pink and red.

June 2*nd*

THOUGH the wise console us with philosophies profound — no man knows from whence we come and whither we are bound. All we know is this : that we are pilgrims passing by. So why waste time in asking questions . . . . Where and how and why.

June 3rd

LOOK at life through sunlit windows and you'll always see — something lovely, something good wherever you may be. Clear away the dust of fear and let no smear remain. Look at every problem through a sunny windowpane.

∘ ∘ ∘ ∘ ∘ ∘

June 4th

IN the garden of your life may Junetide joys remain. Roses never wither and the summer never wane. And should the winter ever come and bring the cold winds blowing — May you never fail to find the flowers of friendship growing.

∘ ∘ ∘ ∘ ∘ ∘

June 5th

SAINTS and sages tell us what to do and how to live. Many clever books are written. Good advice they give. But the secret in one little phrase can be enshrined . . . . Just be kind.

June 6th

STATELY tree ! Look down on me and teach me how to grow — in grace and strength from year to year. Your secret I would know. Teach me how to stand and face a storm with head unbent — patient and contented with a slow development.

o   o   o   o   o   o

June 7th

SEEK the silent places where no jarring sound is heard — and nothing breaks the stillness but the singing of a bird . . . . Nature tells her secrets not to those who hurry by — But to those who walk with quiet heart and seeing eye.

o   o   o   o   o   o

June 8th

WE can't expect fine weather and good fortune all the way. The clouds will come, the storms will break and skies will turn to grey. But when you're looking at a cloud that's thick and black and wide — Don't forget the sun is shining on the other side.

June 9th

AS days go by we live and learn and with the years grow wise. We sift the false things from the true and see with clearer eyes. As each birthday comes along we find that we can say— that Time has left a trail of blessings all along the way.

o   o   o   o   o   o

June 10th

NEVER think you're wasting time in planning lovely things. Dare to reach out for the rainbow. Let your thoughts take wings. Keep on building all the time your castles in the blue. Keep on dreaming. That's the way to make your dreams come true.

o   o   o   o   o   o

June 11th

WHO has had the worst of it and who has had the best? None can say for each must pass his individual test. Covet nothing, envy none, for all have things to bear. Everything is balanced, God is good and life is fair.

June 12*th*

IF it were always summertime how weary we
should grow — of the fadeless roses and the
sun's unfailing glow. We'd never stop and listen
if the birds could always sing. It's twice as sweet
because we know that time is on the wing.

○   ○   ○   ○   ○   ○

June 13*th*

DISAPPOINTMENTS oftentimes are blessings
in disguise. The thing you thought you
wanted might have proved a worthless prize.
The shining hopes that came to nothing . . . . Someday you may see — It was all a part of your unfolding destiny.

○   ○   ○   ○   ○   ○

June 14*th*

IF you let a patch of ground get overrun with
weeds — You can't expect to raise the blooms
that come from goodly seeds. It's a law that
runs through life. You gather as you sow. So
do not plant a thistle and expect a rose to grow.

June 15th

Y OU can smile your way through life or you can fume and fret. It will all depend upon the way your thoughts are set. If they're turned towards the sun you'll always face the light— and you will be guided to horizons broad and bright.

o o o o o o

June 16th

H ERE and there along the road Fate offers you a chance — to change your life and make it something fresh and glorious . . . . A bright new hope comes tapping at the doorways of the heart — bringing Opportunity to make another start.

o o o o o o

June 17th

S UMMER is the festival of bloom and song and light. The gardens blaze, the air is sweet, the corn is green and bright. It's as if God bids us rub our eyes and look and see — His glory in the loveliness of field and flower and tree.

June 18*th*

MAKE a little time each day for putting wrong things right. For breaking up the gloomy clouds and letting in the light. Make the time for making friends and take some time each day — for counting up the blessings that you've gathered on the way.

*   *   *   *   *   *

June 19*th*

YOU'LL never see the sunshine if you always draw the blind. You'll never make new friendships if you close up heart and mind. You can't expect that happiness is going to come to you. You've got to go and look for it from every point of view.

*   *   *   *   *   *

June 20*th*

CLOSE the Gates of Memory. Come back, my heart, come back. You dare not stray too far along that old forgotten track. There's no returning to the past, so cling not to its sorrow —lest you miss the path that leads unto a bright Tomorrow.

June 21st

WE'D like to bid this moment stay — with meadows green and gardens gay. Roses bloom at sill and door. Midsummer Day is here once more. The beauty of the Spring has fled and Autumn's glory lies ahead. How lovely is this golden time — when the year is at its prime !

*   *   *   *   *   *

June 22nd

THIS my wish for you that you will have the power to see — a gleam of gold through every shadow of adversity. For if you bring a happy heart to each experience — you will always walk the sunlit paths of Providence.

*   *   *   *   *   *

June 23rd

THIS is your day : the day when you can turn a clean new page. You can always start afresh whatever be your age. You're never too old to step out on the road of heart's desire — and change yourself into the kind of person you admire.

June 24th

TRY to find out what you have been sent on earth to do. Find out what your mission is then vow to see it through. Try to find out why you're here and why you've come *this* way. No-one else can fill the part that you were meant to play.

June 25th

LIFE, like Summer, hurries by : a swiftly passing show. But it is useless to regret. It passes. Let it go .... Who knows ? Perhaps you'll knock upon Tomorrow's secret door — and find within a happiness you never knew before.

June 26th

STORE the sunshine in the secret places of the heart. Then should shadows fall and all the golden hours depart — you'd still be happy for you'd have the brightness stored away — to bring the memory of June into a winter's day.

June 27th

AGE can hold no threat for you — if you've loved the good and true. Time's swift pace you'll not lament. You'll be happy and content—gleaning with a quiet mind—what the years have left behind.

∘ ∘ ∘ ∘ ∘ ∘

June 28th

THOUGH the pattern of events is hidden from your view. Rest assured God has a purpose and a plan for you. Someday in the tapestry you'll see the gold threads shine — discovering the beauty of the ultimate design.

∘ ∘ ∘ ∘ ∘ ∘

June 29th

HOW God must have loved the world to make such lovely things ! Roses, stars and butterflies and birds with painted wings. Rainbows, dawns and sunsets, tree and stream and waterfall. Surely there is Love behind the beauty of it all.

June 30th

O N the wings of Memory we rise and fly away—
back into the ever-lovely lands of yesterday
—We live again the sweetest moments of the bygone years — disappointments are forgotten—
sorrow disappears. Time draws golden veils
across the scenes of grief and pain. Birthdays
come and birthdays go, but memories remain.

o   o   o   o   o   o

July 1st

G IVE Life time to spin the unseen threads of
destiny. Give Life time to solve your
problems. Trust and wait and see. Providence
has plans for you. Of that there is no doubt.
But they can't be hurried. Give Life time to work
them out.

o   o   o   o   o   o

July 2nd

I F we cannot see beauty on sunless days when
the sky is grey and cold — we'll never see much
when the sky is blue and the earth all green and
gold . . . . If we cannot see God in the daily round
as we hurry here and there — it's doubtful whether
we'll ever really find Him anywhere.

July 3rd

EVERY year has its seasons. Every season
has its mood. Wild and stormy, gay and
happy. Tranquil, quiet and subdued. Every
year brings a birthday and it marks another phase
—and every season of life is sweet : High Summer
. . . . and Autumn days.

July 4th

MAKE your life a house of sunshine, beautiful
and gay. A life that shines and gives out
light to all who pass your way. Even though you
live where there's a grey and gloomy view. You
yourself can be a window that the sun comes
through.

July 5th

WOULD you really wish to live again those
bygone years ? Would you think the joy
recaptured would be worth the tears ? We cover
the past with rosy veils of glamour and romance.
But would you want to live it again if you could
have the chance ?

July 6th

GETTING all you've prayed for doesn't always bring content. Learn to take with gratitude what Providence has sent. Often God withholds from us the things for which we pray — and in the end we find that something better comes our way.

- - - - - -

July 7th

WE'RE only here a little while. We're only passing by. Time has wings and quickly do the golden moments fly. So do not waste a single minute of the precious days. There is something to be gathered out of every phase.

- - - - - -

July 8th

HOW can you cling to a grief that is old— when God paints the morning all rosy and gold? How can you hold to a sad old regret— when Nature is saying—Rejoice and forget.

- - - - - -

July 9th

LIFE is full of boons and blessings. Every day they come anew. You will find them if you seek them where you go . . . . There's a blue patch way out yonder where the clouds are thinning out. Keep on looking and you'll find that it will grow.

July 10*th*

IT doesn't do to plan too carefully,
 To be too sure, too clever or too wise.
Tomorrow's door is locked. God holds the key
Behind it there may be a big surprise.

*   *   *   *   *   *

July 11*th*

ONE who has a birthday on this day,
 From Summer's store can pluck a bright
 bouquet,
Cornflowers, asters, marigolds and stocks,
Lilies and delphiniums and phlox.
Canterbury bells and cherry pie,
All the garnered glory of July.

*   *   *   *   *   *

July 12*th*

THINGS work out if given time so do not
 strive and strain — in a frantic effort to
undo a tangled skein. If your life is fraught with
problems, leave them for today. There are
threads you can't unravel in a hurried way.

July 13*th*

EVERY day make someone glad or someone's faith sustain — and then you'll always know you have not lived the day in vain . . . . Go out of your way to warm a heart that's hard and cold. Give out love and you will find it comes back sevenfold.

*   *   *   *   *   *

July 14*th*

IT was never meant that we should have an easy task — getting always what we want and having all we ask . . . . Set-backs check our progress, slow us down at every turn — but they give us time to think and that's the way to learn.

*   *   *   *   *   *

July 15*th*

DO not fill each passing moment of each busy day — with the thoughts of worldly matters, pleasure, work and play. Make a little pause before the evening shadows fall — to think about the things that really matter most of all.

July 16th

LOOK for beauty and for goodness. Seek them day by day. You will find them on your path wherever you may stray. Don't go looking round for faults and troubles, flaws and woes. We find what we go searching for . . . , for that's the way life goes.

July 17th

WORK is not the thing that makes you old and tired and grey. It's the little cares that press about you every day. It's the pin-prick worries that annoy you and depress— robbing you of zest and youth, of health and happiness. Kill them at the very start. Turn them out of mind and heart.

July 18th

NEVER shrink from taking a responsibility. Do what is expected of you well and willingly. Do not shirk the extra task but do it with a smile. Bear the added load, if asked, and go the second mile.

July 19th

THERE'S one choice that's always right, one road that's always clear — That's the path of duty. Follow this and have no fear. Other signposts may direct to prospects good and gay —Heed them not, but go ahead where duty points the way.

o   o   o   o   o   o

July 20th

DO not build a wall around your garden of content.
Life can't be enjoyed alone, and happiness was meant
For all to share, so let your gate stand ever open wide
Someone will be glad to see what's on the other side.

o   o   o   o   o   o

July 21st

GIVE me a calm and steadfast will to meet whatever is to be — facing the future unafraid with courage and serenity . . . . Give me tranquillity of mind, a heart content, with all at peace. Lead me, O Lord, down quiet ways. My strength sustain, my faith increase.

July 22nd

SEEK your happiness in things on which you can depend. Nature offers to her children pleasures without end : rosy dawns and golden sunsets, fields and forest bowers. Hills and mountains, streams and meadows, gardens, birds and flowers.

◦ ◦ ◦ ◦ ◦ ◦

July 23rd

WAIT before you wonder what tomorrow may unfold.
Wait before you worry what the future days may hold.
Live in hope and confidence. By nothing be depressed.
Then you'll draw unto yourself the good things and the best.

◦ ◦ ◦ ◦ ◦ ◦

July 24th

YOU never know what's waiting at the turning of the road. Or what the bend is going to bring in view. When you're least expecting it a blessing is bestowed. Another vista opens out for you.

July 25th

IF you put your faith in God you won't be at a loss — when you reach the fateful signpost where the roadways cross. You will feel an unseen hand upon your shoulder laid. The right direction will be seen, the wise decision made.

July 26th

DO not fret and worry over things you cannot change. What's the use of beating at a wall ? Accept the things that have to be — with humour and philosophy. For worrying will do no good at all.

July 27th

CAN this be the garden where a few brief months ago — the bare trees stood with branches bent beneath a weight of snow ? Can this be the little pool that Winter glazed with ice ? Some magic wand has turned it all into a paradise : a fairyland of butterflies, of birds and humming bees. Of fragrant bowers, of gorgeous flowers, green grass and shady trees.

July 28th

L EAN upon the Word of God and it will take your weight. Giving you the strength to face whatever be your fate. It will always hold you up when evil powers assail you. Lean upon the Word of God and it will never fail you.

July 29th

I F we could be given that for which our hearts now ache — would it really prove a blessing, or a big mistake ? It's as well we have no choice. It's not for us to say — But to make the best of whatsoever comes our way.

July 30th

L IFE is like a field in which we sow from day to day — seeds of good or evil by the thing we do and say . . . . Some will garner sheaves of joy and some will reap in tears — when they come to gather in the harvest of the years.

July 31*st*

SWIFTLY go the happy days like birds upon the wing. Quickly fly the shining hours when heart and spirit sing. Youth must pass. But why regret when life has passed its prime. Every phase is sweet. It can't be always summer-time.

August 1*st*

IF one road is closed to you another you will find. If the way is barred don't give up hope and fall behind. God directs our steps and has a plan for every soul. There are paths you never dreamed of leading to your goal.

August 2*nd*

OFTEN with the years across our eyes a veil is drawn — and we cease to see the vision granted with the dawn . . . . But we never lose it if we wake with gratitude — thanking God each morning for the gift of life renewed.

August 3rd

WHEN a kindred soul we see. We feel that it was meant to be. It seems the work of Providence — and not of blind and fickle chance. For surely it is God who sends — the happiness we find in friends.

❦ ❦ ❦ ❦ ❦ ❦

August 4th

IT would be a dreary world, a place of gloom and greed — were it not for those who try to live the Christian's creed . . . . These things keep us linked with God wherever we may be — and glorify this bad old world : Faith, Hope and Charity.

❦ ❦ ❦ ❦ ❦ ❦

August 5th

MANY yearn for better things but shrink from sudden change — because they lack the courage for adventures new and strange . . . . Grasp your opportunities in faith and not in fear. Nothing worth the having can be won without a tear.

August 6th

S HOW the spirit of good-will in all you do and
say. Let your life your inner faith express
. . . . Put your heart into your task, your creed
into your day — and let your work proclaim
what you profess.

• • • • • •

August 7th

W HEN things turn against you and there's
nothing left but dreams. When unlucky
circumstances cut across your schemes. Turn
it to advantage. Snatch a pearl out of the dust.
Make misfortune teach you how to wait and
hope and trust.

• • • • • •

August 8th

T HERE'S no need to wander far for opportunity. Look around just where you are
and you will surely see — Somebody in need of
someone. Might it not be you ? Somebody in
need of something . . . . something you can do.

August 9th

WHETHER life be calm and fair or winds of sorrow blow — Trust .... though every hope be lost to view. In the deeps and in the shallows be content to go — where the winds of God are driving you.

•   •   •   •   •   •

August 10th

IT is foolish to lament the passing of the years. Useless to regret the wasted hours with sighs and tears. Round and round the clock will go whatever you may say. So take with grateful heart what Life bestows on you today. The present hour is yours to live. Enjoy all that it has to give.

•   •   •   •   •   •

August 11th

IT'S the little things of life that prove just what we are. What we say can charm and please or it can hurt and jar. It's the little things that test — and show us at our worst or best.

August 12th

FROWN into your mirror and you'll see what others see — when you are disgruntled or depressed . . . . Don't help Time to draw the wrinkles. Live life cheerfully — and show the world your bright side and your best.

∘　∘　∘　∘　∘　∘

August 13th

THE things that you anticipate and plan for eagerly — will often disappoint you bitterly. While the unexpected thing the greatest thrill of all will bring — and leave behind the sweetest memory.

∘　∘　∘　∘　∘　∘

August 14th

HUMAN hearts need sympathy and that is why God sends — consolations through the understanding of our friends . . . . Trouble would be twice as hard with nobody to share it — no good companion at your side to help you grin and bear it.

August 15th

TURN your thoughts to other people when your life looks blank and drear. There is always someone needing strength and comfort, hope and cheer . . . . Help yourself by helping others ill in body or in mind. Easing someone else's pain your own salvation you will find.

o o o o o o

August 16th

OUT into the unknown future be prepared to move — even though it means you have to leave your cosy groove. Fresh conditions may confront you. Face them hopefully. Changes often force the door of opportunity.

o o o o o o

August 17th

THERE'S always a solution when a problem you've been set. There always is a way in which the challenge can be met. There always is a means of getting over every fence — with just a little patience and a bit of common sense.

August 18*th*

TAKING all things into account life's really not so bad — though there are so many people who are sour and sad . . . . The picture has another side. Much happiness you'll find — if you look with seeing eyes and seek with open mind.

- - - - - -

August 19*th*

IF you can't smile a lot smile a little. Though it's only a few times a day. If the smiles never come — you'll get solemn and glum — and your face will start growing that way.

- - - - - -

August 20*th*

TROUBLES come ; that is true. But the blessings come too. And whatever God sends we must take it . . . . There are hills to ascend, but you find in the end — That life is as good as you make it.

August 21st

FACE the problems of today. That's all you need to do. Deal with them according to the strength that's given you. Don't anticipate the hour until you hear it chime. We were meant to live this life just one day at a time.

- - - - - -

August 22nd

UP and down the countryside the golden sheaves now stand. And a rich fulfilment crowns the labours of the land. Satisfying to the heart and pleasing to the eye : the pattern of the harvest fields beneath the August sky.

- - - - - -

August 23rd

WE all arrive by different roads at the appointed place. Each one has his star to follow and his path to trace. It's not the pace that matters as we go upon our way. It's what we really are when we get home at close of day.

August 24th

NO secret key will open the Gates of Yesterday — when once they've closed behind us. We have to make our way — along the path that opens upon the present scene — Not gazing back in longing on things that might have been.

o   o   o   o   o   o

August 25th

HEAVEN would be out of reach
    And God would be a God afar,
If Faith had never set a ladder
Up against the highest star.

o   o   o   o   o   o

August 26th

I RECALL the happiness — no heartaches and no tears. Only what was best and sweetest of the golden years. I remember all the rapture and forget the pain. It is always Summer when I walk in Memory Lane.

August 27*th*

THE Inn of Friendship lights the way along life's winding path. The door stands ever open and a fire burns on the hearth. The lamp gives forth a glow of welcome and a kindly ray. Comforting the hearts of all who travel by that way.

* * * * * *

August 28*th*

THANK you for your friendship. It has meant so much to me. Thank you for your understanding, love and sympathy. You have helped and guided me through many an anxious day. How different life would be if you had never come my way.

* * * * * *

August 29*th*

TIME from our eyes wipes the tears away. A miracle happens. We wake one day — to discover that life has much to give. We find new hope and the will to live. From out of the shadows sweet voices call. The voices that tell us that Time heals all.

August 30th

SUNLIGHT breaking through the mist. The birches turning gold. Crimson dahlias tall and lovely. Sunflowers bright and bold. Fruited branches in the orchards with their burdens bend. Peace and plenty crown the golden days at Summer's end.

- - - - - -

August 31st

WE do not climb high mountains by gazing in a dream — At the heights above us where the bright crags gleam. Great tasks are not accomplished within a single day. We have to work with patience and struggle all the way.

- - - - - -

September 1st

NOW the orchard boughs are hung with apples ripe and bright — russet, red and yellow in the mellow golden light .... Once again the ladder stands against the laden spray — a touch of Autumn in the air : the first September day.

September 2nd

IT'S the root that is the strength of any plant or flower or tree : the root that feeds the fruiting bough, the secret part that none can see . . . . We, too, must have roots in life, and when the storms blow wild and cold — we shall not break, but stand up straight . . . . because the hidden roots will hold.

September 3rd

" BEAR ye one another's burdens "
  Seeing the unspoken need,
Do your part to ease the strain
By kindly word and gracious deed.

September 4th

ISN'T it a blessing that you can't spend all day long — thinking of the many things that keep on going wrong . . . . Always there are jobs that must be done without delay. If it weren't for work we'd very soon grow old and grey.

September 5th

SOULS, like babes, are weak and small. Unless God holds us up we fall. How can we find the strength to stand — if we do not take His hand ?

o o o o o o

September 6th

LEARN to take things easily. Don't fuss and fume and fret. When your will is thwarted and your plans are all upset — Don't push at a bolted door and dry to force a way. Just accept the situation. Live from day to day.

o o o o o o

September 7th

LIFE'S a jig-saw puzzle and when first you look at it — You wonder how you're ever going to make the pieces fit . . . . But take your time and bit by bit the picture you will see — as the fragments come together, fitting perfectly.

September 8th

OLD friends may be dear, but let us never turn away — from the chance to make new friends — for there may be a day — when changes come as come they must. Time passes. Ways divide. Grateful we may be to find a new friend at our side. So never say that it's too late another heart to win. Another door to open, a new friendship to begin.

September 9th

THIS is my birthday. A new year beginning, I'm tired of the goals that are not worth the winning.
I want a new hope, a new song, a new part
I want a new road, a new life, a new heart.
And this is the moment to drop the old theme,
To make a fresh start and to dream a new dream.

September 10th

IF along the path of life we've sown the hidden seeds — Of friendship, love and sympathy, good thoughts and kindly deeds . . . . Always there'll be flowers to pick, a fresh bloom every day — from the seeds we've sown between the stones along the way.

September 11th

IF endless happiness is your aim
   A joy that will burn with a lasting flame,
It's a garden you're needing, a patch of ground
To love and to work for the whole year round.

• • • • • •

September 12th

YOU'VE got to put your back into the work
   you want to do — and put up with the part
of it that is a bore for you. You've got to do
the drudgery and make the sacrifice. For success
in anything you've got to pay the price.

• • • • • •

September 13th

IF smiling lips and shining eyes in the looking
   glass you see. You need not fear the passing
years for young you'll always be. Joy imparts a
beauty Time can't touch, and that's a truth.
Happiness is better than the passing bloom of
youth.

• • • • • •

September 14th

SEASON of fruitfulness ! Golden September
   Summer's bright splendour we swiftly forget,
Autumn brings plenty and peace and fulfilment.
There is no time to repine or regret.

September 15th

TIME grant to you the harvesting of dreams.
And the success of all your dearest schemes.
And after harvest when the fields seem bare — O
may you glean and find a blessing there.

* * * * * *

September 16th

I WOULD hold this Autumn beauty. Bid
the lovely season stay. I would halt the
striding year and keep it at this golden day. But
the glory must depart ; the leaves must fade and
fall to earth — that Nature may commence her
work of resurrection and rebirth.

* * * * * *

September 17th

FORGET the times of trouble, but not the
truths they taught. Forget the days of
sorrow, but not the strength they brought. Forget
the storms you battled through beneath a heavy
load — but not the light that led you safely
down the unknown road.

September 18*th*

WE worship not a God remote but One who loves us here and now. A King with wounds upon His hands and crown of thorns upon His brow . . . . The Friend of man ! He stands and watches at the gateways of the heart—Waiting to be called upon when other comforters depart.

September 19*th*

HOPE needs no staff to lean upon,
    No helping hand, no guiding star,
Over horizons lost to view, outstripping dreams
Hope travels far.

September 20*th*

MAY your good ship soon come home upon the evening tide
Sailing into harbour with her canvas spreading wide.
Laden with the things for which you've sighed and worked and prayed,
The cargo that you thought was lost ; the blessing long delayed.

September 21st

FROM the eyes of God I cannot hide. I feel
His Presence ever at my side. What is this
Love that holds and haunts me so ? What is this
thing that will not let me go ?

* * * * * *

September 22nd

LOOKING out into the future down the pathway of the years. You won't see the bright
horizon if your eyes are blurred with tears. You
will miss the wayside flowers around your present
pathway set — if you cling to memories that fill
your heart with vain regret.

* * * * * *

September 23rd

JUST a few brief weeks ago the fields were gold
with ripened grain. Now across the bare
brown stubbles ploughs are moving once again—
Making furrows for new sowings, getting ready
for the Spring. So that in the days to come
there'll be another harvesting.

September 24th

IN the gardens leaves are turning. Bright leaves whirl about the square. Along the windy street they dance. A festal touch is in the air . . . . Up the walls and round the sills in city street and country lane — Autumn hangs her glowing garlands as the creepers fade again.

September 25th

A GATE that opens in the shadows often proves for you — to be a place of blessedness where life begins anew . . . . The very thing that causes trouble, heartache and distress — often brings much benefit and ends in happiness.

September 26th

DOORS may close, but windows open, letting in the sun. God never leaves us in the dark, but gives to everyone — the power to look with eyes of hope towards a brighter view. Though He bolts and bars the door, He opens windows too.

September 27th

IF the heart is young — you'll always keep your dreams. Through the darkest cloud you'll catch the golden gleams. If with every dawn your hopes and prayers ascend. Life will be for you a Summer without end.

*   *   *   *   *   *

September 28th

I PRAY that I may always hold to all the faith that I profess. That I may do my Master's bidding, serving Him in steadfastness. That Life might be a pilgrimage towards the highest and the best ; a sacrament, a bold adventure and a great and glorious quest.

*   *   *   *   *   *

September 29th

KEEP on singing though there's none to hear. Keep on smiling though there's none to cheer.
Keep on ploughing though you've reaped no crops.
Keep on marching if the drummer stops.

September 30th

THERE will be higher hills to climb and stronger foes to conquer yet. There will be greater loads to bear and more temptations to be met. Do not suppose the road gets smoother as the winding way you wend. You will need God's help and guidance right on to the journey's end.

October 1st

NONE need go without refreshment in the heat of day.
It is there for all who thirst upon the dusty way.
Comfort for the weary heart and joy for all who weep,
Pardon for the penitent. The wells of God are deep.

October 2nd

JEWELS of wisdom are locked in The Book. The riches are hidden. But if we will look With patience and faith and a diligent mind The treasure is there for the seeker to find.

October 3rd

MEMORY casts a golden ray in every secret place. We see old scenes out of the past, a loved and smiling face. The friendship long remembered and the name forever dear. We recall when birthdays come to mark another year.

∘ ∘ ∘ ∘ ∘ ∘

October 4th

THE ear of Faith can hear the music coming from afar — even when there's discord, words that hurt and sounds that jar . . . . The eye of faith can range beyond the place where shadows fall — seeing sunshine in the dark . . . . and God's love over all.

∘ ∘ ∘ ∘ ∘ ∘

October 5th

"BETTER country farther on." So said the pioneers — who beat a trail into the wilds and tamed with toil and tears — the hostile land. They fought with Nature, challenging her hold— wresting slowly from her grasp, the grass, the grain, the gold. In their hearts a great faith shone — in better country farther on.

October 6th

BURN what summer leaves behind in the autumn hours. Broken stalks, decaying weeds, dead wood and faded flowers. Burn the rubbish of the past. Pile it on the pyre. Grievances and grudges . . . . Fling them all upon the fire.

October 7th

GIVE me the happy things of life.
A heart that's merry all the way.
An outlook that is broad and bright,
A spirit that is brave and gay.

October 8th

THE kind of person you will be depends in every way — on the sort of person you are being now, today. Have a warm and kindly heart and when your hands you fold — You'll be happy — You'll be wanted . . . . Loved when you are old.

October 9th

DO the thing you have to do and do it faithfully. Consecrate the commonplace wherever you may be. Someone may be influenced by what you say and do. Somebody may learn a lesson just by watching you.

*   *   *   *   *   *

October 10th

EVERY day's a new adventure, never lived before. Fresh experience awaits you. New things lie in store. You can ask to be set free from every binding chain. You can be forgiven and can start your life again.

*   *   *   *   *   *

October 11th

THE choice is yours to fall or rise, to injure or to bless. To fill a room with gloom or light it up with happiness. To use or waste the precious hours, to work or take your ease. To walk the path of duty or to go the way you please.

227

October 12th

TIME unfolds our destiny
    As the years go by we'll see
If our way was wrong or right.
Time will bring the truth to light.

• • • • • •

October 13th

THERE are times when it's hard to keep fighting.
    There are times when you'd like to give in,
But the one who holds on when the last hope has
    gone
Is the one who is certain to win.

• • • • • •

October 14th

HAPPINESS is catching ! smile and give it
    out. Other folks will take it once it gets
about. Laughter is infectious ! Gloomy moods
suppress. Start an epidemic, spreading happiness.

• • • • • •

October 15th

THERE'S something to be gained from every
    loss we have to bear — something to be
garnered from the harvests of despair. There's
something to be prized in every friendship that
we make. There is something we can give and
something we can take.

October 16th

WHAT if you're not quite so young as you were — and there is grey in the gold? Time's passing swiftly for everyone else. Why should you mind growing old? We should be able to say in our hearts, nearing the end of the way. "Thank You, dear God, for a wonderful time. It's been a beautiful day."

* * * * * *

October 17th

DO not cross your bridges before they come in view.
Wait until you're there before deciding what to do.
Wait before anticipating trouble, tears and loss.
The bridge you dread may prove to be an easy one to cross.

* * * * * *

October 18th

THE Master came on earth to save the Gentile and the Jew. He came to lift our vision to a wider, grander view. He came to turn the thoughts of men away from self and sin — and to tell the tidings that God's kingdom is within.

October 19th

DO not cling too closely to the human reckonings,
Time is nothing when we think of the eternal
things.
Do not count the years as you are looking back
today
But the blessings they have brought you all along
the way.

* * * * * *

October 20th

QUIET are the woods for the song birds are
dumb
Knowing the hint of the winter is come,
Hushed is the garden and silent the lane,
But there'll be sunshine and music again.
This is the promise to which we shall cling
While we are waiting and dreaming of Spring.

* * * * * *

October 21st

NEVER drop out of the race before the course
is run. Don't admit of failure or defeat to
anyone. And if a thing looks difficult — Don't
say it can't be done . . . . before you've tried.

October 22nd

IN God's love we find an answer to the restless thought : and we find the peace for which our weary minds have sought. In the silence we are quietened by a touch divine. When we bow our heads and say, Not my will, Lord, but Thine.

October 23rd

TIME proves the worth of friends, tests them and tries them. Life alters many things, changing our view. Tearing the mask from the false and the trivial. Making us value the real and the true.

October 24th

YOU can't afford to stoop or falter underneath the strain — of long remembered grievances and unforgotten pain .... God offers you the future. You refuse or you accept. You can make your choice. It's yours to take or to reject.

October 25th

THE sun is fickle and uncertain going in and out. But we can make a little bit of sun to spread about — by friendliness and cheery words, bright looks and merry ways — to hearten and to help each other through the sunless days.

October 26th

WHEN we see the changing seasons pass before the eye. We feel there are unfailing laws on which we can rely. We sense a Mind behind it all when Nature's work we scan — We feel there is a meaning and a purpose and a plan.

October 27th

EVERY passing phase of life brings something to remember. April dreams, the joys of June, the harvests of September. Autumn with its mellow beauty has its compensations. Winter, too, brings to the heart its own quiet consolations.

October 28th

MANY chance acquaintances are met from day to day. Many fall in step with us along life's winding way — But few there are to whom we give the sacred name of friend. They who with unfailing love keep faith unto the end.

✿ ✿ ✿ ✿ ✿ ✿

October 29th

IT is love and love alone that makes life bearable. Lifts it from the commonplace and makes it beautiful. Gives to it a meaning and a motive high and fine — touching it with something that is more than half divine.

✿ ✿ ✿ ✿ ✿ ✿

October 30th

FROM my window I can see
    The stark bare branches of a tree.
It seems no sap could ever flow
Through those boughs. And yet I know
That when I see the April rain
The tree will come to life again.

October 31*st*

THE Spring has its glory of daffodil gold,
  When primroses open and green buds
    unfold.
But sometimes I think as I watch the leaves fall
That Autumn's fair days are the fairest of all.

*   *   *   *   *   *

November 1*st*

WELCOME what each season brings, the
  sunshine or the snow. The Summertime
was sweet, but it has gone, so let it go . . . . Happy
is the heart that sings when skies are dark and
grey — hearing on November winds the nightingales of May.

*   *   *   *   *   *

November 2*nd*

IN everything give thanks to God. Look round
  you and behold — unremembered benefits and
blessings manifold . . . . Strokes of fortune, lucky
chances, mercies of past days. You will find
you have been led and blessed in many ways.

November 3rd

THERE'S always the garden to keep you young when days turn bleak and cold. Folks who love a garden are a long time growing old. Never do their minds grow weary weaving lovely schemes. Planning in the winter hours the garden of their dreams.

November 4th

"LEAVE it till tomorrow" says the tempter cunningly — knowing when tomorrow comes that there will surely be — something to divert us from the course we would pursue. An excuse for putting off the good we meant to do.

November 5th

NO-ONE wants to weep with you if you are always sad. Lonely you will never be if you are brave and glad. Search the clouds. You're bound to spot a gleam of light to follow. Though today looks grim and grey. Remember there's tomorrow !

November 6th

THERE comes a time when courage falters and your spirits fail — When happiness seems far away and faith of no avail . . . . When hopes trail in the dust like faded banners once so bright. That is just the moment when you have to stand and fight.

∘ ∘ ∘ ∘ ∘ ∘

November 7th

NATURE does not rush from summer blue to winter grey.
We are given time to watch the glory fade away.
Time to see the changing colours of the countryside
As we stroll along the golden lanes of Autumntide.

∘ ∘ ∘ ∘ ∘ ∘

November 8th

FORTUNE brings to happy harbours all whose sails are rightly set — if a strong hand's on the wheel and every gale is bravely met . . . . Dream your dream. You'll be rewarded when you watch with joy and pride — the argosies you launched returning — homeward on the evening tide.

November 9th

WITS' End Corner is the place where many roadways meet. For some it means catastrophe, disaster and defeat . . . . For others it's the place where first they learn to kneel and pray. Here God puts a fingerpost to show lost souls the way.

•   •   •   •   •   •

November 10th

THEY who lay aside their weapons on the battlefield — instead of struggling on with broken sword and shattered shield — do not know the glow of pride that crowns a fight well won : a goal achieved, a task completed and a duty done.

•   •   •   •   •   •

November 11th

DOWN the lanes and in the woodlands leafy carpets have been spread : rust and russet, bronze and amber, gold and copper, brown and red. Stripped of all their autumn glory, trees stand stricken and austere — just as if they stood in silence for the dying of the year.

November 12th

WHEN Youth has had its shining hour and Love its golden day. Time may fade the colours and the glory pass away — But something of the magic lingers, never to depart — deep down in the secret places of a quiet heart.

November 13th

DON'T assume you've lots of time for all you mean to do. Though the future seems to stretch away into the blue . . . . Maybe you intend to scale those summits far away — but all that matters is the hill you've got to climb today.

November 14th

OTHER people's problems . . . . What are they to you ? Maybe you could solve them if you wanted to. Do not shrug your shoulders and turn the other way. Other people's troubles might be yours one day.

November 15th

NEVER doubt God has a purpose. Someday you will see — the pattern He is working on the looms of destiny. Much is hidden. All the colours cannot show and shine — But every thread is needed to complete the great design.

November 16th

WE cannot find Life's treasure if we're rushing here and there — chasing shadows through the crowds and beating at the air . . . . Draw apart. Be still and pray when weary and hard-pressed. " Come unto Me " the Master said, " and I will give you rest."

November 17th

ON the hills and in the valleys
        Sorrows fade and hopes ascend,
All roads lead to bright horizons
In the company of friends.

November 18th

Y OU were not put into this world mere pleasure
to pursue — or to gain material success . . . .
But to find the work that God intended you to do.
This alone brings lasting happiness.

* * * * * *

November 19th

T HERE is a philosophy in flower and forest,
field and fen — higher than the lofty thoughts
upon the lips of learned men . . . . There's a gospel
of salvation in the song of every bird — for those
whose hearts can understand the hidden truth,
the secret word.

* * * * * *

November 20th

B ELIEVE in your God and lean on Him in
failure and success. This is the secret of a
life of hope and happiness. This is what brings
a magic meaning to all happenings. This is the
truth that glorifies dull days and common things.

November 21st

USE your gifts. Don't let them rest or they will rust away. Take the opportunities that come with every day. By perseverance, self-reliance and self-discipline — You can be what you desire. The kingdom is within.

o   o   o   o   o   o

November 22nd

NO good deed is ever wasted and no kind word said in vain. The good we do to other people Life returns to us again. No good deed is lost to God although it may be lost to view. Cast your bread upon the waters. Time will bring it back to you.

o   o   o   o   o   o

November 23rd

NOWHERE'S too far for a dream to go.
For a dream can outrun the winds that blow
And take a rainbow in its stride,
Waiting not for time or tide.

November 24th

LIFE without love is a meaningless story.
Love is the answer, the power and the glory.
Love is the lamp on the untrodden road,
Lighting the way to the heart's true abode.

*　*　*　*　*　*

November 25th

THE last leaves lie upon the grass. Why, oh
why must Beauty ? Why must all the glory
go ? Such is the law ; it must be so. The
leaves must fall at Winter's breath — and trees
stand stricken, feigning death . . . . And yet I
hear the robin sing. He knows there'll be another
Spring.

*　*　*　*　*　*

November 26th

STOP and lend a friendly hand
To heal the hurt and ease the strain,
Be the good Samaritan.
You will not pass this way again.

November 27th

DO not try to drift along through life without a creed. Cultivate your own philosophy .... Something that will give you in the moment of your need : wisdom, courage and serenity.

✦ ✦ ✦ ✦ ✦ ✦

November 28th

IT is folly to be out upon life's crowded road— if you do not know the meaning of the highway code .... Read the rules. They're in the Bible, there for you to learn. You will need to follow them at every twist and turn.

✦ ✦ ✦ ✦ ✦ ✦

November 29th

THE turning points of life aren't always noticed at the time. Close against the ear the hour of destiny may chime — and we unheeding may not be aware that it has struck. Afterwards we see the point at which we changed our luck.

✦ ✦ ✦ ✦ ✦ ✦

November 30th

OFTEN in this life we don't appear to travel far. We want to get ahead and hitch our wagon to a star — but it's God who sets the pace. In time we realise — the hindrance we resented was a blessing in disguise.

December 1st

FAR away the Winter seemed, a thought I could not entertain — when the roses threaded garlands through the hedges in the lane . . . . But now it's come I'm well content, for knowing that it must be so — I seek again the quiet joys of home and hearth and firelight glow.

o o o o o o

December 2nd

ROUND the gates of Winter when the fogs come thick and grey — the lovely late chrysanthemums their gorgeous blooms display. Nature, ever provident, has paused to scatter here — flowers for the burial of the departing year.

o o o o o o

December 3rd

HAPPY thoughts can change our lives. They're stronger than we guess. Happy thoughts uplift the heart with power to heal and bless . . . . Happy thoughts are magic forces working secretly — to establish in our lives health peace and harmony.

December 4th

BENEATH the bleak and bitter skies — Grey and still the garden lies — But out there in the damp and cold — There is a spray of fairy gold — a touch of beauty in the gloom. The Winter jasmine is in bloom.

December 5th

SOMEDAY you'll recall how nothing went the way you planned — and everything seemed cloaked in hopelessness . . . . But looking back you'll find it was a Providential hand that guided you to ultimate success.

December 6th

THIS is a world where people do and say the strangest things. So do not be surprised at bark or bite. This is a world that's all mixed up, a world of smiles and stings — So try to see it in a kindly light.

December 7th

I F you scan the sky and cannot see a golden glow — Make some sunshine for yourself and take it where you go. When there's none up there amongst the clouds as grey as stone. Try to make a little bit of sunshine of your own.

* * * * * *

December 8th

E VERY time temptations you defy
By being firm and keeping standards high,
When good is done, peace kept and kind words said,
The devil loses . . . . And you win instead.

* * * * * *

December 9th

I T doesn't cost much to do the kindly and the gracious thing — To strike the note that puts an end to strife and quarrelling . . . . It doesn't take long to do those little acts of courtesy — that lift the tone of life and make it run harmoniously.

December 10*th*

THE habit of hurry, the habit of worry when things are not going your way. That is what makes life dim and dull instead of rich and gay . . . . The habit of moping when you should be hoping — no matter how hard be your case. These are the habits that draw the telltale wrinkles on the face.

• • • • • •

December 11*th*

LITTLE mustard seeds of faith can work great miracles — Moving mountains that you thought were mighty obstacles — Breaking down old barriers and making all things new . . . . Little mustard seeds of prayer can change the world for you.

• • • • • •

December 12*th*

EACH to his path. By many ways
        God guides all pilgrim feet.
And somewhere in His kingdom
There's a place where all roads meet.

December 13th

D O you look for snags or for the good in everything? Do you give your thoughts an upward or a downward swing? Life is what you make it by your mental attitude — and blessings come to those who face it in a hopeful mood.

∘ ∘ ∘ ∘ ∘ ∘

December 14th

W E'RE all outward bound on a voyage to a country far away. To a haven beyond the horizons where the darkness meets the day. But whether we drift in the doldrums or must fight with the gale's full force — We all need to pray for the Pilot to keep us on our course.

∘ ∘ ∘ ∘ ∘ ∘

December 15th

Y OU cannot walk the same road twice. Your steps you can't retrace. By tomorrow you'll be heading for some other place . . . . So carry out that good intention now without delay. You won't pass by this way again; so take your chance today.

December 16th

GOD gives us memories for our Decembers
   Something to comfort when darkness
   descends,
Things to recall as we dream by the embers,
Heart-warming thoughts of old times and old
 friends.

* * * * * *

December 17th

THE days grow short . . . . The garden now is
 stripped of leaves and flowers — but there
are other joys to cheer the heart and speed the
hours . . . . Though Winter be unwelcome it is
Wintertime that brings : the peace of Christmas
and the dear delight of homely things.

* * * * * *

December 18th

TIME moves on and changes come, for no one
 can stand still. Yet it is upon our past we
build for good or ill. All whose paths have
crossed our own upon life's winding way — have
helped to shape us and to make us what we are
today.

December 19th

THIS is the time to think of giving. Nigh two thousand years ago — To the world God gave His Son. What greater gift could Love bestow ? We, then, with a willing hand should share the good that we possess — passing on our boons and blessings, giving help and happiness.

* * * * * *

December 20th

THE merry days, the happy days, the days of long ago — come back in remembrance when we watch the red logs glow. The April days, the autumn days, the gold days and the drear ; mingle in the dreams that haunt this season of the years.

* * * * * *

December 21st

IF you have been wandering down many dark and doubtful ways. Let the Babe of Bethlehem now lead you back to childhood days . . . . If life's treasure you would find — the peace that lasts for evermore — Go you with a childlike heart and knock upon the stable door.

December 22nd

IN the wide warm chimney-corner there's an inglenook of dreams ; a secret place, a quiet place, where shadows play and firelight gleams— and if the dreamer speaks no word, but waits and listens silently — Someone to his hearth will hasten : one whose name is Memory.

December 23rd

JUST as April brings new life to every sleeping tree. Joy is quickened at the time of the Nativity. Life and faith are now renewed by thoughts of holy things. Christmas brings to every door the sound of angel wings. Though wintry storms around us roll. It is the Springtime of the soul.

December 24th

CHRISTMASTIME is like a lamp that lights the closing year. A lamp that radiates a glow of charity and cheer. A lamp that burns at every window with a golden ray — and warms the heart in winter when the world seems cold and grey.

December 25th

ONCE again it is the birthday of the King of
Kings
Once again we meditate on high and holy things.
Once again we hear great tidings ringing round
the earth
The wondrous and amazing story of a Saviour's
birth.

*　　　*　　　*　　　*　　　*　　　*

December 26th

WE never reach horizons for they fade into
the blue. They recede as we advance
towards the distant view. That's the way it is
in Life. There's always something more. Some
new dream to spur us on and fresh fields to
explore.

*　　　*　　　*　　　*　　　*　　　*

December 27th

LET the Old Year pass away. Mourn not, but
greet the New. Turn your eyes in faith
towards the peaks that beckon you. Know that
you'll be guided safely down the unmapped road
—given light to see your way and strength to
bear your load.

December 28th

IF we build high walls around the gardens of our lives — no root of love puts forth a bloom, no seed of virtue thrives . . . . God is Light and light we need to make Life's colours glow. Without the sunshine in our hearts how can the flowers grow ?

December 29th

AS December dies away you turn your thoughts again — to all that it has brought to you of pleasure and of pain. And as you cast a backward glance on all that lies behind — Do you not feel thankful as the blessings come to mind ?

December 30th

LIFE offers compensations for our troubles and our care. Consolations shed their light around us everywhere. Things that make life worth the living : blessings great and small. The things through which God speaks to us . . . . Take comfort from them all.

December 31st

THE garden sleeps, the woods are bare. No song breaks through the trees. No golden note comes rippling on the cold and bitter breeze. But the music is to come ! We know it to be true. There'll be thrushes on the bough and skylarks in the blue.

PATIENCE STRONG'S
FRIENDSHIP
BOOK

To gather roses for this book
My wayward thoughts have wended
In and out and round about.
I trust I've not offended,
By stepping on forbidden ground
With this or that quotation,
Straying down the thorny path
That leads to litigation.
Here a bud and there a blossom
From an old friend's garden
I may have picked in error,
And if so, I beg for pardon.
And hereby make acknowledgment.
My trespass overlook,
Remembering that after all
It is a friendship book.

PATIENCE STRONG

JANUARY

January 1st

When I think about the future all seems dark to me
  Everything is veiled in shadows of uncertainty.
But when I think about my friends my heart is comforted
  I am given strength to face whatever lies ahead.

There'll be burdens to be borne along the unknown road,
  But always there'll be somebody to help me bear the load,
Or someone somewhere needing *me*.
  And so my prayer ascends,
On the threshold of the year I thank God for my friends.

January 2nd

GRIEF GROWS OLD

God is good and griefs grow old,
  Time plays its gentle part
Laying healing hands upon the red wounds of the heart.
The secret scars grow fainter with the passing of the years
Faith returns and joy comes back to wipe away the tears.

Gleams of sunlight steal in at the windows of the mind.
Hope revives. The future beckons. Once again we find
Life has something sweet to offer.
Grey skies turn to gold.
Memories remain, but sorrows end.
  And grief grows old.

January 3rd

"I awoke this morning with devout thanksgiving for my friends, the old and the new."

EMERSON

January 4th
BETWEEN YOUR HEART AND MINE

Between your house and mine, my friend, there is a well-worn way—a path made by our footsteps, coming, going, day by day . . . Between your soul and mine there is a strange affinity—we are closely bound by unseen threads of destiny . . . This is something that I cannot fathom or define—this mystery of love, my friend, between your heart and mine.

January 5th
WINTER ROSES

Winter has its compensations though no sunlight gleams—there are many consolations: firelight, friendship, dreams . . . Thoughts of old and lovely things that comfort, cheer and bless—bringing unto weary hearts a secret happiness.

January 6th
THE EPIPHANY

"Lo, the star which they saw in the east, went before them, till it came and stood over where the young child was.

When they saw the star, they rejoiced with exceeding great joy."

MATTHEW 2.9–10

January 7th
DOORS HAVE FACES

Doors have faces, some look kind, inviting to the eye—others seem to scowl and to repel the passer-by. Some are dark and look forbidding. Some are bright and gay. Some say "Won't you step inside?" and some say, "Keep away" . . . At the doorway of the heart oh may there always be—a ray of light outstreaming from the lamp of charity.

January 8th
"And the Lord spake unto Moses face to face, as a man speaketh unto his friend."

EXODUS 33.11

January 9th

Gather up your memories. Like lavender they'll keep—fresh and fragrant when the earth is wrapped in winter's sleep . . . Happy is the heart that can rejoice when skies are grey—hearing on the bitter wind the nightingales of May.

January 10th

"Greater love hath no man than this, that a man lay down his life for his friends.

Ye are my friends, if ye do whatsoever I command you. Henceforth I call you not servants; for the servant knoweth not what his lord doeth: but I have called you friends: for all things that I have heard of my Father I have made known unto you."

JOHN 15.13–15

January 11th

THE TIMELY DEED

A little touch of kindliness when it is needed most. That's the kindness that you don't forget. The gesture of true sympathy that's made in all sincerity and comes when you are weary or upset . . . The understanding word that reaches down into your heart—at the very moment of your need. When someone shows concern for you by doing a good turn for you. How much it means, that good and timely deed! . . . A well-timed act of friendliness can save you from despair—even though it may be something small. The love that we appreciate is that which does not come too late to help us when we need it most of all.

January 12th

"There can be no friendship where there is no freedom. Friendship loves a free air and will not be penned up in straight and narrow enclosures. It will speak freely, and act so too; and take nothing ill where no ill is meant; nay, where it is 'twill easily forgive, and forget too, upon small acknowledgments."

WM. PENN

January 13th

TOLERANCE

I tread the road where I've been led and good it seems to me. I wish that you could come along and keep me company, but it's MY road, my road not yours. Perhaps it wouldn't do—if I should turn you from the path where God was leading you. By many strange and wondrous ways He guides the pilgrim's feet—and somewhere in His kingdom there's a place where all roads meet.

January 14th

ONE OF THESE DAYS

One of these days I'll make amends—to all my long-neglected friends. I'll drop a line to Mrs. C—and ask the Joneses round to tea. I'll ring Miss Brown and Maude and May. I really must . . . but not today.

One of these days I mean to make—the opportunity to take some flowers to poor old So-and-So. I should have done it weeks ago . . . Truly at the time I meant—to carry out my good intent—but it's fatal when you say—One of these days, but not today.

January 15th

"And the scripture was fulfilled which saith, Abraham believed God, and it was imputed unto him for righteousness: and he was called the Friend of God."

JAMES 2.23

January 16th

ALONE

Alone, yet never quite alone, I face an empty chair. But sometimes in the silence I imagine you are there. The good companion of the past, no longer here with me—and yet in some mysterious way you keep me company.

Ghost or angel? Does it matter? Words are meaningless. I only know that in my times of greatest loneliness—I feel that you are somewhere near though nothing's seen or said. The bitter moment passes and my heart is comforted.

GOOD LUCK, GOD BLESS

Ours has been a lovely friendship. Many happy times we've had. Now you're getting married and I want to tell you I am glad. I wish you well and may the future be a rosy one for you. All you hope for be fulfilled and every little dream come true.

When you've gone there'll be a gap, but that's the way it has to be. I shall miss you quite a lot for you have meant so much to me—but changes come. Life can't stand still; and on your day of happiness—I'll be saying in my heart: Goodbye, my friend, good luck, God bless.

January 18th
THE MEDICINE OF LIFE

"A faithful friend is a strong defence: and he that hath found such a one hath found a treasure. A faithful friend is the medicine of life."

ECCLESIASTICUS

January 19th
IN YOUR COMPANY

Why is our friendship such a dear and precious thing to me? I think it is because when I am in your company—my better self comes uppermost in all I say and do. Through your eyes I see things from a higher point of view.

My weaknesses you overlook, my failings you ignore. You draw out what is best in me and bring it to the fore . . . Through the radiance of your mind a different world I see. I'm something more than just myself when in your company.

January 20th
AFFINITY

Friendships do not come by chance. Upon the looms of circumstance Fate weaves an intricate design—and threads of other lives entwine to make a pattern with our own. We were not made to walk alone . . . How strange it is when pathways lead—to where we meet a friend in need. It seems that it was meant to be. We can't explain affinity—or understand the mystery of minds that blend in harmony.

January 21st
"Faithful are the wounds of a friend; but the kisses of an enemy are deceitful."

PROVERBS 27.6

January 22nd
A cottage in the country is the place where Winter yields—its deepest measure of content. The quiet of furrowed fields—seeps into one's consciousness. The fallow earth conveys—a healing peace you never found in Summer's busy days . . . Nature rests and you too catch the mood of her repose. Even though the cold is bitter and the wild wind blows—there are joys to compensate for fog and frost and sleet. The world of firelight, friends and books is cosy and complete.

January 23rd
CHARLES LAMB TO HIS SISTER, MARY

> "Thou to me didst ever show
>   Kindest affection; and would oft-times lend
>   An ear to the desponding love-sick lay
>   Weeping my sorrows with me, who repay
>   But ill the mighty debt of love I owe,
>   Mary, to thee, my sister and my friend."

January 24th
RUTH TO NAOMI, HER MOTHER-IN-LAW
"And Ruth said, Intreat me not to leave thee, or to return from following after thee: for whither thou goest, I will go; and where thou lodgest, I will lodge: thy people shall be my people, and thy God my God. Where thou diest, will I die, and there will I be buried: the Lord do so to me, and more also, if aught but death part thee and me."

RUTH I. 16–17

January 25th
YOU NEVER KNOW
You never know what's waiting at the turning of the road.
You don't know what you'll see beyond the bend . . . Keep
that thought in mind though rough the path and hard the
load. Round the corner you may find a friend.

That's what makes life so exciting. One can never say—
what Tomorrow's turn may bring in view . . . Just as you are
feeling that it's humdrum all the way—another vista opens
out for you.

January 26th
SHARING YOUR HAPPINESS
There is really no such thing as private happiness. If it is
not shared it quickly dies . . . Do not build a wall around the
heaven you possess. If you do the bird of joy soon flies.

Do not make a closed-in garden of the heart's content.
Leave the gate ajar and let it swing . . . Someone weary-
hearted down your pathway may be sent—and find through
you some good and lovely thing.

January 27th
"The soul of Jonathan was knit with the soul of David, and
Jonathan loved him as his own soul . . . Then Jonathan and
David made a covenant, because he loved him as his own
soul . . . And Jonathan stripped himself of the robe that was
upon him, and gave it to David, and his garments, even to
his sword, and to his bow, and to his girdle."

FIRST BOOK OF SAMUEL

January 28th
TO A SNOWDROP
"Lone flower, hemmed in with snows, and white as they
　　But hardier far, once more I see thee bend
　Thy forehead, as if fearful to offend,
　　Like an unbidden guest."

WORDSWORTH

MAKING NEW FRIENDS

Sometimes it's a change of job that brings a friend your way
—a journey or a party or a summer holiday. You turn a bend
upon the road and suddenly you find—you've met a kindred
spirit. Thus the threads of fate unwind. Your path in life is
crossed by someone who was meant for you—and everything
takes on a sweeter tone, a brighter hue.

Old friends may be dear but you must never turn away—
from the chance to make new friends, for there may come a
day—when dearest friends must leave you, death or distance
may divide—and then how grateful you will be for new friends
at your side.

LAURA TO MARIANNE

"She stayed but half an hour and neither in the course of
her visit, confided to me any of her secret thoughts, nor
requested me to confide in her, any of mine. You will easily
imagine therefore my dear Marianne that I could not feel any
ardent affection or very sincere attachment for Lady
Dorothea."

JANE AUSTEN

THE GARDEN SLEEPS

The garden sleeps. No splash of colour stains the fallow
mould. The trees are stark, the hedge is bare, the air is damp
and cold—and Nature on the quiet earth has spread a quilt of
snow—as if to cover and protect the life that lies below.

How still it is! No sound disturbs the silence of the day. No
sign or hint reveals that underneath the frozen clay—are
bulbs and roots and seeds from which there'll come at Winter's
close—a blaze of bloom, flame, gold and crimson, ivory and
rose.

FEBRUARY

February 1st

There is something about the word February that stirs the heart with an irrational but irrepressible joy. The arrows of the rain fall sharp and cold from a wintry sky and the doors of the north are not yet barred against the threat of snow, but once January has slipped off the calendar nothing can ever be quite the same again. A ghost of a snowdrop flutters in the grass. A blue light lingers on thé edge of the lengthening days and the voice of "February's thrush" comes pouring down the wind.

February 2nd

SOMEONE NEEDS YOU

Life is never hopeless when there's someone needing you. Life is never futile when there's something you can do—something you can do to help and something you can say—to lighten someone's burden or to brighten someone's day.

Don't give way to loneliness, depression or despair—just because you find you have to face an empty chair . . . The world is full of people. There is much for which to live. Someone needs you. Someone wants the things that you can give.

February 3rd

"The vision of Christ that thou dost see
Is my vision's greatest enemy,
Thine is the friend of all mankind;
Mine speaks in parables to the blind."

WM. BLAKE

February 4th

RETIREMENT

Well and truly have you done your work throughout the years. You've had your ups and downs, your trials and troubles, hopes and fears—and Time has called a halt. The job is finished now for you. But though it is an ending it's a new beginning too . . . You will miss the old routine and the familiar ways—but life will start afresh and bring good friends and happy days—a future full of interests in which we hope you'll find—the blessings of contentment, health and joy and peace of mind.

February 5th
THE GOSPEL OF FELLOWSHIP

It's sometimes good to get away from all the noise and din—to dwell upon a quiet thought and find your peace within. Is it good to seek too much the joys of solitude—in a place where other people's troubles can't intrude? . . . We were meant for fellowship for that's the Christian creed—scattering the seeds of friendship, meeting someone's need. Doing what you can for others. Sharing lovingly. Getting out into the world and helping somebody.

February 6th
"This is my commandment, that ye love one another, as I have loved you."

JOHN 15.12

February 7th

LIGHT FOR TODAY

Light for today is light enough for me. One step ahead is all I need to see. Light for the doing of the daily task. Light for the present. That is all I ask.

I do not seek to know what lies ahead—out in the dark beyond the road I tread. Why should I fear for what the years may bring? God giveth light for each day's journeying.

February 8th

CONTENTMENT

Don't despise contentment for it's something rich and rare—in an age of restlessness, frustration and despair. It is an achievement, in itself a victory—to make a world within a world and live contentedly . . . Heaven's where you make it and its treasures you will find—wherever you may seek with thankful heart and quiet mind.

February 9th
BEN JONSON,
INVITING A FRIEND TO SUPPER

"Tonight, grave sir, both my poor house and I
  Do equally desire your company:
Not that we think us worthy such a guest.
But that your worth will dignify our feast."

February 10th
SOMEONE'S WAITING FOR A LETTER

Someone's waiting for a letter. Do not be unkind. Take that pen and write that line to ease somebody's mind. It's hard to pick up broken threads when once you let them go. Someone's waiting for a letter. Somebody you know. Mother, father, family, the old friend or the new. Someone's waiting. Someone's hoping for a line from you.

February 11th
PAUL REMEMBERS HIS FRIENDS
IN A LETTER TO TIMOTHY

" . . . without ceasing I have remembrance of thee in my prayers night and day; greatly desiring to see thee, being mindful of thy tears, that I may be filled with joy.

When I call to remembrance the unfeigned faith that is in thee, which dwelt first in thy grandmother Lois, and in thy mother Eunice. Salute Prisca and Aquila and the household of Onesiphorus. Eubulus greeteth thee, and Pudens, and Linus, and Claudia, and all the brethren. Grace be with you."

JOHN TO GAIUS, THE WELLBELOVED

"Beloved, I wish above all things that thou mayest prosper and be in health, even as thy soul prospereth. For I rejoiced greatly when the brethren came and testified of the truth that is in thee . . . I trust I shall shortly see thee, and we shall speak face to face. Peace be to thee. Our friends salute thee. Greet the friends by name."

February 13th

RELIGION

The path to Heaven is the path where daily duty lies. The road to glory is the road that runs before your eyes . . . Where you are is where God comes to meet you face to face. Where you are is where you'll find His blessing and His grace.

Do not say religion is too high and rare for you. Work it into everything you think and say and do . . . Every day is Sunday if you take it where you go—for every day is holy if you choose to make it so.

February 14th

LEAST SAID

Least said, soonest mended. It's trite but it is true. Learn this bit of wisdom and keep it well in view. Don't let your tongue betray you. Remember when upset—it's better to say nothing than something you'll regret. Never go on talking when everything's been said—That only worsens matters and brings them to a head.

A little altercation can have a bitter end—and make a deep division with family or friend . . . The less you say about it the easier it will be—to forget it and to let it fade from memory.

February 15th

"Do not keep on with a mockery of friendship after the substance is gone—but part, while you can part friends. Bury the carcase of friendship: it is not worth embalming."

WM. HAZLITT

OLD FRIENDS RETURNING

Welcome are the snowdrops on a cold and wintry day—
like old friends returning from somewhere far away.

BURIED GOLD

Beauty lies hidden, a captive bound—deep in the dungeons
of the ground. Down in the cells of the frozen clay—where the
riches of Spring are stored away.

The crocus was locked behind earthy walls—where never
a gleam of sunlight falls—but see how she breaks through the
prison bars—and points a bright finger to the stars!

THE TIDES OF PROVIDENCE

It's not what you gather but what you sow that gives the
heart a warming glow. It's not what you get but what you
give decides the kind of life you live . . . It's not what you
hoard but what you spare. It's not what you take but what
you share—that pays the greater dividend and makes you
richer in the end . . . It's not what you spend upon yourself or
hide away upon a shelf—that brings a blessing for the day. It's
what you scatter by the way. A wasted effort it may seem—
but what you cast upon the stream—comes back to you in
recompense, upon the tides of Providence.

REGRETS

Sometimes it's too late to say the thing you meant to say—
too late to say you're sorry or some kindness to repay. Too late
to speak the loving word or lend the helping hand—to show
appreciation or to give the gift you planned.

Thus we pile up vain regrets that haunt the years ahead:
memories of all the things we might have done or said . . .

Save yourself that pain and take each opportunity—of doing all that's in your power for friends and family.

GIVING HAPPINESS

Giving opens doors in hearts and makes affections glow. Giving stirs the fires of friendship when they're burning low. All too often through our lives there runs a selfish theme. Thoughts turn inwards seeking the fulfilment of a dream— but if we thought of others more and self a little less—a wider world we should discover, giving happiness.

NO FRIEND LIKE AN OLD FRIEND

There's no friend like an old friend who has walked life's road with you—easy to get on with like a worn well-fitting shoe . . . There's no friend like an old friend. When blows fall and troubles brew—it's good to turn to somebody who knows you through and through.

LAMB TO COLERIDGE

"And now, when shall I catch a glimpse of your honest face-to-face countenance again; your fine dogmatical sceptical face by punch-light? Oh! one glimpse of the human face, and shake of the human hand, is better than whole reams of this cold, thin correspondence; yea, of more worth than all the letters that have sweated the fingers of sensibility, from Madame Sévigné and Balzac to Sterne and Shenstone."

A SENSE OF HUMOUR

If you see the funny side, you'll stroll along the sunny side while other folks are walking in the shade. Things will never harass you, embitter or embarrass you. A sense of humour is the finest aid—to wisdom and philosophy—in trouble and adversity—it brings you smiling through the stress and strife. So cultivate the power to see—the humour and the comedy— behind the trials and tragedies of life.

February 24th
NOT SO LONG AGO

Not so long ago it seems the snow lay thickly here. Is this not a good and lovely moment in the year—when across the garden crocus carpets are unrolled: white and purple, mauve and yellow, ivory and gold.

February 25th
FRIENDS IN MISFORTUNE

There are many people who are charming, good and gay— but you do not want them near when blue skies turn to grey. When the soul is sorrowful you shun their company—going where the heart directs for warmth and sympathy.

In the dark and grievous hours instinctively you turn—to the ones you love and trust for with the years you learn—where to look for consolation when the shadows fall. The friend with whom you share your troubles is the best of all.

February 26th
YOUR BIT OF THE ROAD

You cannot travel every road or carry everybody's load, but on your own bit of the track—you can take upon your back—a part of someone's else's cross of misfortune, pain or loss . . . You can't light lamps of charity on every long dark road you see, but on the path that now you tread a little brightness you can shed.

February 27th
A FRIEND AT YOUR SIDE

Perhaps you travel faster when you take the road alone— and reach the goal a little sooner climbing on your own—but isn't it a better thing as on the way you fare—to have some-body at your side the ups and downs to share.

It's not the pace that matters as the path of life you tread. It's having courage faith and hope to face the miles ahead . . . How much easier it is to plod on to the end—in the happy company of a beloved friend.

February 28th

February is a month of intimations and anticipations. There is a peculiar blueness in the twilights which lengthen with the widening arc of the sun. The blackbirds are nesting. The crust of the soil is pricked with green pins. The sallow willow lifts its budded wands of silvery fur above the hedges where the hazels shake their yellow catkins in the wind and the banks are starred with celandines. Spring is not yet come, but the mind which is in tune with the moods of nature is aware of the banked up forces of life breaking through at every point.

February 29th

AN EXTRA DAY

When it is a Leap Year—Time doles out an extra day. Four and twenty precious hours are gained for work and play . . . As the first sweet songs of love amongst the birds are chanted—a gift is given to this month; another dawn is granted.

MARCH

March 1st

When Wordsworth saw that host of daffodils "fluttering and dancing in the breeze" by Ullswater it was, no doubt, a sight most marvellous, but when a flower is at its fullest and brightest point of beauty it is nearest to its moment of dissolution, that is why I love best the time when the thin pointed buds of the daffodils begin to break from the sheaths in which they have been folded like tightly rolled umbrellas. The anticipation of beauty yet to come is sweeter than the contemplation of perfection.

March 2nd

> "Daffodils,
>   That come before the swallow dares
>   And take the winds of March with beauty;
>   Violets, dim,
>   But sweeter than the lids of Juno's eyes,
>   Or Cytherea's breath."

> SHAKESPEARE'S PERDITA,
> FROM *The Winter's Tale*

March 3rd

"I looked, and behold, a door was opened in heaven: and the first voice which I heard was as it were of a trumpet talking with me; which said, Come up hither, and I will show thee things which must be hereafter."

> REVELATION 4.1

March 4th

MEMORIES

Memories . . . not in the brain, for cells could never hold—the record of a story that no tongue has ever told. Memories

. . . through memories we tread the secret way—across the silent borderlands of Now and Yesterday. Memories evoke for us the face, the words, the smile—of those whom we have "loved long since and lost awhile."

March 5th

Never make an enemy by word or deed or thought. Offer good for evil in the way the Master taught. Pocket pride and you will be rewarded in the end—by seeing an opponent change and turn into a friend.

March 6th

TOMORROW NEVER COMES

It's fatal to procrastinate—until you find it's just too late—and then to put the blame on Fate . . . Tomorrow never comes. The putting right of some mistake—the gesture that you meant to make—the habit that you vowed to break . . . Tomorrow never comes. So do it now for Life can play—some funny tricks. Time slips away. Tomorrow will become TODAY. Tomorrow never comes.

March 7th

Folks are queer, but oftentimes you find they're not so bad. You may be mistaken in the view that you have had. Sometimes when with unkind word they snarl and show their teeth —it's because the better self is hidden underneath . . . Try to get at what is there behind that ugly frown. Look beyond the barriers and try to break them down. Many people hide their better selves behind a wall. Do not judge in haste, but better still . . . don't judge at all.

March 8th

WANTED

WANTED—men with willing hands to do God's urgent work.
WANTED—those who will not falter, quail or shrink or shirk.
WANTED—sympathetic hearts to ease the world's distress.
WANTED—helpers for the job of spreading happiness.

March 9th

GIVE THANKS

Give thanks when every morning breaks and thank God every night for strength and health and precious gifts of hearing and of sight. For all the daily blessings that too often we forget. We owe Him more than we can give. We're always in His debt . . . We cannot make a just return for what we take each day—for all the benefits received we never can repay—but gratefully and gladly we can make acknowledgment—for all the good and lovely things a loving God has sent.

March 10th

ONLY PASSING BY

We are only passing by so doesn't it seem madness—to fill the world with things that make for evil, strife and sadness! . . . Men for money, pride or power will fight and kill and lie. Is it worth it when you think we're only passers-by—passing through this world but once with all its sin and sorrow. Here today, not here to stay, but here and gone tomorrow.

March 11th

JUST A LITTLE

Just a little sympathy can go a long long way—to help a breaking heart to face a world that's hard and grey. A little snatch of melody can fill the world with song—and put some music into life when things are going wrong. Just a little friendliness, a little bit of praise—can urge some tired discouraged soul to live the dreary days. A golden streak of sunlight in a sky that looks like rain—can make a weary traveller look up and smile again.

March 12th

ABOVE ALL THINGS

"But the end of all things is at hand; be ye therefore sober, and watch unto prayer. And above all things have fervent charity among yourselves: for charity shall cover the multitude of sins."

I PETER 4.7-8

March 13th
SILKEN THREADS

Love is like a silken thread that holds us heart to heart—a silken thread, yet strong as chains. We cannot draw apart. We are tied to those we love for all eternity—held in bondage of affection, gently, tenderly.

Day by day and year by year the unseen ties are wound—in and out between our hearts until we're closely bound—by ties as light as gossamer. In fairy webs we're caught—in the tangled meshes of the silken threads of thought.

March 14th
A SIXPENNY PACKET

From the contents of this little packet I shall see—green shoots thrusting through the soil and someday there will be—pansies, asters, scented stocks and marigolds ablaze. All the fragrance and the glory of the summer days . . . Isn't this a lesson that we'd all do well to heed? God brings forth his wonders from a tiny speck of seed. Small the seed of faith may be in dark and troubled hours—but from small beginnings He can bring the sweetest flowers.

March 15th
ST. PETER WRITING TO THE STRANGERS AND THE PILGRIMS
"Use hospitality one to another without grudging."

March 16th
IS IT TIME?

Is it time to open? says the primrose in the lane. Is it time to venture out into the world again? Underneath the crinkled leaves the folded petals stay—hesitating in the bud, so bitter is the day.

Is it time for nesting? asks the songbird looking round.
There's a keen edge on the wind and grey frost on the ground,
but day by day I feel a joy that rises like a tide. Is it time to
sing, or must this rapture be denied?

March 17th
THE RUNE OF ST. PATRICK

At Tara today in this fateful hour
I place all Heaven with its power,
and the sun with its brightness,
and the snow with its whiteness,
and fire with all the strength it hath
and lightning with its rapid wrath,
and the wings with their swiftness along their path,
and the sea with its deepness,
and the rocks with their steepness,
and the earth with its starkness:
   All these I place,
by God's almighty help and grace,
between myself and the powers of darkness.

March 18th
ST. PAUL, WRITING TO THE CORINTHIANS

"Though I speak with the tongues of men and of angels and
have not charity, I am become as sounding brass, or a tinkling
cymbal. And though I have the gift of prophecy, and understand all mysteries, and all knowledge; and though I have all
faith, so that I could remove mountains, and have not charity,
I am nothing."

March 19th
BONE OF CONTENTION

Is it worth contending for that silly little bone? Why not
drop the argument and let the thing alone. Does it really
matter who was wrong and who was right? If it breaks a
friendship then it isn't worth the fight.

Life's too short and sweet to spoil. The only thing to do—
is to try and understand the other's point of view. Either halve
the bone and to an equal share agree—or one must be mag-
nanimous and give in graciously.

In any case, no matter what the quarrel is about—it's not
worth hanging on to and it's not worth holding out . . . It isn't
so important as it seems as Time will show. The bone's not
worth the struggle. Think again and let it go.

March 20th
THEY NEVER GROW OLD

They never grow old, the young who die before their years
are spent. They never grow old and tired and grey beneath
life's burdens bent. Always in our memories their faces will
remain—as they were, untouched by Time, unmarked by age
or strain.

They never grow old. We recollect them as we knew them
here. Whether it was long ago or only yesteryear. They never
change as we must change in looks and character. For them
it's always Springtime and we see them as they were.

March 21st
"The good alone can be friends. The friendship of the good
is alone superior to calumny; it not being easy for men to
believe a third person respecting one whom they have long
tried and proved. There is between good men mutual confidence, and the feeling that one's friend would never have
done one wrong, and all other such things as are expected in
friendship really worthy the name."

ARISTOTLE

March 22nd
ALL IN ALL

All in all you've been to me. My comfort in adversity. My
sunshine when the skies were grey. All the while and all the
way.

Everything you are to me: my hope, my help, my destiny.
The joy at every journey's end—My good companion,
dearest friend.

March 23rd
THE REASON WHY
We do not know the reason why there always seems to be—
a dark thread running through the gold upon life's tapestry—
but there it is. And sorrow comes at last to everyone. Shadows
fall across the path and clouds obscure the sun . . . Can it be
that if this life were one long rosy way—the soul would never
learn to climb, to strive, to grow, to pray . . . If everyone were
satisfied and no one had a care—none would ever need to help;
there'd be no loads to share.

March 24th
THE RECONCILIATION
Let us remember what was best, the good times, not the bad
—the happiness, the golden hours, the blessings we have had.
Let us forget the angry word, the bitter memory. Let us renew
our sacred pledges of fidelity.

Let us put far from heart and mind, the doubts, the tears,
the pain. Take up the broken threads of life together once
again . . . Let us remember only this: the things we meant to
do. Let us recall our dearest dream and make that dream
come true.

March 25th
THESE THREE
Have you ever thought of what this world of ours would be
—without these three great Christian virtues, faith, hope,
charity? . . . They put the salt and savour and the meaning
into life—without them it would be all sorrow, doubt and sin
and strife.

It would be an ugly world, a place of gloom and greed—
were it not for those who try to live the Christian creed . . .

These things keep us linked with God wherever we may be.
These are our salvation: faith and hope and charity.

March 26th
PAUL TO THE CORINTHIANS

"And now abideth faith, hope, charity, these three; but the
greatest of these is charity."

March 27th
THE LESSONS OF MISFORTUNE

It's easy to be grateful for the good and happy days—to lift
the heart in joyous prayers of thankfulness and praise—when
everything is going well with not a cloud in view—when all
the roads run smoothly and our dreams are coming true . . .
But we must learn to thank God for the things that bring us
low—if we never suffered then the soul would never grow.
That which wounds the vanity and curbs the selfish will—is
an opportunity for wresting good from ill.

March 28th

"This communicating of a man's self to his friend, works
two contrary effects; for it redoubleth joys, and cutteth griefs
in halves. For there is no man, that imparteth his joys to his
friend, but he joyeth the more; and no man, that imparteth his
griefs to his friend, but he grieveth the less."

FRANCIS BACON

March 29th
THE UNEXPECTED

The unexpected pleasure sometimes gives more happiness—
than those that we have planned for many a day . . . An
unexpected bit of fun is like a sudden flash of sun—a burst of
brightness breaking through the grey.

March 30th
PURE RELIGION

"If any man among you seem to be religious, and bridleth

not his tongue, but deceiveth his own heart, this man's religion is vain.

Pure religion and undefiled before God and the Father is this: to visit the fatherless and widows in their affliction, and to keep himself unspotted from the world."

JAMES TO THE TWELVE TRIBES SCATTERED ABROAD

March 31st

Whether March comes in like a lion and goes out like a lamb or comes in like a lamb and goes out like a lion I let it go without a pang of regret. The domed blossom of the almond tree is like a pink parasol. The floor of the copse is carpeted with wildflowers. The chiffchaff has arrived and the daffodils have danced along the garden path, but it is good to stand on the threshold of Spring with March over and April at the gate.

APRIL

April 1st

> "April, April,
>   Laugh thy golden laughter,
>   But, the moment after,
>   Weep thy golden tears!"
>   WM. WATSON

April 2nd

WEATHER WISDOM

"April wet, good wheat."

"A cold April brings us bread and wine."

"When the elm leaf is like a mouse's ear, then to sow barley never fear."

April 3rd

FOOTPRINTS

In the footprints of the Winter sunlight falls and buds unfold. April follows in its track and strews the path with fairy gold.

Where the morning frosts have glittered and the bitter snows have lain—Spring comes dancing, young and lovely, bringing primroses again.

April 4th

CLOSE THE GATE OF MEMORY

Close the gate of memory. Come back, my heart, come back. You dare not go too far along that old unhappy track . . . Keep sacred every well-loved name, but cling not to the sorrow —lest you miss the way that leads you to a bright Tomorrow. You can't take one step back upon the road of destiny. Forward to the future. Close the gate of memory.

April 5th
PAUL TO THE SAINTS AT EPHESUS

"Let all bitterness, and wrath, and anger, and clamour, and evil speaking be put away from you, with all malice.

And be ye kind one to another, tenderhearted, forgiving one another, even as God for Christ's sake hath forgiven you."

EPHESIANS 4.31–32

April 6th

TO STAY FOR EVERMORE

If I could live one day again, one day out of the past, I'd choose the day that we two met—for when my mind I cast across the landscape of the years it stands out bright and bold. The memory is evergreen although the tale is old.

A blue and golden afternoon, a clear and cloudless sky. A garden by the water with the white sails moving by, and someone coming up the path I'd never seen before—walking straight into my life to stay for evermore.

April 7th

"Ho, every one that thirsteth, come ye to the waters, and he that hath no money; come ye, buy and eat; yea, come buy wine and milk without money and without price.

Wherefore do ye spend money for that which is not bread? and your labour for that which satisfieth not? hearken diligently unto me, and eat ye that which is good, and let your soul delight itself in fatness."

ISAIAH 55.1–2

April 8th

> "A primrose by a river's brim
> A yellow primrose was to him,
> And it was nothing more."

WORDSWORTH

April 9th

WHEN IT'S APRIL

What could be more lovely than to wander up and down—

a street of quaint old houses in a quiet country town, where Time has stained the mossy roofs to russet gold and brown . . . In England when it's April?

What could be more beautiful than watching sunlight fall— on little cottage lattices, oak, stone and weathered wall? There's a sort of magic in the beauty of it all—in England when it's April.

April 10th

A very dear friend has beguiled me into accompanying her in her pretty equipage to her beautiful home, four miles off. Talking with her is like being in the Palace of Truth described by Madame de Genlis; and yet so kindly are her feelings, so great her indulgence to the little failings and foibles of our common nature . . . that with all her frank speaking, I never knew her make an enemy or lose a friend.

MARY RUSSELL MITFORD
FROM *Our Village*

April 11th

THE RAINBOW

"I do set my bow in the cloud, and it shall be for a token of a covenant between me and the earth. And it shall come to pass, when I bring a cloud over the earth, that the bow shall be seen."

GENESIS 9.13–14

April 12th

THANKING YOU

You helped me when I needed help, and did it willingly. I never shall forget the kindness that was shown to me. I owe a debt of gratitude that I can never pay. Thank you, thank you from my heart is all that I can say.

April 13th

SET-BACKS

Set-backs you are bound to have,
On every road you meet,

Hindrances and obstacles
Disaster and defeat,
But do not be surprised when things don't work the way you
  plan
That's the way that life has been since first the world began.

April 14th

Dear friend, when bored with humdrum ways
  I think about those happy days
When we went laughing and down
  The magpie streets of Shrewsbury town,
Then it seemed our feet had wings.
  Oh the many lovely things
We shared and talked of, you and I
  Underneath the Shropshire sky.
Through the old old town we went,
  So young, so gay, so innocent,
With faith afire and heart aglow,
  But that, my friend, was long ago.

April 15th

Just as the flowers need rain and sunshine to strengthen their
roots for the bringing forth of the best and loveliest blooms, so
do our friendships need the warmth and refreshment of kindly
remembrances. A friendship neglected will wither like a plant
starved of air, light and water, but even if a friendship is
remembered only in prayer it lives, for there will be life in its
roots.

April 16th

THE GARDEN TOMB, JERUSALEM

Still it stands, that little garden near the city wall. Still the
olives spread their branches and the sparrows call. All may
stand where Jesus stood and all may come to pray—where He
rose in glory on the Resurrection Day. The place where Christ
was seen of Mary in the morning hour. The garden of the
miracle of Love's transcendent power.

"Now in the place where He was crucified, there was a garden."

JOHN 19.41

April 17th

Life's not the same without you. The waiting seems so long. So hurry up. Get better—and come back well and strong. More than you guess you're wanted. Have faith and you will see—that God will work the wonder. "The best is yet to be."

April 18th

THE FACES OF THE FLOWERS

Just like humans, flowers have faces with expressions grave and gay. Some appear to smile at you and others turn their heads away. Some look pious and remote as if engaged in secret prayer. Some look wild and frivolous and others have a homely air . . . Each one has its own sweet meaning and its message to convey. Each one has its place and purpose and its little part to play. Though we mass them into beds and crowd them in a tiny space—let us sometimes stoop and see the beauty of each separate face.

April 19th

I REMEMBER

I forget the big adventures of the years now gone: the ecstasies, the agonies—and yet this still lives on: that quiet room, the clock, the beams, the window with a view. The willow-pattern china and the table set for two. Time in passing steals so many memories away—but I'll remember till I die that lovely April day.

April 20th

BLESSED ARE THE PEACEMAKERS:
FOR THEY SHALL BE CALLED
THE CHILDREN OF GOD

MATTHEW 5.9

April 21st
THE BOND OF BREAD AND SALT
"He went forth, and brought some food, and put it before him, saying to him, Eat, oh my master, that the bond of bread and salt may be established between us; and may God (whose name be exalted) execute vengeance upon him who is unfaithful to the bond of bread and salt."

The Arabian Nights

April 22nd
SOMEDAY YOU WILL UNDERSTAND
Bear you now what must be borne. Accept and not rebel. Know that in the end all will come right and all be well. You're in the dark. You question why such things as this should be, but someday you will understand it. Someday you will see.

April 23rd
LEAVING HOME
The time has come to spread your wings and leave the family nest—your own way in the world to make. O may that way be blessed—with happiness and all success. This is our wish for you—that you'll fulfil the highest hopes and reach the goal in view.

Write as often as you can and tell us how you fare. There'll be problems and temptations all around you there—but never let your standards fall. Be good and straight and true—remembering the faith and trust that has been placed in you.

April 24th
TACT
Tact will help you round life's awkward bends. If you have no tact you'll have no friends. Without intention you will give offence by being clumsy, indiscreet or dense.

Tactless people always seem to be—up against some animosity—because they do not know how to convey—their meanings in a wise and gracious way.

No matter what the others do or say—you'll find a little tact will always pay ... At home or work when trouble looms in sight—a tactful word will often put things right.

April 25th
THE MAKING OF A RAINBOW
Take some lovely thought out of a poem or a prayer. Turn it over in your mind and let it linger there. Don't sit watching at the window for the clouds to part—there'll soon be a rainbow if you start one in your heart. Work your own small miracle and make the dull day glow. Put some sunshine into life and let the glory show.

April 26th
A BIG MIND IN A LITTLE HOUSE
"When Socrates was building himself a house at Athens, being asked by one that observed the littleness of the design, why a man so eminent would not have an abode more suitable to his dignity he replied, that he should think himself sufficiently accommodated, if he could see that narrow habitation filled with real friends."

SAMUEL JOHNSON

April 27th
THE BOW OF PROMISE
What is this thing called a rainbow, so lovely, so fair to behold—circling the earth with a glory of indigo, orange and gold? What is this wonder, this marvel, that none can describe or define. Useless to try and explain it. To me it is something divine ... I care not for dull explanations. I know it's God's bow on the cloud. A symbol of faith to the faithless, a silent rebuke to the proud.

"I will look upon it that I may remember the everlasting covenant between God and every living creature."

GENESIS 9.16

April 28th
THE VICTORY OF SPRING
The rulers of this world for all their proud and vaunting words—can't halt Spring's invasion or cry Silence to the birds. Nature presses on. Her great green armies take the field—every living thing to her dominion now must yield. The hosts of Spring victoriously with banners all unfurled—move in triumph out across the unresisting world.

April 29th
SINGING THROUGH THE SHOWERS
Sun and rain, they come together all along the way. Life with all its tears and joys is like an April day . . . Cloud and shadow, changing with the changes of the hours. O for faith with which to go a-singing through the showers! knowing that the glory's there behind the gloomy pall—knowing that the love of God is in and over all.

April 30th
So much is happening in garden and countryside that I run this way and that trying to hold everything at once: the wallflowers, the tulips, the lilac and the apple-blossom. I should like to stay the pace of Time here at this point and to linger over the last of April, but all around life rises like a tide and I am carried forward into the exciting anticipation of pleasures to come.

MAY

May 1st

Dare I sit here grieving in a dream-world of my own
—thinking back across the years of happiness once known—
when outside the window on this bright and lovely day—
miracles are happening, the miracles of May: the hawthorn
in the hedges and the bluebells in the wood? Can I now deny
that life is sweet and God is good?

May 2nd
THE BLESSINGS OF THE YEARS

Sometimes when the fates conspire to cheat you of your
heart's desire—you quite forget the good things gained, the
gifts received, the goals attained . . . That is just the time when
you—should struggle on and see it through—remembering
not trials and tears—but all the blessings of the years.

May 3rd

There are numberless occasions which may render an
absence between friends highly expedient; and to endeavour,
from an impatience of separation, to prevent it, betrays a
degree of weakness inconsistent with that firm and manly
spirit, without which it is impossible to act up to the character
of a true friend.

CICERO

May 4th
SOMEONE IS THINKING OF YOU

Someone remembers—and somebody cares. Your name is
mentioned in somebody's prayers . . . Keep the bright hope of
the future in view. Someone is thinking of you.

May 5th
BETWEEN THE STONES OF TIME

Seasons pass in Love's green garden and the years their changes bring—but beneath the fallen blossoms griefs are buried, new hopes spring.

Round the arbours of remembrance Youth's unfading roses climb—and the mosses of affection grow between the stones of Time.

May 6th
SITTING AT THE GATE

The lazy man sat at his gate—fortune's favours to await. He did not stir to dig or plant—but waited for the gods to grant the wishes that he wished all day. But no good angel came his way . . . He sat until his back grew bent beneath his load of discontent. He envied others, railed at fate. But all he did was sit and wait—So Time just left him high and dry. Friends and fortune passed him by.

May 7th
THE OLD TREE BEARS NEW BLOSSOM

The old old tree has bloomed again. In the sunlight and the rain—it stands once more, a lovely thing—in the bridal white of Spring . . .

Year by year its leaves are shed and every year we think it dead—but in the roots beneath the clay—life remains and May by May—the gnarled old branches flower and spread—a dome of blossom overhead.

May 8th
HAPPINESS IS CATCHING

Happiness is so infectious once it gets about—Do not keep it to yourself but always give it out . . . Happiness is catching! How the joy germs thrive! If you're feeling grateful just to be alive—don't suppress your feelings. Let them effervesce. Start an epidemic, spreading happiness.

May 9th
WHEN BLOSSOM FALLS
When upon the orchard grass the fallen blossoms lie—a shadow steals across the mind and with a passing sigh—you wish it could have lasted longer. Transient and brief—is the glory that precedes the coming of the leaf . . . Blossom falls to make way for the green and swelling shoot—that conceals within the bud the pledge of summer's fruit.

May 10th
FORGET-ME-NOT
Flower of friendship! Every year—when forget-me-nots appear—around the borders, hazy blue. My long lost friend, I think of you . . . These tiny flowerlets of May—take me back to yesterday—and walking in my garden plot—I hear you say, Forget-me-not.

May 11th
"Why are thou cast down, O my soul? and why art thou disquieted within me? hope thou in God: for I shall yet praise him who is the health of my countenance, and my God."

PSALM 42.11

May 12th
IS IT REALLY TIME TO GO?
Is it really time to go? Must we part? Time hurries so.

Friend, when in your company—the clock becomes my enemy. In vain we try the hours to hold—but before the tale is told—the moment comes to say goodbye, so quickly do the moments fly. It seems we're always saying Oh!— is it really time to go?

May 13th

BRIDGES
Do not cross your bridges till they come in view. Don't waste time in wondering what you're going to do—when you meet

disaster or adversity. It may never happen. It may never be . . .
It is more than foolish to anticipate—trouble in the future.
Why not let it wait—till you're up against it? Fate may
intervene. Something unexpected, something unforeseen—
may be round the corner, changing everything. Situations
alter while you're worrying.

May 14th
CELTIC RUNE OF HOSPITALITY

I saw a stranger yestreen,
I put food in the eating place,
Drink in the drinking place,
Music in the music place,
and in the sacred name of the TRIUNE,
He blessed myself and my house, my cattle and my dear ones,
    and the lark said in her song
Often, often, often, goes the Christ in the stranger's guise.

May 15th
NEVER MEASURE TIME

Never measure Time, but if you want a sum to do—count
the many mercies that the Lord has granted you. Count the
boons and benefits, the things you're thankful for. Keep on
adding to the list. There's always something more—something
to be glad about whatever may betide—another item to be
marked upon the credit side . . . Never measure out the miles
as down life's road you tread. Do not count your birthdays up
but count your friends instead.

May 16th
THE BEAUTY OF THE LARCH

Gracefully the larch boughs stretch as if they felt in every
vein—the tender searching of the wind, the warm caress of sun
and rain . . . From far wild mountains it has come—now
rooted here as if at ease. No stranger, but a happy guest, content amongst our English trees.

May 17th
POT-POURRI

My lovely memories of you are gathered up and stored away
—like faded petals that retain the sweetness of a summer day
... Without you Winter lingers long—yet often in my heart it
seems—I catch the perfume of the past, the breath of unforgotten dreams, like fragrance rising secretly—from the bowl
of memory.

May 18th
PEN PALS

We've never met and yet we've come to know each other
well. It may be that the written word says more than tongue
can tell ... Just a paper friendship that you'd think would fade
away—with the changes in our lives that come from day to
day. Much has happened, things have altered. Friends have
come and gone—Time has passed, but this our lovely friendship still goes on.

May 19th

"Let the words of my mouth, and the meditation of my
heart, be acceptable in Thy sight, O Lord, my strength and
my redeemer."

PSALM 19.14

May 20th
IS IT FAR?

Is it far to the end of this long long road? Is it uphill all the
time? Yes, it's steep and hard and with every yard—it's a stiff
and steady climb.

Is there no quiet inn where a man can rest when the load
bears heavily?

Not, my friend, till you reach the end of your road of destiny.

May 21st
TOWARDS A BRIGHTER VIEW

There's many an anxious thought behind a smiling face

today. There's many a heartache underneath expressions grim or gay—so speak a kind word where you can, it doesn't cost a cent—to give a little bit of comfort or encouragement . . . Many could be helped and strengthened by a word from you —a word that turns the eyes towards a broader brighter view.

May 22nd
THE FIRST OF THE ROSES
The last rose of Summer brings Autumn's chill breath—the thought of farewell, of decay and of death—but the first of the roses that opens for me—speaks of the joy of the Summer to be —straight out of Heaven it seems to appear—at this most glorious time of the year.

May 23rd
> "Who goes to bed and doth not pray,
> Maketh two nights to every day."
>   GEORGE HERBERT

May 24th
ROSES HAVE THORNS,
BUT THORNS HAVE ROSES
Roses have thorns, but thorns have roses. Birds peck the cherries, but they sing . . . Bees carry poison, but make honey. God has a use for everything.

Life has its times of grief and sorrow. Sharp is the thorn of tribulation—but from the same stem as the thorn there comes the rose of resignation.

May 25th
FLOWERS OF FRIENDSHIP LEFT TO FADE
All the roadways of the past are strewn with the mistakes we've made—with opportunities we've missed and flowers of friendship left to fade.

O if we could only turn and go back just a little way—to do the thing we meant to do and say the things we meant to say!

WHO'LL EVER GET TO PARADISE?

Do not make a hasty judgment. Seize on what is fine and true. Ignore the worst, bring out the best and take the charitable view.

I hope God does the same for me and sees the virtue not the vice . . . If He remembers only faults—who'll ever get to Paradise?

May 27th
I KNOW A LANE

I know a lane walled in by hedges, flowery, deep and green —a lane where beauty waits to take your breath at every scene—where every bend reveals some pleasing prospect to the eye: a cottage hung with roses or a spire against the sky. A meadow where in quietness the grey sheep come to graze— fields of golden buttercups that hold the sun's bright glaze. Sunlight sifting shadows through the trees that arch above . . . I wonder when I'll walk again the little lane I love.

May 28th
SPEAK NO ILL

Speak no ill of friend or neighbour. Let your words be kind and true. Speak of others in the way that you would have them speak of you . . . Weight the scales of your opinions on the side of sympathy. Temper justice with compassion and the breath of charity . . . Better silence than reproaches. Bitter words affections kill. If you cannot praise say nothing. Cast no stone and speak no ill.

May 29th

"I had three chairs in my house; one for solitude, two for friendship, three for society. When visitors came in larger and unexpected numbers there was but the third chair for them all, but they generally economised the room by standing up . . . I have had twenty-five or thirty souls, with their bodies, at once,

under my roof, and yet we often parted without being aware
that we had come very near to one another."

THOREAU'S *Walden*.

May 30th

KEEPSAKES

A cross, a fan, a photograph, a watch beyond repair. A
flower pressed in a Bible, beads and books and locks of hair.
Meaningless to strangers, things they would not look at twice—
but to you who keep them they are treasures beyond price.

May 31st

To months like January, March or November you say
goodbye as you would to a disagreeable guest, one whom it has
been a trial to entertain, but May means buttercups in the
meadows, bluebells in the woods, glory in the garden and
hallelujah choruses of birdsong at sunrise and sunset. You
cannot watch the passing of May without an agonising sense
of the swiftness of Time and the transience of all things lovely.

JUNE

June 1st
TIME SIFTS OUR FRIENDSHIPS

Time sifts our friendships and our friends, for Time alone can be the test. With the passing of the years we lose the false and keep the best.

And when beyond the last long hill the golden sun of life descends—we find God's greatest gift has been the love of true and faithful friends.

June 2nd
THE CRAZY PAVING OF THE YEARS

Here and there upon the road a broken stone appears—but Time is kindly. In the crazy paving of the years—it covers up the ugly cracks concealing them from sight—with the mosses of remembrance ever green and bright.

June 3rd
REMEMBER THE BEST

Remember the best, friendly words, kindly deeds. Remember the roses and not the weeds. Remember the pleasure, forget the pain—then only sweet memories will remain.

Remember the sunshine, forget the rain. Remember the blessing, the boon, not the bane: the prayers that were answered, the goals achieved—the wishes fulfilled and the good received.

June 4th
Birthdays keep the links of recollection bright and strong—Life would be a lonely road and each mile twice as long without the dear remembrances of friendships old and new—proven through experience, the best, the good, the true . . .

Happy is the heart that finds at every journey's end—the comfort of companionship, the blessing of a friend.

June 5th
NEW HORIZONS
There's always something to live for—as clouds and shadows clear—Time opens up fresh vistas with every passing year . . . The view beyond is hidden—but thank God you can say—There's always a new horizon. There's always another day.

June 6th
"Sweet language will multiply friends: and a fair-speaking tongue will increase kind greetings. Be in peace with many: nevertheless have but one counsellor of a thousand.

If thou wouldst get a friend, prove him first, and be not hasty to credit him. For some man is a friend for his own occasion, and will not abide in the day of thy trouble."

THE APOCRYPHA

June 7th
THIS IS MY WISH FOR YOU
Strength for the task you have in hand,
  Time for the lovely things you've planned,
Hope to sustain you day by day,
  Laughter and sunshine all the way.
Wisdom to guide and light to lead,
  Courage and faith in time of need,
Health never-failing. Friends to bless
  And love to complete your happiness.

June 8th
JUNE BRIDE
Married in the month of roses when the year is at its prime —Lucky girl whose wedding bells ring out at this most glorious time! . . . when the days are long and brightest and the year is at its noon. Lovely is a Summer wedding. Happy is the bride of June.

June 9th

"I had often occasion to notice the use that was made of fragments and small opportunities in Cranford; the rose-leaves that were gathered ere they fell to make into a pot-pourri for someone who had no garden; the little bundles of lavender flowers sent to strew the drawers of some town-dweller, or to burn in the chamber of some invalid. Things that many would despise, and actions which it seemed scarcely worth while to perform, were all attended to in Cranford."

MRS. GASKELL

June 10th

OVERHEARD

It was only a voice that I overheard—in a jostling crowd, but my heart was stirred. Words that were meant for a stranger's ears—banished my doubts and calmed my fears . . . The speaker passed on through the busy throng—but in my soul he left a song—a message of hope on a hopeless day—something that sent me on my way—feeling elated instead of sad—thinking that things weren't quite so bad.

June 11th

LIFE IS AS GOOD AS YOU MAKE IT

Hold to your faith and whatever Fate sends—Rough weather or fine, you must take it . . . It isn't what happens—it's how you react—for Life is as good as you make it.

June 12th

"Few friendships would continue to exist if each man knew what his friend says of him in his absence, even though it is said in all sincerity and without vindictiveness."

PASCAL

June 13th

HAPPY THE HOME

Love bears no malice for love understands. Love is warm-hearted and gives with both hands. Love speaks with charity showing goodwill—passes no judgment and harbours no ill.

Happy the home where love makes its abode, easing the burden and sharing the load—making the best of whatever life brings—seeing the beauty in commonplace things.

June 14th
THINKING OF OTHERS
Thinking of others . . . it's easy to say—but harder to carry it out—we who are Christians we like to appear unselfish, sincere and devout—but if we're absorbed in our own little lives and blind to our neighbour's distress—our failure in practice will prove we have missed the point of the creed we profess.

June 15th
"Add to your faith virtue; and to virtue knowledge; and to knowledge temperance; and to temperance patience; and to patience godliness; and to godliness brotherly kindness; and to brotherly kindness charity."

II PETER 1.5–7

June 16th
GROWING OLD
There are things that grow in beauty as the ages pass. Furniture and tapestries, oak, silver, gold and glass. Houses, churches and cathedrals, colleges and halls. Jewels, pearls and paintings, lawns and trees and weathered walls.

O that we might grow in virtue, kindliness and grace—as Time draws its pencilled marks about the ageing face, growing calm and happier instead of cross and cold—growing sweeter, kinder, wiser as we're growing old.

June 17th
THE ROAD TO EMMAUS
There is Someone at our side on every road we travel. Falling into step with us He helps us to unravel—the problems of our lives, the things that baffle and dismay us. Every common road becomes a journey to Emmaus.

"And it came to pass that while they communed together and reasoned, Jesus himself drew near, and went with them. But their eyes were holden that they should not know him."

LUKE 24.15-16

June 18th
THE GRACE OF GIVING IN

Giving in to others is a test of character. In every situation opportunities occur—to push aside your own ideas, deferring graciously. Bowing to another for the sake of harmony. Mental conflicts wear you down. When faced with things unkind—never waste your strength against a hard and stubborn mind. You will only hurt yourself a worthless point to win. Better far to cultivate the grace of giving in.

June 19th
SCHOOL FRIENDS

The friendships of our schooldays linger strangely in the mind—after we have left the world of childhood far behind. Though we make new ties as through the years our lives advance, changing with the buffetings of time and circumstance.

A friendship of those early days will sometimes live and last—remaining when the friendships of the later years have passed. We are hurt and disillusioned when affections cool—and fall back on that dear old friend: the friend we made at school.

June 20th
"Give not over thy mind to heaviness, and afflict not thyself in thine own counsel.

The gladness of the heart is the life of man, and the joyfulness of a man prolongeth his days . . . Envy and wrath shorten the life, and carefulness bringeth age before the time."

ECCLESIASTICUS

June 21st
The arc of the sun has reached its highest point and from now on, though imperceptible at first, the long lovely twilights

of summer will begin to shorten. The hay is stacked in the meadows. The limes are murmurous with bees. The gardens are gay with irises, sweet williams, stocks and poppies, but the first glory of the roses is spent. Young birds are on the wing, but the mistle-thrush has ceased to sing, the cuckoo falters, the robin has lost his voice and soon now a silence will fall upon the drowsy woods of summer.

June 22nd

LIFE MUST GO ON

Life must go on—for God takes and God gives. Our loved ones must go, but the memory lives . . . Hearts may be broken, the dearest thing gone—but Time stops for no man and Life must go on.

June 23rd

A MORNING PRAYER

Use me in Thy service, Lord, and find a task for me. Send me where there's someone needing help or sympathy. Though I know I often fail and sometimes disobey—Surely there is something I can do for Thee today.

June 24th

TITANIA: "Come now, a roundel and a fairy song;
Then, for the third part of a minute, hence;
Some, to kill cankers in the musk-rose buds;
Some, war with rear-mice for their leathern wings,
To make my small elves coats; and some, keep back
The clamorous owl, that nightly hoots and wonders
At our quaint spirits: Sing me now asleep;
Then to your offices, and let me rest."

A Midsummer Night's Dream

June 25th

GEORGE HERBERT TO HIS SISTER, WRITTEN FROM CAMBRIDGE

"Most Dear Sister, Think not my silence forgetfulness, or

that my love is as dumb as my papers: though business may stop my hand, yet my heart, a much better member, is always with you."

June 26th
THE GRACE OF ACCEPTANCE
We are told that it is more blessed to give than to receive, but if there are to be givers there must be recipients. A stubborn independence can upset the balance of friendship and there are occasions when it is more blessed to receive than to give. If in taking something from a friend you are able to make him feel that he has served or pleased you truly, then your pleasure is his and if there be any debt of gratitude it is contracted and discharged on both sides. The joy of giving on the one hand is balanced on the other by the grace of acceptance.

June 27th
THESE THINGS REMAIN
In the world all things are changing—changing with the days. Life has ceased to move along its old accustomed ways. Everything is topsy turvy. Nothing seems secure—but the garden still remains and these things still endure: the familiar structure of the trunks and boughs of trees—morning dews and evening shadows, butterflies and bees. Autumn, winter, spring and summer. Nothing changes here: the rhythm of the seasons and the cycle of the year.

June 28th
YOU DO NOT TRAVEL A LONELY ROAD
You do not travel a lonely road. You do not walk alone. You do not grope unguided through the dark of the unknown. Unseen hands reach out to help you as you struggle on. Unseen friends surround you when you think that all have gone.

June 29th
THE MOVING FINGER WRITES
"The moving finger writes; and, having writ
Moves on: nor all thy piety nor wit
Shall lure it back to cancel half a line,
Nor all thy tears wash out a word of it."

OMAR KHAYYAM

June 30th
Something of the sadness of Omar Khayyám's Rubaiyat hangs about the mind on this last day of June, the philosophical acceptance of what cannot be denied. The year is half over and as you tear the page off the calendar you are disquieted by the questions which seem to rise up from nowhere at the beginning, the middle and the end of a year. What has been achieved? The answer invariably makes you wish you could lure back the moving finger of Time for there is always something to regret, something for which to ask forgiveness of God or man.

JULY

CONTINUALLY TO HAPPINESS

"They that are in the stream of Providence are borne continually to happiness no matter what the appearance of the means."

SWEDENBORG

July 2nd

The building of a friendship is something like the building of a house. If it is to be the real thing it must have strong foundations on which to stand, windows to let in the light and doors for going out and coming in. Like the structure of a building a friendship is subject to stresses and strains, certain things have to be allowed for and taken into consideration. And after the architectural structure has been erected there is always the necessity of maintenance and repair. A neglected house soon goes to rack and ruin. So does a neglected friendship.

July 3rd

LOOK FOR IT

You've got to make an effort and you've got to look around. That's the only way that precious treasure can be found. You'll never catch the sunshine if you always draw the blind. You'll never make a friend unless you open heart and mind. If you want to find the best you've got to search a bit. You'll never see the good in life unless you look for it.

July 4th

COUNT IT ALL JOY

"My brethren, count it all joy when you fall into divers

temptations; knowing this, that the trying of your faith worketh patience. But let patience have her perfect work, that ye may be perfect and entire, wanting nothing."

JAMES 1.2-4

July 5th

GIVING GOOD ADVICE

When you're asked to give advice—weigh your words. Take thought, think twice. Make quite sure that what you say—is not really meant to sway—the opinion of your friend for a purely selfish end . . . Be detached, impersonal, never making capital—out of someone else's plight. Try to help and put things right . . . If you've got a prejudice—or a grudge? Beware of this, lest it warp your reasoned view—when a friend appeals to you. Keep his good before your eyes—when you're trying to advise.

July 6th

"A crowd is not company, and faces are but a gallery of pictures."

BACON

July 7th

THIS IS COURAGE

To hide your griefs and grievances behind a smiling mask. To carry on and sink your sorrows in the daily task . . . To lift your head though brokenhearted; of life's best bereft—making something good and lovely out of what is left.

July 8th

PERFECT UNDERSTANDING

There can be no friendship without perfect understanding. A true friend will never take offence, never force a confidence or harbour a grudge. To love is to make allowances, to suspend judgment, to withhold the uncharitable comment.

July 9th
HORIZONS RECEDE

The place where sky and water meet recede into the blue—as you sail towards it—it will move away from you . . . You never reach the far horizon. So it is, my friend—with horizons of the mind, you never reach the end. There's always something beckoning. There's always something more: new hopes and possibilities, new country to explore.

July 10th
STRUCK BY STORM

In the green bowers of the wood there stands a stricken tree—with stark and broken boughs outspread, a lifeless parody—the victim of the lightning flash that felled the giant oak—the blackened ruin of disaster, shattered at a stroke. No sap moves in the hidden root, no bird comes singing there. No bright leaves whisper to the wind on branches dead and bare. That's what happens to a life when Death strikes suddenly—cleaving friendships like the rending of a stricken tree.

July 11th

"The friends thou hast, and their adoption tried,
Grapple them to thy soul with hoops of steel;
But do not dull thy palm with entertainment
Of each new-hatched, unfledged comrade."
Hamlet

July 12th
FROM GREEN TO GOLD

The corn turns now from green to gold beneath the warm glow of the sun . . . The earth is good and faileth not to give return for work well done.

July 13th
DO YOU REMEMBER, DEAREST FRIEND?

Dear friend, I long to walk again along that little leafy

lane—deep set in banks of ferns and flowers where we two spent such happy hours.

Each twist and turn of it I know—and oftentimes in thought I go—rediscovering anew—the pleasure of those walks with you, retracing every step we took: the bridge that spanned the wayside brook. By church and manor, farm and mill—we climbed together up the hill—to see the view around the bend. Do you remember, dearest friend?

July 14th

HOW COULD I BE SAD?

How could I be sad and friendless in a world where I can see—flowers growing in the garden, green leaves dancing on the tree? . . . How could life seem dull and cheerless in a world so beautiful—garlanded in summer glory, decked as if for carnival?

July 15th

SOMEWHERE OUT THERE

Somewhere out there beyond death's dark door—we who were friends will be friends once more . . . We who in fellowship walked this way—we shall go forth to a brighter day.

We shall discover a greater joy: the gold of true friendship without alloy . . . We shall unravel the tangled skein. We who were friends will be friends again.

July 16th

NEWS FROM HOME

News from home . . . How much it means to those who in some distant place—are thinking and remembering a room, a voice, a smile, a face.

They may look dull in black and white, just little items, odds and ends—and yet in lonely hearts they stir old memories, old times, old friends.

News from home! A few brief words can paint a picture on the mind: the house, the street, the garden seat—and all the dear things left behind.

July 17th

IN THE HOUSE OF MY FRIENDS

"And one shall say unto him, What are these wounds in thine hands? Then he shall answer, Those with which I was wounded in the house of my friends."

ZECHARIAH 13.6

July 18th

HOW MUCH SHALL I REMEMBER?

How much shall I remember when I am tired and old? What threads of recollection will gleam like strands of gold—worked into the pattern of the departed years? Time wears away the colour. It fades and disappears. The things that brought great sorrow get blurred as old I grow—and when with darkness falling I face the sunset glow—What thoughts will come to haunt me with pleasure or regret? How much shall I remember? How much shall I forget?

July 19th

HIGH TIDE

See the golden harvest tide—rolls across the countryside. Oats and barley, wheat and rye—flowing out to meet the sky . . . Tides of plenty. Waves of gold—breaking over weald and wold. Lapping round the town's grey edge—brimming over bank and hedge . . . Seas of blessing broad and wide—coming in on every side. Nature's vast benevolence! The charity of Providence.

July 20th

"Let me not to the marriage of true minds admit impediments."

SHAKESPEARE

July 21st

GOOD FARE

Who shall fear the darkness in the company of friends? Friendship lights a lamp of welcome where the journey ends.

How sweet it is when lost and lonely, weary and hard-pressed
—to come upon an Inn of Friendship, there awhile to rest . . .
Be it night or be it day good fare is offered here: wine of joy
and bread of comfort, charity and cheer.

July 22nd
IN MEMORY LANE

No shadow dims the sunshine when I'm walking there with
you—the day is always lovely and the sky is always blue.
Roses, roses everywhere. No winter, snow or rain. It is always
Summer when we meet in Memory Lane.

July 23rd
ST. PAUL, WRITING TO THE HEBREWS

"Let brotherly love continue. Be not forgetful to entertain
strangers: for thereby some have entertained angels un-
awares."

July 24th
WHEN NOTHING STIRS THE
HEART'S CONTENT

Through all the ever-changing years you've helped me on
and pulled me through—and yet I did not realise until I'd
said goodbye to you—what life would be without you near,
and all that separation meant. We take for granted oh so much
when nothing stirs the heart's content!

July 25th
THE POWER OF PRAYER

Miracles are wrought by prayer, for in some mysterious way
—a mighty source of power is tapped—when someone somewhere kneels to pray.

In times of danger and temptation when the storms of life
descend—we know not how we are protected and preserved
through praying friends.

TILL DEATH US DO PART
"To have and to hold from this day forward, for better for worse, for richer for poorer, in sickness and in health, to love and to cherish, till death us do part."

THE BOOK OF COMMON PRAYER

SONGS OF JOY
Bird, how free of care you are with happy note and soaring wings! Do you know nothing of this world with all its sad and evil things? . . . Nothing. God created me and put me here for this one thing: to fill the air with rhapsody. My commandment is to sing . . . And so the Lord's work I perform. My daily song of joy I raise. For this He brought me from the nest—to sing His glory and His praise.

MARKING THE DAY
Certain dates bring back old griefs. The anniversary—stirs the recollection and recalls the agony—but if each year by some good action we would mark the day—in time the bitterness would pass, the sorrow fade away.

If on someone's path a gleam of sunshine could be shed—as an act of memory for the *beloved dead* . . . It for them would cast a radiance down the passing years—for loving deeds to them would be more precious than our tears.

THE DARK THREAD
We do not know why there should be this dark thread in the twisted strand—but it is all in the design and someday we shall understand.

TO A MINISTER
You have been our faithful friend and helped us through

the changing years . . . With a sympathetic heart you've shared our sorrows, hopes and fears.

By word and deed you've made us feel—the love of God as something real—and many a heart by grief subdued—remembers you with gratitude . . . Long may you continue here to guide, to comfort and to cheer.

July 31st
GIVE US THIS DAY OUR DAILY BREAD

The end of July means the beginning of the corn harvest. The methods of sowing, reaping and threshing the grain have changed with the changing times, but every harvest is still a miracle.

AUGUST

August 1st

The wheat is like a sun-flecked sea beneath the summer sky.
Little ripples break the surface as the wind goes by . . . Here
and there the scarlet poppies with their petals wide—dip and
rise like red-sailed boats upon the restless tide.

August 2nd

AND THEN BEGIN AGAIN

It takes a lot of courage, it calls for strength of mind—to
make a new beginning and leave the past behind . . . To build
upon the ruins, to dream another dream. To set forth in the
darkness towards a distant gleam. To suffer many losses, yet
faithful to remain. To rise above disaster—and then begin
again.

August 3rd

REVERIE IN EXILE

Evening sunlight on the river, dragonflies about the reeds.
Herds in peaceful pastures grazing by the quiet watermeads
. . . In and out between the islets moves a swan with queenly
grace—to a nest amongst the rushes where the willows interlace.

Waking from my reverie I see great mountains range on
range. My dream of England fades away. This place is
wonderful and strange—but I, an exile, see no beauty where
the clouds and summits blend, because in thought I'm walking
there beside the river with my friend—talking as we used to
talk of this and that and everything. Though I'm here my
heart is there—remembering, remembering.

August 4th
THINK
Think before you cut the link that snaps the golden chain.
Pause before you take a step that causes others pain . . . Wait
before you speak the word, the angry thought subdue. Think
before you cast aside affection tried and true.

August 5th
"Hast thou a friend? Visit him often, for thorns and brush-
wood obstruct the road which no one treads."

EASTERN PROVERB

August 6th
TOMORROW BECKONS,
PROMISING A GOOD AND LOVELY DAY
Suppose the road that now we tread led back to Yesterday
—would we wish to turn about and go back all the way? The
heart cries, No a thousand times. Thank God that path is
barred. Although the road before us may be lonely, steep and
hard—we would not have it otherwise no matter what we say.
Tomorrow beckons, promising a good and lovely day.

August 7th
"Bless the Lord, O my soul, and forget not all his benefits:
who forgiveth all thine iniquities; who healeth all thy diseases;
who redeemeth thy life from destruction; who crowneth thee
with loving kindness and tender mercies; who satisfieth thy
mouth with good things; so that thy youth is renewed like the
eagle's."

PSALM 103.2-5

August 8th
HER NAME IS MEMORY
I have a good companion, a true and constant friend. I am
never lonely from dawn till daylight's end, for she with quiet
footsteps walks ever close to me. She follows like a shadow
wherever I may be.

I'm happy in her presence. When other friends depart—
she's always there to comfort and cheer my aching heart . . .
She comes unsought, unbidden—to keep me company. She is
my dear companion. Her name is Memory.

August 9th
IN TIME OF TROUBLE
In time of trouble friends draw near to offer sympathy.
They desire to share our griefs in all sincerity, but human love
is not enough when hearts are desolate. We yearn for a diviner
touch, a love more intimate.

In time of trouble something more than love of friends we
crave. It is God we hunger for, for He alone can save—only
in that gracious Presence can we hope to find—consolation for
the soul and healing for the mind.

August 10th
"The King of Love my shepherd is
    Whose goodness faileth never,
I nothing lack if I am His
    And He is mine forever."
SIR H. W. BAKER

August 11th
THE OLD MILL STANDS
The old mill stands with sails outspread against the summer
sky—a symbol of the home-baked cottage loaf of days gone by
—the days when sails and watermills were used to make the
power—that ground the good grain of the wheat into a whole-
some flour.

We should keep and cherish every mill throughout the land.
Save them from the planners and from Time's destroying
hand—Save them to remind us of the days when we were fed
—and strengthened by the staff of life: the days when bread
was bread.

AWAY FROM IT ALL

Away from the dust and the fume-laden air. Away from the crowds and the din and the blare. Away to the country, the fields and the trees—to the smell of the earth and the health-giving breeze.

Away from the treadmills of daily routines—the noise of the traffic, the roar of machines . . . Away to the sea, to the cliffs and the caves—to the sand and the rocks and the song of the waves.

Away from the news: strikes and strife and unrest—to the quiet of a place where the soul can be blessed—To somewhere unspoilt where the tired eyes can see—this beautiful world as God meant it to be.

August 13th

BROKEN GLASS

A little boy out paddling cut his small foot to the bone. A little girl was gashed when reaching out to grasp a stone. It caused a lot of suffering and spoilt their holidays—all because of carelessness and someone's thoughtless ways . . . If you have a picnic by the sea or on the grass—think of what can happen if there's any broken glass. Don't leave bottles when you go, or throw them anywhere. Children may come there to play Remember and take care.

August 14th

TWENTY-FIRST

The world is yours at twenty-one
   Life offers you the key
That opens up the magic doors of opportunity.
   It is yours to seek and find
That castle in the blue,
   All the lovely dreams of youth are waiting to come true.
Blessings on your twenty-first
   And many more in store,

This my wish that you will find behind Tomorrow's door
   Fulfilment of your heart's desire,
Good fortune and success,
   And best of all, the precious gifts
Of health and happiness.

August 15th
      "Who hopes a friend, should have a heart
      Himself, well furnished for the part,
      And ready on occasion
      To show the virtue that he seeks;
      For 'tis an union that bespeaks
      A just reciprocation."
                              WM. COWPER

August 16th
HOLIDAY MOOD
Give yourself a rest from worry while on holiday. Bolt the door against your troubles and they'll slink away. Take the opportunity of turning out your mind—clearing up the mess and muddle Time has left behind.

Set your mental house in order now while you are free. Dust the corners; overhaul your whole philosophy, and you will find when once again you face what troubled you—that when you swept the rubbish out you swept the worries too.

August 17th
SILVER WEDDING ANNIVERSARY
For five and twenty years you've walked the road of life together. Good companions all the way in every sort of weather. And now the years have brought you to this anniversary. Gifts and greetings there will be from friends and family—and with our congratulations these few lines are sent—to thank you for your friendship and for all that it has meant.

August 18th
"We cannot tell the precise moment when friendship is formed. As in filling a vessel drop by drop, there is at last a

drop which makes it run over; so in a series of kindnesses there is at last one which makes the heart run over."

BOSWELL's *Life of Johnson*

August 19th
FOUR AND TWENTY HOURS

Time is life—so precious. Yet how much of it we spend—on things that do not matter and that serve no useful end. Many golden hours we squander in a reckless way—of the four and twenty we are granted every day.

August 20th
PEACE AT EVENTIDE

These are things that to the mind bring satisfaction and content: a good job done, a task complete, a goal achieved, a day well spent . . . The knowledge of the love of friends. And when we lay our tools aside—these are the thoughts that warm the heart, bringing peace at eventide.

August 21st

"One writes, that 'Other friends remain',
　　That 'Loss is common to the race'
　　And common is the commonplace
And vacant chaff well meant for grain.

That loss is common would not make
　　My own less bitter, rather more:
　　Too common! Never morning wore
To evening, but some heart did break."

TENNYSON

August 22nd
THERE ARE ALWAYS CONSOLATIONS

There are always consolations for our sorrows and our pains. There are always compensations. Much is lost but much remains . . . If we never doubt or falter, never cease to hope and pray—we are led through tribulations out towards a brighter day.

August 23rd
ONCE THE BRANCH WAS ALL BUT DEAD

See the bough is heavy now with apples ripening—green fruit flushes red and golden where the thrushes sing. Once the branch was all but dead, within its sheath of frost. Then Nature worked a miracle and o'er the tree she tossed—a shower of rosy-tinted buds that blossomed with the Spring—promising a heavy bough at time of harvesting.

August 24th

> O Lord, in thee have I trusted:
> Let me never be confounded.
>
> TE DEUM LAUDAMUS

August 25th
THE FIRST TRIP

Shipmate, where does the sea road go, this salty highway hedged with foam? Shipmate, what is it like out there, a thousand miles away from home? . . . Courage, lad, for there is One who watches while men wake and sleep. Fear not. It is He who walked upon the waters of the deep.

August 26th
BE FRIENDS AGAIN

When you feel that someone has been thoughtless or unkind —do not make too much of it, but put it from your mind. Maybe you have often caused a pang or brought a tear—and without intention have been hasty and severe. Maybe all unknowingly resentment you have stirred, wounding someone's feelings by a silence or a word . . . We all inflict on one another needless suffering. Life's so short and yet we waste our time in quarrelling . . . so if you're hurt by something that has caused you pique or pain. Let it pass. Forgive, forget it—and be friends again.

August 27th
TO A COLLEAGUE

I'm no good at saying things with flowery eloquence. I never could convey in words my thoughts and sentiments—but I often feel I'd like to say a word or two—to express appreciation and my thanks to you.

I hope you will not be offended at this little rhyme—but we've worked together now for quite a length of time—and I'd like to let you know what it has meant to me—to have had your help, your friendship and your loyalty.

August 28th

"Virtue cannot live in solitude: neighbours are sure to grow up around it."

CONFUCIUS

August 29th

COURTESY

It smooths the path and oils the wheels, a little courtesy. It sweetens our relationships. How different life would be—if everyone would be polite, considerate and kind. It would warm the chilly soul and ease the daily grind . . . It doesn't cost us anything and yet it means so much: the tone of affability, the sympathetic touch; the civil word, the charming manner, geniality—showing unto friend and stranger simple courtesy.

August 30th

A POOR MAN'S BEQUEST

He had no great possessions. With wealth he was not blessed —No riches for his children, but this was his bequest: he left them all the glories of dawn and sunset skies—the woods, the brooks, the meadows, birds, bees and butterflies—the salt wind on the marshes, the blossom on the tree—the flowers, the fruit, the sunshine. This was his legacy.

August 31st

"Thou crownest the year with thy goodness . . . and the little hills rejoice on every side. The pastures are clothed with flocks; the valleys also are covered over with corn; they shout for joy."

PSALM 65

SEPTEMBER

September 1st
FIRST QUARTER

The new moon sails into the sky with bright stars streaming in her wake. In her path the foaming clouds like silver-crested billows break . . . Thin and slight, a slender crescent, like the paring of a nail—stealing quietly through the heavens over city, field and vale.

Is it not miraculous that this frail vessel of the night—this drifting, floating fairy thing, this tiny bow of golden light—should drag the oceans from the shores, compel great waters deep and wide—hold in check the surging sea and set the rhythm of the tide?

September 2nd
HOPE TRAVELS ON

Hope travels on and far she goes into the darkness undismayed—where none has dared to tread before, she hastens forward unafraid—pressing on and heeding not the mocking voice that cries, "Too late"—striding on beyond the point where others halt and hesitate.

September 3rd
THE RIGHT WORD
AT THE RIGHT MOMENT

"A word fitly spoken is like apples of gold in pictures of silver."

PROVERBS 25.11

September 4th
THE FOOTSTEP

Hush! I thought I heard a footstep fall upon the path. Mere imagination. Just a dream dreamed by the hearth . . . I thought I saw him at the gate, the lamplight on his hair. Foolish, foolish to suppose he could be standing there . . . I thought I saw him as I walked across the moonlit hall. It was nothing—just a shadow moving on the wall—and yet it's always happening. I face an empty chair—and when the house is still there comes that step upon the stair.

September 5th
WAYSIDE ALTARS
Amongst the nettles and the thorns that grow along the rutted way—we raise a little wayside altar every time we pause to pray . . . On the common ground of life we break the bread and drink the wine—when in search of strength and faith we turn in thought to things divine . . .

September 6th
"Friendship is like a debt of honour; the moment it is talked of it loses its real name."

OLIVER GOLDSMITH

September 7th
BRIEF ACQUAINTANCE
In your Book of Memory—please mark a little place for me. A brief acquaintance we have had. O how I wish that I could add—a few more hours, a few more days—before we go our separate ways . . . Meeting you has been so sweet. A tale half told, not yet complete. Though now we take a different road—this strange and happy episode—may have a sequel. We shall see. So, dear friend, remember me.

September 8th
LOVE LEADS THEM HOME
Thoughts go home unbidden when we're somewhere far away. Thoughts need no compelling. Off they wander night or day—to seek the places and the faces dear unto the heart: the spot where all our journeys lead and all roads end and start.

Thoughts go back. They know the way. They need no goad or guide—to cross the distance in between, the chasms that divide . . . And though with friends we may abide as round the world we roam. To the place of heart's desire thoughts turn. Love leads them home.

September 9th

"Master, which is the great commandment in the law? Jesus said unto him, Thou shalt love the Lord thy God with all thy heart, and with all thy soul, and with all thy mind. This is the first and great commandment. And the second is like unto it. Thou shalt love thy neighbour as thyself."

MATTHEW 22.36–39

September 10th
THE LOVE THAT WILL NOT LET ME GO

No atom of the cosmic dust of space—is hidden from the glory of God's face—yet He who holds the sun and moon apart —can make his dwelling in the human heart . . . I cannot hide from those unclosing eyes. I feel His Presence when I sleep or rise, He is within, beyond, above, below. What is this Love that will not let me go?

September 11th
FROM MY HEART I THANK YOU

From my heart I thank you. You have been so good to me. Always in the future I'll remember gratefully—the cheerfulness and helpfulness you never failed to show. How much it has meant to me you'll never ever know.

You've been a pal, you've been a friend. You've gone out of your way—to do so many kindnesses. Believe me when I say, I am truly sorry that the time has come to part. Bless you—and the best of luck. I thank you from my heart.

September 12th
AND MAN BECAME A LIVING SOUL

"And the Lord God formed man of the dust of the ground,

and breathed into his nostrils the breath of life; and man became a living soul."

GENESIS 2.7

September 13th

OUT OF EVIL

Out of evil good must come for only thus can we progress—wresting wisdom from disaster, blessings from unhappiness. Out of things calamitous the heart through dire experience—must turn all evil into that which serves the ends of Providence.

September 14th

CHARLOTTE BRONTE TO MISS WOOLER

"I should grieve to neglect or oppose your advice, and yet I do not feel it would be right to give Miss Martineau up entirely. There is in her nature much that is very noble. Hundreds have forsaken her, more, I fear, in the apprehension that their fair names may suffer if seen in connection with hers than from any pure convictions, such as you suggest, of harm consequent upon her fatal tenets. With these fair-weather friends I cannot bear to rank."

September 15th

LATER, CHARLOTTE BRONTE TO
MR. GEORGE SMITH

"The differences between Miss M. and myself are strong and very marked, very wide and irreconcilable ... In short, she has hurt me a good deal, and at present it appears very plain to me that she and I had better not try to be close friends; my wish indeed is that she should quietly forget me ... I don't want to quarrel with her, but I want to be let alone."

September 16th

THANKFUL

Much have I lost, but I must not lament. My heart must be quiet, my spirit content, not asking too much and not greedy for more. Joys unexpected may yet be in store—but even if Time has no blessings to add—I must be thankful for all I have had.

September 17th
THE HARVEST OF A QUIET HEART

O may the rains of mercy fall on all our follies and misdeeds. The sun of God's forgiveness shine and quicken all our scattered seeds—that we when summer's crop is reaped and life's last sunset rays depart—may stand amidst the sheaves of peace, the harvest of a quiet heart.

September 18th
THE JOYS OF ANTICIPATION

Just before a friend arrives I like to sit and watch and wait— and listen in anticipation for the footstep at the gate—for once the visitor has come Time hurries on, the moments fly— there's hardly time to give a welcome and it's time to say goodbye . . . Anticipate the happy things, thus double pleasures yet to be—and live the lovely moments twice, in thought and in reality—but don't anticipate disasters, trouble, failure or distress—only sunshine and fair-weather, joy, good fortune and success.

September 19th
IN MANY FORMS

In many forms the Christ appears although His face you cannot see. He comes in everything that makes demands upon your charity . . . The sufferers, the destitute, the soul in need of sympathy. Little children, victims of neglect, disease or cruelty. Every friend and every neighbour, every stranger on the road—whose back is breaking underneath the pressure of a heavy load . . . So think before you turn away and pause ere you refuse a plea—for did He not Himself declare, "Ye did it unto Me"?

ROADS

The road that runs out to the world's far end is a road with romance at every bend. Distant horizons beckon us, adventures great and glorious. Restless, we follow the winding path that carries us far from the homely hearth. Bright is the star of fate that gleams over the mountaintops of dreams—but the road to the door of a well-loved friend—is a road that's a good road to the end—green with the moss of remembered years—though sometimes touched with dews of tears. Down many strange roads we love to wend—but the best is the road to the house of a friend.

We're shuffled like a pack of cards. We fall in different places—Jacks and jokers, kings and queens, the numbers and the aces. We are mixed up daily by the unseen hand of chance —jumbled up together by the force of circumstance. But does it matter where we're flung—so long as in the end—we find we're side by side with someone we can call a friend?

GOLDEN SEPTEMBERS

Golden Septembers . . . my heart still remembers—someone who loved this sweet time of the year—pearly grey mornings and amethyst twilights—bring back the thought of a face ever dear . . . Golden Septembers . . . The summer's last embers glow with rich memories, warming my heart. Once more I see her, untouched by Time's finger. She changes not, though the long years depart . . . Golden Septembers . . . My heart still remembers—one whom I loved with a love deep and fond —One who in sunshine of summer eternal—walks in the light of the glory beyond.

WHEN JESUS CAME TO BETHANY

How lovely must have been the house, how clean and gay

and neat—when Jesus came to Bethany, a quiet meal to eat—
in the company of friends. Imagine Martha's pride—in
shining pans and spotless linen—Would she not provide the
best for the beloved guest who graced her humble board? The
Friend she served with loving pride, the Master and the Lord.

THERE IS A FRIEND

September 24th

There is a Friend who knocks upon the door of every heart,
a Friend who comes to comfort when all other friends depart.
A Friend who stands upon the threshhold waiting patiently—
with hands outreaching, hands that bear the marks of Calvary.

September 25th

"Behold, I stand at the door, and knock; if any man hear
my voice, and open the door, I will come in to him, and will
sup with him, and he with me."

REVELATION 3.20

September 26th
BE A GOOD SAMARITAN

The man lay stripped and bruised upon the roadway, left to
die. Two travellers passed on, then the Samaritan came by—
and pitying, he knelt and bound the wounds with loving care
—took him to the inn and paid for food and shelter there . . .
He did much more than give him wine and bathe the wounded
part. He did more than was necessary—for he had a heart of
great compassion; so may we do more than just our share—
to help a brother in distress and for his needs to care . . . Don't
be like the Levite—but obey Love's quick command. Be a
good Samaritan and lend a helping hand.

September 27th
SUMMER'S WANING

Daisies of Michaelmas, giant-headed sunflowers, mist in the
morning and dew in the night . . . Mauve of the heather and
red of the creeper—tell of the waning of summer's delight.

Season of fruitfulness. Golden September! Prelude to Autumn, the opening phase—clothing the woods in a garment of glory—bringing the promise of lovelier days.

Ladders in orchards and ploughs on the stubbles. Summer's bright splendour we quickly forget—borne swiftly on to new views and new vistas. There is no time to repine or regret.

September 28th
THE HARVEST OF THE HEDGES

The corn has all been gathered in and now in every lane—the hedges have their harvest-tide and bring forth once again —nuts and fruits in rich abundance on the tangled sprays—swelling in the yellow sunlight of the mellow days.

Bramble thickly matted with its red and purple load. Scarlet hips like fairy lamps strung out along the road . . . Mauve and red and rosy globes on leafless branches borne—berries on the spindle bush and haws upon the thorn.

September 29th
BE OF GOOD CHEER

"These things have I spoken unto you, that in me ye might have peace. In the world ye shall have tribulation: but be of good cheer; I have overcome the world."
JOHN 16.33

September 30th
The beauty of the English countryside at all times of the year has something to do with the gentle way in which the cycle of the seasons turns. You cannot put a finger upon the exact point of transition nor can you isolate the precise moment of change. It steals upon you so slowly so unobtrusively as to be almost imperceptible. There is no sudden and dramatic change of scene. I should hate to live in a country of climatic extremes. Even though living in England means many days of grey sky and unpredictable weather, it is the country where the grass is greenest and even the periods of transition have their own peculiar beauties, so gently does a beneficent Nature lead us from one thing to another.

OCTOBER

October 1st

SAYS THE SUNDIAL

I record the sunny hours, not the shadows and the showers.
The hours I measure one by one—in the full glow of the sun,
I've no need for bell or chime, in my reckonings of Time.

I am old and quiet and wise. I ignore the cloudy skies.
Foolish folks who frown and fume—Be like me. Ignore the
gloom. Take no account of storm and rain. The sun will soon
be out again.

October 2nd

REMEMBERING THOSE DAYS

Every season brings its special memories to me. Through the
changing year I walk in unseen company—with those I loved
and shared so much—And now with Autumn's phase—I walk
again the golden woods remembering those days.

October 3rd

"Better by far you should forget and smile
Than that you should remember and be sad."
CHRISTINA ROSSETTI

October 4th

IN TUNE

Some are disappointed in their fellow-men and so—seeking
for companionship to animals they go. Dogs and horses, cats
and birds and pets of every kind—but nothing takes the place
of friendship, linking mind with mind.

What a blessing and a boon such fellowship can be: based
on understanding, love and trust and loyalty . . . Only those
who know it know the joy such friendship brings—and what

it means to share the saddest—and the happiest things—with a kindred spirit, one with whom you can commune—somebody with whom you are in harmony . . . in tune.

WAITING TO BE BLESSED
Round the pulpit and the porch, the lectern and the stalls. On the window ledges where the slanting sunlight falls. At the font and in the niches where the shadows rest—lie the good things we have garnered, waiting to be blessed.

Everywhere the colours glow, the yellows, reds and greens. Hops and grapes and wheat and marrows, apples, pears and beans . . . And the faces of the flowers crowd in on every side—as if they too would join us in the hymns of harvest-tide.

RIPPLES
Throw a little stone into the middle of a lake—watch the rings of ripples and the circles that they make—troubling the water just as if a storm had blown. All the deep and hidden depths disturbed by one small stone!

Throw a stone of malice, though it be a whispered word—into someone's life, and how much trouble will be stirred! Other people's lives within the spreading rings are caught. Who can see the end or say what misery is wrought? The effects of words and deeds reach out to the unknown—far beyond today. So think—before you cast a stone.

TO MY GODCHILD
What can I say to you, dear child, what word of guidance give. What wisdom can I offer you to show you how to live? Only this: have faith in God and in the power of prayer. Nothing else can help you when your cross you have to bear. Walk with Christ your Saviour and you'll be victorious. He alone can make life lovely, great and glorious.

October 8th
NOTHING STANDS STILL

Mourn not the fading of leaf, fruit and flower. Life is transition. With each passing hour—we, too, are moving, for nothing stands still. All things are changing for good or for ill.

May every change be a change for the best. When you look back may you find you've progressed—reaching your goals and achieving your ends—gaining new wisdom and making new friends.

October 9th

"Though the life of a man be short of a hundred years, he gives himself as much anxiety as if he were to live a thousand."

CHINESE PROVERB

October 10th
MARTHA'S HANDS AND MARY'S HEART

Give me Martha's hands, O Lord, to do what must be done. Never let me rest until my earthly course is run. Find for me some useful thing to do without delay; a job for every idle hour, a task for every day.

Give me Mary's quiet heart that I may deem it sweet—to watch, to wonder and to worship at the Master's feet. Give me the desire to break the bread of heavenly things—and hear about the kitchen door the beat of angel wings.

October 11th
AUTUMN CROCUS

Underneath the weeping birch where boughs are dripping gold—a drift of autumn crocuses their fairy cups unfold . . . Wraith-like in the grey autumnal dusk they seem to be—other-worldly in their beauty: flowers of fantasy . . . Are they real or mere illusions of the evening mist—Dream-shapes, streaked with lavender and cloudy amethyst? Strange they seem, a ghostly throng, pale spirits of the Spring. Do they hope on Winter's edge to hear the chiffchaff sing?

October 12th
ECHOES OF THE SONG OF SUMMER
High above the fallow fields a lone lark hovers scattering—June-notes on the bare brown earth that seem to melt the frost and bring—a memory of shining hours when days were warm and bright and long. Through the great grey sky there floats the echo of a Summer song.

Thickly now the blue smoke curls from cottage chimneys in the lane—but still my heart is unconvinced that Wintertide is nigh again . . . Though a keen wind sweeps the pastures and the elms stand gaunt and stark—I can hear a Summer song: the lyric music of the lark.

October 13th
SLEEP
Nature's balm. We could not live unless it had its way. Sleep, the friend into whose arms we fall at close of day . . . It's only when our rest is broken and we're counting sheep—we come to know the worth of that good friend whose name is Sleep.

October 14th
NEVER DESPAIR
Though you carry within you a heart fit to break—and your own little world seems to tremble and quake—Remember it's your world to mar or to make . . . Never despair.

Though the thing that you lived for is taken away and you see through the darkness no comforting ray—Remember each night brings another new day . . . Never despair.

October 15th
"When I awake, I am still with Thee."
PSALM 139.18

October 16th
GOING THE SECOND MILE
When compelled to go a mile—Go two, the Master said. It

sounds a hard commandment when the road is dark ahead. The first mile represents your duty, that which must be done, the everyday demands of life that come to everyone. The second mile is duty plus that something we call Love. You forget the weary feet, the stormy sky above, when you walk that extra mile and cheerfully respond—to the little inner voice that bids you go beyond—the post that marks the measurement. Unasked, and with a smile—when you've done what is expected . . . Go the second mile.

October 17th
SHOWERS OF BLESSINGS
"Prove me now herewith, saith the Lord of hosts, if I will not open you the windows of heaven, and pour you out a blessing, that there shall not be room enough to receive it."

MALACHI 3.10

October 18th
ST. LUKE'S LITTLE SUMMER
When the sun shines at the time of St. Luke's Little Summer the country is at its loveliest. The floor of the wood is carpeted with thick layers of leaves in every shade of gold and yellow, red and russet. The hedgerows, hung with fruits and berries, blaze with the fiery banners of the wild cherry. And in the garden if the weather be mild a few butterflies, red admirals, painted ladies, brimstones and peacocks, will flutter fitfully amongst the sorry ruins of the herbaceous borders. The robin, never far from the kitchen door, pours out a silvery song to establish rights of tenancy over his own little patch of territory. St. Luke's Day seems to mark the high point of Autumn's glory, a point from which there is a quickening descent into the depths of the declining year.

October 19th
THE UNSEEN GUEST
There is an unseen Guest at every table, hallowing—and transmuting by His presence every common thing . . . Break

your bread with gratitude your gracious thanks expressing—
for every meal is sacramental when He gives the blessing.

October 20th
THE LIVING BREAD
"The bread of God is he which cometh down from heaven,
and giveth life unto the world. Then said they unto him, Lord,
evermore give us this bread. And Jesus said unto them, I am
the bread of life: he that cometh to me shall never hunger."
JOHN 6.33-35

October 21st
WHEN THE HOUSE IS STILL
When the house is still and the firelight gleams and I draw
the curtains across the pane—Past and present are one, it
seems—and my friend is here at my hearth again—here in the
room where we two once spent—so many winters of content.

October 22nd
LIFE GOES ON
Life goes on in spite of all our human tragedies—Life goes
on in spite of losses and calamities. The leaves fall in the
Autumn lane the same as yesteryear. The sun comes up, the
morning breaks, dusk falls and stars appear . . . They know
not and they care not that for you the best has gone—Yet in
that indifference is solace. Life goes on.

October 23rd
THE WINGS OF THE MORNING
"Whither shall I go from thy spirit? or whither shall I flee
from thy presence? If I ascend up into heaven, thou art there:
if I make my bed in hell, behold, thou art there. If I take the
wings of the morning, and dwell in the uttermost parts of the
sea; even there shall thy hand lead me, and thy right hand
shall hold me."
PSALM 139.7-10

October 24th

CONTENT

Content I pray I'll always be—with home and hearth and family ... Content in my small realm to reign. Happy in my own domain ... Thankful for whatever's there—goodly feast or frugal fare. Every meal a sacrament—when the spirit is content.

Content with what comes to my door—not always wanting something more—but grateful for the odds and ends—that a God of mercy sends.

October 25th

OCTOBER MORNING

Drifting mist and burning bushes all along the garden ways. Blue smoke rising from the chimney through the soft and silvery haze ... Webs upon the spangled hedges. Wisps of gauze upon the lawn. Dying roses wan and lovely in the grey October dawn ... By the pond a white birch weeping. Sighing wind and falling leaf—and a small bird fluting sweetly, heedless of the tree's quiet grief.

October 26th

GOOD ADVICE

"Better to hunt in fields for health unbought,
 Than fee the doctor for a nauseous draught,
 The wise, for cure, on exercise depend;
 God never made his work for man to mend."

DRYDEN

October 27th

BETWEEN THE LINES

When you write a letter to a dear one far away—words fail to express the meanings that you would convey. As the pen moves on the paper recollections start—a face is pictured in the mind, a voice speaks in the heart.

Though you write of humdrum things and everyday affairs—behind the words, though not expressed, are hopes and fears and prayers ... Thoughts outpace the written sentence galloping ahead—and memory between the lines entwines her golden thread.

October 28th
DEAD LEAVES, LIVING ROOTS
The dead leaves flutter from the branches but the roots remain—the living roots from which some day the sap will rise again . . . There will be a resurrection, an awakening— There will be an Easter morning when the birds will sing—a rhapsody of Spring up in the blossom overhead—and daffodils come pushing up where now the leaves lie dead.

October 29th
"He brought me to the banqueting house, and his banner over me was love."

THE SONG OF SOLOMON

October 30th
THE LAST ROSE OF SUMMER
The frost that killed the other flowers has beautified this crimson rose. She wears a string of frosted pearls and in the wintry sunlight glows, red and lovely, standing bravely in a world that's cold and grey. The rose I thought had breathed its last has lived to bloom another day.

October 31st
THE EVE OF ALL HALLOWS
The genius of Christianity is that it takes the secular and transforms it into the sacred. Many of the feasts of pagan times have become the holy festivals of the Church of Christ. In the days of the old Celtic calendar the thirty-first day of October was the end of the year. At night the spirits of the dead were abroad and the witches and the warlocks held their revelries. With the coming of Christianity the Church gathered this festival up into its own calendar as the Eve of All Saints yet something of the macabre and the superstitious still lingers darkly around this time of Hallowe'en.

NOVEMBER

November 1st
THE COMMUNION OF SAINTS

I BELIEVE . . . "in the communion of saints; the forgiveness of sins; the resurrection of the body; and the life everlasting". Amen.

THE APOSTLES' CREED

November 2nd
ALL SOULS

We thought yesterday of the saints, those great souls of all time who by their labours, their faithfulness and their martyrdoms laid the foundations of the Church, known and unknown, acknowledged and unacknowledged, but today we think of all souls, the souls of the ordinary people of this world who were never called to do any extraordinary thing for God. Not for them the halo of the saint or the crown of the martyr, but being of the multitude of believers in the fellowship of the faith they too have their place in the blessed company of heaven.

"And lo, a great multitude, which no man could number, of all nations, and kindreds, and people, and tongues, stood before the throne."

THE REVELATION OF ST. JOHN THE DIVINE

November 3rd
HOPE CLEAVES THE ROCK

When courage fails and troubles loom—like monstrous mountains dark with doom—Hope cleaves the rock and suddenly—a gap appears, a path you see.

November 4th
LOG FIRES

Sometimes when the leaping flames are dancing on the

hearth—I catch the murmur of the trees along a woodland path. I hear the dry leaves rustling as an Autumn wind goes by —and see a tent of summer green against a clear blue sky.

The logs now crumbling into ashes once were sentient things—tremulous with life and with the quivering of wings ... The logs that lend a golden warmth to this November day— have worn upon their living limbs the rosy blooms of May.

November 5th
FRIENDSHIP BETWEEN NATIONS

Friendship between nations is a thing not lightly made. The broad foundations of respect must first be truly laid ... Speech is easy. Deeds are costly. Friendship must be proved. Sacrifices must be made, gaps bridged and mountains moved.

November 6th

"Friendship is a disinterested commerce between equals; love, an abject intercourse between tyrants and slaves."

OLIVER GOLDSMITH

November 7th

Common calamities level us all. Troubles unite us and barriers fall. Obstacles vanish. Strange things come about. People are kindly. The best side shows out. Goodness comes uppermost. Grievances fade. Feuds are forgotten and friend-ships are made.

November 8th
THERE WHERE YOU BELONG

Yearning for familiar things, and all you've left behind. Haunted by the memories that linger in the mind. Thinking thinking all the time of home and family—the place that seems so far away, the friends you never see. Looking forward to the day when you can go once more—up that path you know so well, to knock upon the door—to knock and know that you'll be welcome, in your heart a song—happy in the knowledge that you're there where you belong.

November 9th

"Now stir the fire, and close the shutters fast,
Let fall the curtains, wheel the sofa round,
And while the bubbling and loud-hissing urn
Throws up a steamy column, and the cups,
That cheer but not inebriate, wait on each,
So let us welcome peaceful evening in."

WM. COWPER,
FROM *The Winter Evening*

November 10th

PARTINGS AND GREETINGS

When on the eyes of dearest friends—the marble touch of death descends—we see them in their last repose—but when to us those eyelids close—they open somewhere to the light—the glory out beyond the night . . . They wake where life's dark journey ends—to other joys and other friends—who stand before their opening eyes—while we are saying our goodbyes.

November 11th

REMEMBER THEM

In known and unknown graves they rest,
The young, the bravest and the best.
They too loved well what life could give
And yet they died that we might live.
Twice in half a hundred years
The price was paid in blood and tears,
Twice we faced the German threat
Twice the challenge has been met.
Let not Memory's lamp burn low.
As generations come and go
Sing out their glorious requiem.
Remember them,
Remember them.

November 12th
OUT OF GREAT TRIBULATION
"And one of the elders answered saying unto me, What are these which are arrayed in white robes? and whence came they? And I said unto him, Sir, thou knowest. And he said to me, These are they which came out of great tribulation."

REVELATION 7.13-14

November 13th
WHITE CHRYSANTHEMUMS
Far into November when the fogs are thick and grey—the lovely white chrysanthemums their perfect blooms display. Pure as virgin snow they look. My passing glance they hold—more than all the gorgeous tones of copper, wine and gold . . . Startling in their wintry whiteness, restful to the eyes—after all the brilliant colours of the autumn dyes . . . Nature like a reverent mourner surely placed them here: white flowers for the burial of the departing year.

November 14th
While November yet can show a splash of colour bright and bold—I won't admit that Winter's here or that the year grows sere and old . . . I do not want to let it go or watch the last pale petal die. I do not want to face the truth. I do not want to say goodbye.

November 15th
"But of all plagues, good Heaven, thy wrath can send,
Save me, oh save me, from the candid friend!"

GEO. CANNING

November 16th
TO AN ABSENT FRIEND
Friend of my heart, we walk no more the roads we loved so well—and when we'll pass that way again—alas, I cannot tell. Perhaps we never shall retrace that old familiar path—or share our hopes and thoughts and dreams beside a firelit

hearth . . . But somewhere we shall fall in step and swing into our stride—and find another road to travel, for the world is wide. Though now apart, but close in thought, our separate ways we wend—you will always be to me by best and dearest friend.

November 17th
THE IMPUDENT INTRUDER
A robin redbreast perched upon the mossy headstone of a tomb; an impudent intruder in a place of silence and of gloom, in the shadows where the yew stretched out its sombre canopy —as if to guard the grey old graves of those who slept beneath the tree.

The robin, looking pleased and perky with his gaudy bib of red—hopped around the crumbling stones and sang his song amongst the dead . . . and some sad mourner kneeling near looked up and heard and understood—the meaning of the robin's song: that life could still be glad and good.

November 18th
"If a man does not make new acquaintance as he advances through life, he will soon find himself alone. A man, Sir, should keep his friendship in constant repair."

DR. JOHNSON

November 19th
STRIPPED
It is not until it is stripped of its leaves that you can see the peculiar characteristics of each individual tree: the massive and generous bough structure of the beech, the majesty of the oak, the straightness of the larch and the grace of the birch. And so it is with our friends. It is not until we have shared some great experience that we see one another as we really are. It is when the winters come and the big winds blow that superficialities and pretences are stripped away revealing the bare bones of true affection in all their strength and beauty.

STORMCOCK

What does he care for the shrieking gale, the blustering gusts and the driving hail? High in the tossed and straining tree— he sings his song defiantly . . . Tuning his note to the wind's wild scream—loudly repeating his own set theme—singing his part in the high-pitched key—of the tumultuous symphony . . . Scorning the hedgerows safe and warm—seeking no shelter from the storm . . . High on the topmost twig he swings. The rougher the weather the better he sings!

November 21st

"When thou art bidden, go and sit down in the lowest room; that when he that bade thee cometh, he may say unto thee, Friend, go up higher."

LUKE 14.10

November 22nd

ST. CECILIA'S DAY

"Music, when soft voices die
Vibrates in the memory."

SHELLEY

November 23rd

THE DESERTED HOUSE

Dustsheets shroud the furniture, no step sounds on the stair. The beds are stripped, the house is cold, for there is no one there—to open up the windows letting in the light of day— To wind the clock and light the fire and sweep the dust away.

In thought I often wander like a ghost lost in the gloom— opening the doors and cupboards, looking in each room— noting every well-loved object. Round the house I roam— followed by a voice that says, "When are you coming home?"

November 24th

"Man is a social animal."

SPINOZA

345

November 25th
LOVE IN ACTION

Virtue without love is like a flower without a scent—not a mere emotion, not a cloying sentiment—but love that cannot rest while there is work that must be done—wounds to bind and friends to help and errands to be run.

Without the warming grace of love our hearts grow hard and chill. The impulses of charity of kindness and goodwill—spring out of the seed of love. So let it be expressed. Charity is love in action, love made manifest.

November 26th
TO A SICK FRIEND

My friend, it won't be very long—before once more you're well and strong . . . The sun is going to shine for you. You're getting well, you're coming through. Hopeful thoughts your strength sustain. Have faith! You'll soon be home again—your own place in the world to take—a new and happy life to make.

November 27th

"There is no duty we so much underrate as the duty of being happy."

ROBERT LOUIS STEVENSON

November 28th
THE ROSARY OF LIFE

No good seed is ever wasted, no good deed unheeded goes. No true praying is unheard for there is One who sees and knows. Every loving word or act that satisfies a brother's need —adds to the rosary of life another bright and lovely bead.

November 29th
OUT OF DANGER

Silence, suspense—and the night hours ahead. Waiting and praying—a life on a thread . . . What is that radiance that lights up the gloom? Are angel presences here in this room? Who is the Third who is watching with me? No voice can I hear and no face can I see—but Someone is here. See, the grey morning breaks! And out of danger, the patient awakes.

November 30th

"Life is to be fortified by many friendships. To love, and to be loved, is the greatest happiness of existence . . . It is not that a man has occasion often to fall back upon the kindness of his friends; perhaps he may never experience the necessity of doing so; but we are governed by our imaginations, and they stand there as a solid and impregnable bulwark against all the evils of life."

SYDNEY SMITH

DECEMBER

December 1st
THE MONTH OF THE SHORTEST DAY

The month of the longest night is the month of the shortest day. Drear December wrapped in ragged cloak of sombre grey. Though unlovely, ever welcome for she comes to bring—the greatest gift of God to man: the birthday of the King . . . From her frozen hand we take this thing most wonderful—that crowns the ending of the year: the Christmas miracle.

December 2nd

BRAILLE

Darkness is a necessary part of God's great plan. Out of darkness life is born, plant, animal and man. Though the blind may seem to dwell in everlasting night—shut away from all the glow and glory of the light—there's a means by which they can escape and wander free—in imagination. Braille has turned the magic key—and so unlocked the treasures to be found within the mind. Fingers read the written word, a blessing to the blind.

December 3rd

> "My friend, the things that do attain
> The happy life be these, I find:
> The riches left, not got with pain;
> The fruitful ground, the quiet mind."
>
> HENRY HOWARD, EARL OF SURREY

December 4th

TEA-TIME

I have drawn the curtains close upon the day's last light— and piled the logs to make a blaze, sufficient for the night.

Shadows flicker red and golden on the ingle wall. The tray is on the table and the clock chimes in the hall.

There are crumpets piping hot with butter thickly spread—cherry cakes and ginger snaps and home-made jam and bread . . . The copper kettle on the hearth is singing merrily—a welcome to the dear old friend who's coming in to tea.

December 5th

"When to the sessions of sweet silent thought
I summon up remembrance of things past,
I sigh the lack of many a thing I sought
And with old woes new wail my dear times' waste:
Then can I drown an eye, unused to flow,
For precious friends hid in death's dateless night,
And weep afresh love's long since cancell'd woe,
And moan the expense of many a vanish'd sight:
Then can I grieve at grievances foregone,
And heavily from woe to woe tell o'er
The sad account of fore-bemoaned moan,
Which I new pay as if not paid before.
But if the while I think on thee, dear friend,
All losses are restored, and sorrows end."

SHAKESPEARE

December 6th
WHAT IS LIFE WITHOUT A FRIEND?

What is life without a friend to help you get along—to strengthen you when troubles come and things are going wrong . . . When problems loom like mountains and the sudden storms descend—When everything looks hopeless—what is life without a friend?

December 7th
ANGELS IN REGENT STREET

Above the roar of Regent Street where traffic rumbles by—shining angels lift their trumpets to the wintry sky. Past the lighted windowpanes the jostling people gaze—reminded of the meaning of these high and holy days ... The glitter of the herald seraphs, beautiful and bright—lends an artificial glory to the London night—but he who comes with faith will listen for a heavenly chord—and hear above the tinselled choirs the angels of the Lord.

December 8th

> "Good thoughts his only friends,
>   His wealth a well-spent age,
> The earth his sober inn,
>   And quiet pilgrimage."
>
> THOMAS CAMPION

December 9th

WINTER SUNLIGHT

The sun is like the smile of God upon the earth below—as the year grows old, when days are short and bleak winds blow ... When suddenly the grieving sky is touched with gold and blue—a blessing seems to fall as clouds roll back and light breaks through.

December 10th

CHEERFUL GIVERS

"But this I say, He which soweth sparingly shall reap also sparingly; and he which soweth bountifully shall reap also bountifully. Every man according as he purposeth in his heart, so let him give; not grudgingly, or of necessity: for God loveth a cheerful giver."

II CORINTHIANS 9.6–7

December 11th

STEADFAST IS THE LOVING HEART

The loving heart is like a fire that gives a quiet glow. All who come within its range can feel its warmth and know—the comfort and the beauty of a never-failing flame. Steadfast is the loving heart unchanged by praise or blame.

December 12th

JUST THE FAMILY

What will your Christmas programme be? The usual . . . just the family. We shall spend our Christmas Day in the old accustomed way. The children and an aunt or two. Grandma and Grandpa. Lucky you!

Lucky you at Christmastide to have your own folks at your side. Many will face an empty chair—not belonging anywhere—and many a lonely soul will be—a stranger in strange company.

And there'll be those in hospital—trying to be comical, but recollecting near to tears, the Christmases of other years . . . Remember them and grateful be—for home and hearth and family.

December 13th

"A few of us are endeavouring to raise a fund to buy the poor some meat and drink, and means of warmth. We choose this time because it is a time, of all others, when Want is keenly felt and Abundance rejoices. What shall I put you down for?"

"Nothing!" Scrooge replied.

DICKENS

December 14th

THE TOY CUPBOARD

Look into the cupboard where the broken toys are put—the engine with a missing wheel, the doll without a foot—the story book no longer read, the fairy with no wings. Surely something could be done with these discarded things.

Could they not be mended well enough to give away? Empty stockings they would help to fill on Christmas Day. Brush that shabby teddy, paint the bricks and wash the swan. Bring the old toys back to life. Don't keep them. Pass them on.

December 15th

THE LITTLE WHITE GATE

There is a friendly look about a small white wooden gate

especially when it leads to a cosy old cottage along a lavender-bordered path of weathered bricks. It has no airs and graces. Its simple beauty lies in the fact that it is the right thing in the right place, homely and unpretentious. One does not hesitate to lift the latch. "Come right in," says the little white gate. And in you go, sure of a welcome.

December 16th

ADVENT

"Hark the glad sound!
  The Saviour comes,
The Saviour promised long!
  Let every heart prepare a throne,
And every voice a song."

P. DODDRIDGE

December 17th

HEARTS AND PURSES

We have to open hearts and purses at this time of year—and give beyond the cosy circle of our own small sphere . . . We have to think of others and of self a little less—choosing presents, writing letters, giving happiness.

December 18th

HOW WERE THEY TO KNOW?

The man in the crowd going up to Bethlehem for the census saw a young woman on a donkey and thought it was Mary of Nazareth. How was he to know it was the handmaid of the Lord?

The stranger tethering his beast at the inn saw the glow of a lantern across the yard. He thought he was looking at a stable. How was he to know that it was a Throne Room?

The beggar at the gate saw a child being carried into the Temple for the ceremonial offering of two turtle doves and two young pigeons. He thought he was looking at an ordinary Jewish baby. How was he to know that it was God?

December 19th

SO BUSY!

"Lord, Thou knowest how busy I must be this day. If I forget thee, do not Thou forget me."

THE PRAYER OF SIR JACOB ASTLEY
BEFORE THE BATTLE OF EDGEHILL,
1642.

December 20th

ALREADY ON THE WAY

When Mary and Joseph were preparing to leave Galilee and go up to Judea for the census the three wise men were already on the way. They had seen the Star of prophecy and had set out in faith on the long long journey to Bethlehem. Had they doubted or delayed they would have missed their moment and arrived too late to see the King.

In five days' time we too must be at the manger with our gifts of praise and adoration. Spiritually, we should already be on the way for there will be many things between now and then to waylay and detain us. We make costly elaborate and exhausting preparations to entertain ourselves and our friends, but how much time do we spend in preparing to meet the King?

December 21st

"Small, busy flames play through the fresh-laid coals and their faint cracklings o'er our silence creep like whispers of the household gods that keep a gentle empire o'er fraternal souls.

. . . Many such eves of gently whispering noise may we together pass."

KEATS, TO HIS BROTHERS

December 22nd

THE SUN STANDS STILL

It is the shortest day of the year. The sun for a few days appears to halt at its winter solstice. It has reached the lowest point in the downward curve of what appears to be its journey round the earth. The night can never be longer or darker than it is now. Minute by minute from now on the days will lengthen as the earth in its annual course around the sun moves towards the vernal equinox. May there not be some parabolic meaning in the fact that at this time of the winter solstice when the sun appears to be standing still the earth is actually nearer to the sun that it is on midsummer day, for is it not true that we seem to be nearer to the Sun of the soul in the deep winter of our greatest griefs.

December 23rd
WHAT IS CHRISTMAS?

What is Christmas without a child to make the meaning clear? What is Christmas without the children? In their joy we hear—the echo of our own lost faith. God speaks to us through them—and turning back we find once more the road to Bethlehem . . . What is Christmas without a thought of the Nativity? Nothing but a foolish farce, a hollow mockery. What is Christmas without the Christ? A throne without a king. He turns the tinsel into gold and hallows everything.

December 24th
STRANGE AND WONDERFUL

Strange and wonderful it was that God the Lord of all—should show Himself unto the world as something weak and small, choosing for this miracle a Jewess undefiled—to be the wise and gentle Mother of the Holy Child.

Cradled in a stable! the incarnate Deity. Love itself. The Word made flesh—yet none was there to see—except a few poor shepherds and the Magi from afar—bringing gifts and guided by the glory of a Star.

Strange and wonderful indeed! Too marvellous for me. I could not hope to understand so great a mystery . . . Such a truth I cannot fathom or such love conceive—but I can kneel on Christmas morning saying, I BELIEVE.

December 25th
GOOD TIDINGS OF GREAT JOY

"And the angel said unto them, Fear not: for, behold, I

bring you good tidings of great joy, which shall be to all people.

For unto you is born this day in the city of David a Saviour, which is Christ the Lord."

December 26th

"It is a beautiful arrangement, also, derived from days of yore, that this festival, which commemorates the announcement of the religion of peace and love, has been made the season of gathering together of family connections, and drawing closer again those bands of kindred hearts, which the cares and pleasures and sorrows of the world are continually operating to cut loose: of calling back the children of a family, who have launched forth in life, and wandered widely asunder, once more to assemble about the paternal hearth, that rallying-place of the affections, there to grow young and loving again among the endearing mementos of childhood."

WASHINGTON IRVING,
FROM *Christmas at Bracebridge Hall*

December 27th

SICK AND TIRED

I'm sick of the old paths that led me astray. I want a new road, a new route, a new way—a new star to follow, a new world to find—a new dream to dream, a new heart, a new mind.

I'm tired of my failings, my faults I would mend. Here at the point where the year nears its end—I ask for forgiveness. Lord, help me I pray—to work out my life in a new kind of way—To do more, to give more, to love more, not less—and put into practice the faith I profess.

December 28th

NOW IS THE TIME

The year now dying once was young and much it promised you. Hopefully you greeted it when it was fresh and new. So do not let it pass away without a thankful thought—of the happy times and all the blessings that it brought . . . Forget the disappointments and the hopes that missed the mark—and before the poor old year goes out into the dark—Light a penitential candle. Let a tear be shed—for the good deed left undone, the kind word left unsaid.

Now is the moment to confess, the time to look within—at the uncorrected fault—the unforgiven sin.

December 29th
IF WE KNEW

If we really knew just how much time was left for us—how many years or months or weeks we'd cease to fret and fuss about the unimportant things that fill our lives today—using every precious hour before it slipped away.

If we knew exactly what the span was going to be—we should value Time and live each minute gratefully—wasting nothing of its treasure, sifting false from true—making up for all the time we've squandered . . . if we knew.

December 30th
THE PASSING OF THE YEAR

What did you do for me? said I as I watched the dying year. I would settle accounts with you before you go from here. You failed to bring me all the things you promised at the start: the fulfilment of my hopes, the wishes of my heart.

The Old Year opened his fading eyes and said reproachfully, I gave you all I had to give, but what did you do for me? I gave you opportunities and chances that you spurned—many mercies undeserved and happiness unearned.

Had you only known, he said, I was a friend to you. And as the Old Year breathed his last I knew his words were true . . . I had been ungrateful, but it's too late now, I said. Forgive me, Lord, and make me wiser in the year ahead.

December 31st

"Old things are passed away; behold, all things are become new."

"Be ye transformed by the renewing of your mind."

ST. PAUL